S0-EKI-524

ABRAHAMIC BLESSING

American Society of Missiology Monograph Series

Series Editor, James R. Krabill

THE ASM MONOGRAPH SERIES provides a forum for publishing quality dissertations and studies in the field of missiology. Collaborating with Pickwick Publications—a division of Wipf and Stock Publishers of Eugene, Oregon—the American Society of Missiology selects high quality dissertations and other monographic studies that offer research materials in mission studies for scholars, mission and church leaders, and the academic community at large. The ASM seeks scholarly work for publication in the Series that throws light on issues confronting Christian world mission in its cultural, social, historical, biblical, and theological dimensions.

Missiology is an academic field that brings together scholars whose professional training ranges from doctoral-level preparation in areas such as scripture, history and sociology of religions, anthropology, theology, international relations, interreligious interchange, mission history, inculturation, and church law. The American Society of Missiology, which sponsors this series, is an ecumenical body drawing members from Independent and Ecumenical Protestant, Catholic, Orthodox, and other traditions. Members of the ASM are united by their commitment to reflect on and do scholarly work relating to both mission history and the present-day mission of the church. The ASM Monograph Series aims to publish works of exceptional merit on specialized topics, with particular attention given to work by younger scholars, the dissemination and publication of which is difficult under the economic pressures of standard publishing models.

Persons seeking information about the ASM or the guidelines for having their dissertations considered for publication in the ASM Monograph Series should consult the Society's website—www.asmweb.org.

Members of the ASM Monograph Committee who approved this book are:

PREVIOUSLY PUBLISHED IN THE ASM MONOGRAPH SERIES

David P. Leong, *Street Signs: Toward a Missional Theology of Urban Cultural Engagement*

Christopher L. Flanders, *About Face: Rethinking Face for 21st Century Missions*

Stephen Pavey, *Theologies of Power and Crisis: Envisioning/Embodying Christianity in Hong Kong*

Abrahamic Blessing

A Missiological Narrative of Revival in Papua New Guinea

Sarita D. Gallagher

American Society of Missiology Monograph Series vol. 21

PICKWICK *Publications* • Eugene, Oregon

ABRAHAMIC BLESSING
A Missiological Narrative of Revival in Papua New Guinea

American Society of Missiology Monograph Series 21

Pickwick Publications
An Imprint of Wipf and Stock Publishers
199 W. 8th Ave., Suite 3
Eugene, OR 97401

www.wipfandstock.com

ISBN 13: 978-1-61097-928-3

Cataloguing-in-Publication Data

Gallagher, Sarita D.

Abrahamic blessing : a missiological narrative of revival in Papua New Guinea / Sarita D. Gallagher.

American Society of Missiology Monograph Series 21

xii + 264 pp. ; 23 cm. Includes bibliographical references and index.

ISBN 13: 978-1-61097-928-3

1. Christianity—Papua New Guinea—Urapmin. I. Title. II. Series.

BR1495 N5 G10 2014

Manufactured in the U.S.A. 10/23/2014

This book is dedicated to my dad,
Robert L. Gallagher,
and my sister,
Luisa J. Gallagher,
whose encouragement and late night telephone conversations
made this book possible.

And to the CRC pastors and leaders in Papua New Guinea,
who heard God's voice and responded with such passion and
dedication
that the future of Papua New Guinea was changed forever.

Holi Spirit kom long mi olsem paia
Kukim ol pasin no gut
Kom insait na klinim mi O Lord
Kom insait na wokim wok

Holi Spirit kom klinim mi

Holy Spirit come to me like a fire
Burning all my sins away
Come inside, and clean me O Lord
Come inside and do your work

Holy Spirit, come clean me

Contents

Tables and Figures

Acknowledgments

God's plans are so much bigger than ours. When I first walked onto the Bethel Center property in Port Moresby in 2004, I could never have imagined the journey that God had planned for me. A first-term missionary, I was welcomed by a Christian community that was deeply dedicated to their savior Jesus Christ, and who had been forever transformed by the power of the Holy Spirit. It was during these first few months in Papua New Guinea (PNG) that I learned about the 1970s–1980s revival and was intrigued about the possibility for further research. I now have the privilege of publishing this book and the stories of the revival in honor of the pastors and leaders of the CRC movement[1] in Papua New Guinea.

It is with deep appreciation that I thank the revival leaders of the CRC movement for inviting me into their homes, their lives, and their families. And for sharing with me the testimonies of God's power, faithfulness, and love that have shaped their collective spirituality. I would like to especially thank the revival leaders that I interviewed for this project: Fuwe and Rhoda Hageyo, Richmond Tamanabae, Thomas Tamanabae, Peter Igarobae, Margaret Sete, John Togawata, Barnabas Tabara, Robert Tamanabae, Alkin Orona, Aria Hegame, Geua Wari, Kila Laena, David and Manoka Jaruga, Elijah and Beverly Umeume, Ai and Gabi Wari, Thelma Garao, Uvau and Katie Amani, Geno and Elena Kanage, Priscilla Ban, Micky and Alu Purinau, Jennifer Zairere, Pikal Gela, John Marmar, Kelly Lotu, Numba Puri, Arthur Jawodimbari, Sebastian Peremo, Henry Nigel, Ivan Avowari, Sylvestor Barai, Nelson Barai, Hilarion Mairaro, and Kingsford. Thank you for opening my eyes anew to the wonder of God's love for the nations. I am likewise grateful to the CRC missionaries who served as my guides in this research: Barry and Rosalie Silverback, Norm and Cathy Reed, Kevin and Brenda Hughes, Marilyn Teague and Barry Chant.

1. Originally called the Christian Revival Crusade.

This book would not exist without the constant encouragement, love, and kindness of Papa Fuwe and Mum Rhoda Hageyo, who welcomed me into their home in Papua New Guinea as their own daughter. Thank you for loving me and inviting me into your family. The many nights that we told stories, ate rice together, laughed, and mucked around, refreshed my soul and my heart. Thank you also to all my brothers and sisters in the Hageyo tribe—Enoch, Sammy, Gwen, Jerry, Simon, Malcolm, Chris and Jill—mi laikim yu tru.

I would also like to thank Chuck E. Van Engen, my mentor at Fuller Theological Seminary, for his unwavering support and expert advice, and R. Daniel Shaw who served as my mentor in all things Papua New Guinean. Your encouragement and wise counsel strengthened not only my research but also my heart as I completed this project. Additionally, I am grateful for the expertise and editing prowess of Paula Hampton at George Fox University, who with great perseverance and dedication edited my final manuscript. And Hayley Delle, my fantastic teaching assistant at George Fox, who took on the enormous task of preparing this book for publication. Without both of you, this book would still be a manuscript on my desk.

My final and greatest thanks is to my family: to my father, Robert L. Gallagher, who taught me what it means to be a Spirit-led scholar, and to my sister, Luisa J. Gallagher, who tirelessly edited my original dissertation, and modeled for me the love of Christ in action. And, to my mum, Dolores M. Gallagher, who through her example taught me how to pursue God with all my heart.

PART I

Abrahamic Blessing in Scripture

1

Setting the Stage

The cool tropical air of Lae drifted through the house as we settled down to begin the interview. Surrounded by cups of black tea, Pastor Peter Igarobae began sharing the story of revival that forever transformed his life and the lives of his community in Oro Province. A stronghold of sorcery, Kurereda village was originally evangelized by Anglican missionaries but despite their Christian witness it held adamantly onto the black magic and sorcery practices passed down for generations. A thin layer of Christianity hid the routine animistic rituals of burying bones and hair on fields for a prosperous harvest, and practicing sorcery to bring both blessing and curses to one's neighbors. Pastor Peter as a student at the University of Papua New Guinea in Port Moresby himself perpetuated this syncretistic life; serving as the president of the Anglican Student Society while simultaneously experimenting in the world of sorcery, magic, and the paranormal.[1]

The spiritual history of Kurereda however took a dramatic turn in the early 1970s. Pastor Peter described the miraculous events that took place when his own family members, influenced by the teaching at Bethel Center in Port Moresby, returned to the village with the gospel message. I was listening to Pastor Peter's account with growing interest, when he mentioned that as Abraham[2] had done centuries before, the clan leaders of Kurereda decided to cut a covenant with the God of Abraham. Igarobae

1. Igarobae, interview by author, August 1, 2009.

2. For reasons of consistency the use of Abram's name "Abraham" will be used throughout this book to refer to the patriarch both before and after his name change in Gen 17:5.

explained, "When we turned to the Lord we had to cut our bridges with [the evil forces] . . . and cut a new covenant with the Lord. Not only with the Lord but also with each other." He continued, "When the whole family turns and commits. Then their land, their homes, their village, [and] their clan becomes the Lord's."[3]

My interview with Pastor Peter Igarobae that day was just the beginning of a growing correlation between the life and journey of Abraham and the 1970s–1980s Christian Revival Crusade (CRC) revival in Papua New Guinea (PNG). As I followed the missional connection between Abraham and the PNG CRC revival, I realized that God's blessing to the nations through Abraham was far from over. The parallels could be incorporated into several categories including the motivations of participants, agents of mission, the message shared, the methods of mission, and the patterns of missional expansion. With each additional interview, I confirmed my initial findings as the missional relationship with the Abrahamic blessing motif became more prominent. This discovery altered the course of my research as the PNG CRC revival movement emerged not only as a case study, but also as an extension of the biblical Abrahamic blessing motif.

As my research developed, my goal was to identify the missional patterns of the Abrahamic blessing motif in Scripture and in the Papua New Guinean case study of the CRC missionary movement. The following questions served as the foundation of my research and form the outline of my study. The research questions that I answered included:

1. What is the foundation for the Abrahamic blessing motif within Genesis?
2. How is the motif of God's people as a blessing to the nations developed in Scripture?
3. How have missiologists and theologians historically interpreted the Abrahamic blessing motif?
4. What occurred during the CRC mission outreaches in PNG during the 1970s–1980s?
5. What parallels exist between the Abrahamic blessing motif and the 1970s–1980s PNG CRC movement?
6. What are the missional patterns of the Abrahamic blessing motif in Scripture and in the Papua New Guinean case study of the CRC missionary movement?

3. Igarobae, interview by author, August 3, 2009.

While the biblical and PNG CRC contexts are unique, during my research I found that they shared similar missional patterns related to the Genesis 12:3a promise. Van Engen likens these missional patterns within Scripture to a tapestry "with the woof (horizontal threads) of various themes and motifs interwoven in the warp (vertical) of each historical context."[4] In comparing the Abrahamic blessing motif in Scripture with that in the PNG CRC revival movement, I found that this analogy still stands as the missional patterns surrounding the blessing motif in Scripture are also found in the new historic context of PNG. However, as David Bosch wisely notes, a complete one-on-one correlation between biblical faith—and I would add missional patterns in Scripture—cannot be made directly with contemporary society.[5] Therefore, although clear associations between the two contexts were evident in my research, an exact correspondence was not the goal of my data analysis. Instead, as biblical faith is incarnational—"the reality of God entering into human affairs"[6]—both the unity and uniqueness of the Abrahamic blessing motif in Scripture and the PNG context was explored.

In order to compare and contrast the two contexts I used standard theology of mission categories to analyze the data. In Gerald Anderson's definition of theology of mission, he identifies these foundational categories as "the motives, message, methods, strategy and goals of the Christian world mission."[7] While not changing the data itself, these categories provided a general structure within which to sort and compare the biblical data with the historical events of the PNG CRC revival. It is significant to note that these categories were also independently evident in the PNG field research data. In the process of doing grounded theory I first noticed these broad missional categories in the PNG interview transcripts and later identified them as common theology of mission constructs. The presence of these missional categories in both the theology of mission literature and the PNG interviews led to my adapting them to this research project.

4. Van Engen, *Mission on the Way*, 41.

5. Bosch, *Transforming Mission*, 181.

6. Ibid.

7. Neill et al., *Concise Dictionary*, 594. Additional authors who reference these missional categories include Van Engen, *Mission on the Way*; Verkuyl, *Contemporary Missiology*; Thomas, "Following the Footprints"; Hedlund, *God and the Nations*; and Dyrness and Kärkkäinen, "Theology of Mission."

As my acceptance of the missiological categories was based upon both mission theology literature and the categories which emerged from my field data analysis, I have revised Anderson's original list to also reflect the uniqueness of the PNG data. The revised list thus additionally includes agents of mission and combines the original strategy and goals of mission categories under the one title of "missional expansion." The five missional categories are thus: agents of mission, motivation for mission, message shared, methods, and missional expansion. Also, due to the contextual diversity of the Hebrew Scriptures, the New Testament, and the CRC revival narratives, I defined the missional categories broadly to allow for the distinctive characteristics of the varied contexts.

TABLE 1
MISSIONAL CATEGORIES

Agents of Mission	Characteristics of the individuals and/or groups who missionally shared the blessing of God.
Missional Motivation	Motivational factors leading to individual and/or group participation in the *missio Dei*.
Message Shared	Tenets that were verbally expressed by God or human beings regarding the Abrahamic blessing, the *missio Dei* and/or the gospel of Christ.
Evangelistic Methods	Methods used to spread the blessing of God within communities and also geographically.
Missional Expansion	Local and foreign acceptance and physical expansion of the blessing of God.

As I explored the Abrahamic blessing motif through Scripture, I used narrative theology as the framework of my biblical hermeneutic. While there are many diverse approaches within the field of narrative theology,[8] there are certain characteristics that define the method. The key foundational assumptions of narrative theology are that: (1) the focus of biblical narrative is God, (2) Scripture should be viewed both holistically and independently, (3) narrative penetrates and influences the real world, (4) the narrative's message cannot be separated from the narrative itself, (5) narratives have cyclical interpretations and that (6) God still speaks through biblical narrative.

8. Van Engen, *Mission on the Way*, 51.

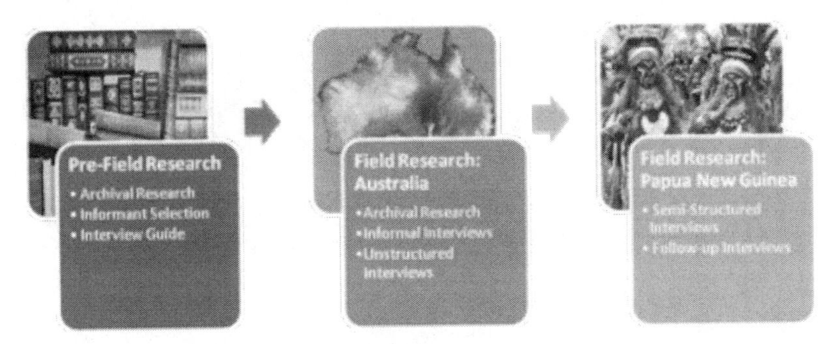

FIGURE 1
STAGES OF QUALITATIVE RESEARCH

The Australasian field research took place in three basic stages: (1) pre–field research design; (2) archival research and preliminary interviews in Australia; and (3) ethnographic semi-structured and follow-up interviews in PNG. First, in order to gain an historical overview of the PNG CRC's national and international mission work for my case study, I explored a variety of primary and secondary materials. My primary archival resources included letters written by Australian CRC missionaries regarding the mission work in PNG and in particular the missionary outreach patrols emerging from Bethel Center in Port Moresby. In addition, I reviewed the "New Guinea News" reports within the CRC denominational magazine *The Revivalist* (from its inception in 1962), as they related to the indigenous mission movement in PNG and Australasia. The final primary resources I referenced were the original CRC pamphlets and sermons which focused on international mission during the 1970s–1980s such as the "Prayer Invasion Booklet" (1980s) and Barry Silverback's "Run with the Vision" (1980s) which were both distributed in Australia and PNG.

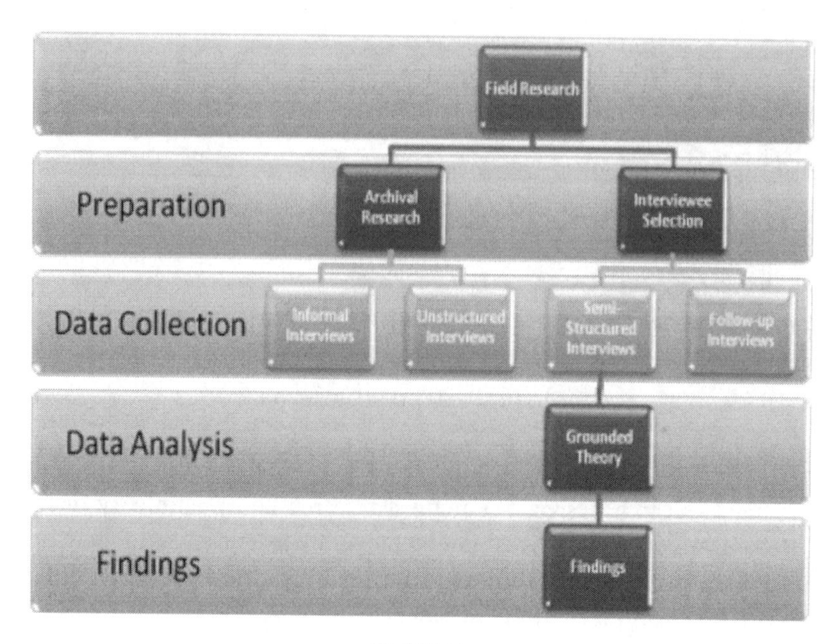

FIGURE 2
FIELD RESEARCH DESIGN

The primary method used during my field research in Australia and PNG was ethnographic interviewing. Within the context of my research, I conducted a series of unstructured and semi-structured interviews in each country respectively in addition to collecting archival data. Two phases of interviews were conducted during my research; the first was unstructured interviews with former CRC missionaries to PNG. The selection of interviewees in Australia was limited to former Australian CRC missionaries who were based at Bethel Center in Port Moresby during the 1970s and 1980s and who participated in the provincial missionary outreach patrols and/or citywide crusades. Additionally, former Australian missionaries to PNG who are currently working for the CRC mission office in Adelaide were contacted in regard to accessing archival data focusing on the initial denominational mission work which emerged from Port Moresby starting in the early 1970s.

The second phase of interviews were semi-structured interviews with former and current national PNG CRC leaders and pastors who participated in the missionary outreach patrols, citywide crusades and/or were involved in national or international mission work during the 1970s and 1980s. The selection criteria for the semi-structured interviews were based upon the following factors: interviewees must be

- PNG nationals.
- Current or former leaders within the CRC International denomination.
- Active within the CRC denomination during the 1970s–1980s.
- Former participants in the 1970s–1980s provincial missionary outreach patrols, city crusades, and/or national or international missionary endeavors.

The goal of this series of interviews with PNG CRC leaders was to record the personal stories of the participants of the 1970s–1980s revival and mission movement, and to identify their motivations for participating in the *missio Dei*. This collection of oral history therefore seeks to reconstruct "the past through the experiences of those who have lived it."[9] As such, "many of the surviving participants" of the CRC revival were given "the opportunity to tell their personal stories—all of which together [will] form a mosaic representation of the event."[10] However, as each individual's experience is unique, data saturation was sought after in regards to the revival events but not the informants' rationale for mission involvement.

The time period of the 1970s–1980s was selected due to the large church growth of the CRC denomination within PNG during that period. From Barry and Rosalie Silverback's arrival in Port Moresby in January 28, 1972, the CRC expanded from consisting of two individuals to having 24,000 active members in 1990, more than a 10,000 percent increase. While the CRC did continue to grow numerically after 1990, the main growth spurt and national and international missionary endeavors took place during the first two decades.

In part 1, Abrahamic Blessing in Scripture, I explore the Abrahamic blessing motif in Scripture. I start my analysis of the missional theme in chapter 2 as I investigate God's universal blessing in Genesis 1–11, the origin of the Abrahamic blessing in Genesis 12:1–3 and the development of the Abrahamic blessing in Genesis 12–50. In chapter 3 I follow the Abrahamic blessing motif through the Old Testament, exploring its fulfillment through the Abrahamic line and through the prophets of Israel.

9. Angrosino, *Doing Ethnographic*, 46.

10. Ibid.

In chapter 4 I examine the Abrahamic blessing motif in the New Testament, focusing on its significance within the ministry of Jesus and his followers. Finally, in chapter 5 I analyze the Abrahamic blessing motif in Scripture through the missiological lens of standard mission theology categories. These missional categories include: agents of mission, motivational factors, the message shared, the methods of mission, and missional expansion.

In part 2, Abrahamic Blessing in Context, I provide a historical and socio-cultural background for understanding the PNG CRC revival movement within its context. I also present a missiological categorization of the PNG field research data. First, in chapter 6, I outline the significant historical events that most influenced the development of the PNG CRC movement and also highlight the key socio-cultural values and beliefs that uniquely shaped the CRC revival. In chapter 7 I introduce a historic overview of the CRC revival movement in PNG based upon my archival research and ethnographic interviews in Australia and PNG. Finally, in chapter 8 I analyze the PNG interview data with the same standard mission theology categories used in the biblical data analysis: agents of mission, motivational factors, the message shared, methods of mission, and missional expansion.

In part 3, Abrahamic Blessing in Application, I compare my data analysis of the Abrahamic blessing motif in Scripture with that of the PNG CRC revival movement. Using the standard mission theology categories which I have incorporated throughout my data analysis, in chapter 9 I compare and contrast the Abrahamic blessing motif in Scripture with its representation in the PNG case study. In my final chapter, chapter 10, I present the conclusions of my biblical and integrative research and suggest recommendations for further study.

While a missiological exploration of both the Abrahamic blessing motif and the PNG CRC revival independently contribute to mission theory, their interrelationship has the potential to significantly alter not only contemporary mission theory but also mission praxis. The significance of this research is multifaceted in that it contributes to the contemporary church's understanding of the *missio Dei*, records an unexplored chapter of Melanesian indigenous mission history, and impacts the foundational motivations and methodology of contemporary mission theory. It is in this final contribution that I hope to both encourage and motivate indigenous mission movements worldwide to continue their participation in the *missio Dei*.

2

Genesis: Declaration of God's Blessing

In researching the Abrahamic blessing within Genesis, it is significant to observe that the theme of blessing does not originate with the Abrahamic narrative in Genesis 12:1–3. Instead, the motif of blessing is a strong thematic thread whose origin in Genesis 1 extends throughout the text. In order to gain an understanding of the Abrahamic blessing, it is first necessary to look at the origins and the development of this blessing motif within the primeval history of Genesis 1–11. In the subsequent section I present the purpose of Genesis 1–11 and the unfolding of the blessing motif as God blesses all creation, humankind and Noah and his family. I additionally mention the role of the flood and Tower of Babel events as precursors of the Abrahamic blessing.

Purpose of Genesis 1–11

While often simply dismissed as the "prologue" or "background" to the patriarchal history of chapters 12–50,[1] Genesis 1–11 holds great importance as it serves not only to introduce major themes but also to provide a rationale for the major developments that follow. Allen P. Ross notes that the principal purpose of the primeval events of Genesis 1:1—11:26 is to explain "why God called Abram and inaugurated a program of blessing through his covenant."[2] He explains:

> [Gen 1–11] demonstrates convincingly and graphically the need for God's blessing in the world; for ever since humankind

1. Whybray, *Introduction*, 35.
2. Ross, *Creation and Blessing*, 99.

> acquired the knowledge of good and evil, evil became the dominant force, bringing corruption and chaos into God's creation and incurring the divine curse.[3]

While Ross' argument does rightly acknowledge the need for human redemption, the fact that God's blessing antedates the Fall directly contradicts the core of Ross's hypothesis. According to the Genesis account, all of God's creation had already been blessed by God prior to the introduction of Abraham in Genesis 11; thus Abraham was not the first or only means of God's blessing. Gordon J. Wenham instead points to the continued sinfulness of humankind as the rationale behind the presentation of Abraham. He writes: "The succession of catastrophes that befell humanity prior to Abraham's call show just why the election of Abraham and in him, Israel, was necessary."[4] It is thus the combination of this "succession of catastrophes" within Genesis 1–11 coupled with the general disobedience of humanity that leads to the climactic entrance of Abraham. While God had formerly blessed his creation at its conception, a new era had arrived where God's blessing to the nations would emerge through one chosen people.

In addition to setting the stage for the patriarchal narratives, Genesis 1–11 also introduces the primary motifs of the Genesis text. Of these key motifs, the themes of promise, blessing/cursing, order/chaos, obedience/sin, creation/destruction, life/death, and forgiveness/judgment are especially evident in the opening chapters. David J. A. Clines calls attention in particular to the theme of "promise" or "blessing" within Genesis. He argues in *The Theme of the Pentateuch* that the partial fulfillment of the promise/blessing of Israel is in fact the overarching theme of the entire Pentateuch.[5] Clines demonstrates that the threefold promise of posterity, divine-human relationship and land are present within the Books of Genesis (posterity), Exodus and Leviticus (divine-human relationship), and Numbers and Deuteronomy (land).[6] He further claims that Genesis 1–11, while not containing any reference to a patriarchal promise, contains distinct evidence of God's intentions to later bless humankind.[7]

3. Ibid.
4. Wenham, *Genesis*, xxii.
5. Clines, *Theme*, 29.
6. Ibid.
7. Ibid., 78.

With this insight into the text we turn to the motif of blessing within Genesis 1–11.

Blessing Motif in Genesis 1–11

The Hebrew term "to bless" used in Genesis, *brk*, is complex in both its original meaning and application. Used more frequently within Genesis and Deuteronomy than anywhere else in the Old Testament, the act of blessing within Genesis 1–11 refers to a divine act wherein God imparts "vital power" to creation or human beings.[8] The tangible results of blessing impacted both the material and spiritual realms leading to prosperity in life and health, and in the fertility of the people, their animals, and their land.[9] Derek Kidner refers to divine blessing as "God turning full-face to the recipient . . . in self-giving."[10] This supernatural essence of blessing has also been described as the imparting of one's soul into another.[11] It is this act of imparting power and life that so distinguishes the pronouncement of blessing from that of speaking mere words.

As the act of blessing is multileveled in nature, the blessing itself, *brk*, is likewise multifaceted. Blessings—"bestowed, transferred from one party to another in an almost palpable way"[12]—have multiple functions within the Genesis text. The divine blessings of God as expressed in Genesis 1–11, impart the power of fertility, dominion and resources. First, in Genesis 1:22, 28, and 9:1, 7, both the land and womb are promised abundant fruitfulness with expectations to "fill the earth" (1:28; 9:1)[13] and to "abound on the earth and multiply in it" (9:7 NRSV). This divine blessing of fertility upon the land and humankind illustrates the core of the blessing of God. Not only does God's blessing affect the phases of life, but it actually brings literal life.[14] In addition to the promise of fruitfulness, the blessings of God to humankind are coupled with the promise of dominion over creation (1:28; 9:2) and the gift of natural resources (1:29; 9:3). These blessings of God in Genesis 1–11 are spoken upon creation

8. Westermann, *Blessing in the Bible*, 29, 18.

9. Mowinckel, *Religion and Kultus*, 66.

10. Kidner, *Genesis*, 52.

11. Westermann, *Blessing in the Bible*, 18.

12. Brueggemann, "Ministry Among," 24.

13. Unless otherwise indicated, all Scripture references are from the NIV.

14. Westermann, *Blessing in the Bible*, 18.

and humankind leading the reader to a deeper understanding of the blessings to come.

Within the narratives of Genesis 1–11, there are four specific divine acts of blessing.[15] The creator God blesses: (1) every living creature (Gen 1:21–22); (2) humankind (1:27–29; 5:1b–2); (3) the seventh day (2:3); and (4) Noah and his sons (9:1–6). Interwoven between these four blessings are three major consequences of humankind's disobedience: the banishment from the garden of Eden (3:24), the flood (7:11–24), and the scattering of humanity due to the Tower of Babel (11:8–9). Although there is a temptation to identify all three punishments as divine curses, Genesis only records that one of them, the disobedience of Adam and Eve, involves individuals and creation being "cursed" (*qalal*). Giving exception to these passages, Claus Westermann concurs that

> the Old Testament speaks frequently and in varied contexts of Yahweh's activity in bestowing blessing, but nowhere does it speak of the curse of Yahweh or of Yahweh's putting a curse on someone or something. Instead of speaking of Yahweh's curse, the Old Testament tells of his judgment and punishment. That is to say that in Israel the curse was never theologized the way blessing was.[16]

While the essential essence of "being cursed" is present within Genesis 1–11, Westermann is correct in his observation that besides Genesis 3:17 and 4:11 there are no references to God cursing creation in the primeval history. However, as expressed later in Genesis 12:3—"I will bless those who bless you and the one who curses you I will curse" (NRSV)—the combination of blessing and cursing is not absent from the book of Genesis. Therefore for the purpose of this study, I make a distinction between God's punishment and God's cursing of humankind as it is distinguished in the narrative text.

In the following section, the most significant of the blessings of Genesis 1–11—the blessings of creation (Gen 1:21–22), humankind (1:27–29; 5:1b–2), and Noah and his sons (9:1–6)—is explored as they present insights into the later blessing of Abraham (12:1–3). In addition, the critical turning points of the flood (7:11–24) and the Tower of Babel (11:8–9) are also discussed in light of their preparatory position in the Genesis narrative.

15. See appendix B, Blessing of God in Genesis 1–11.

16. Westermann, *Blessing in the Bible*, 23–24.

Blessing of All Creatures

The first act of divine blessing in Genesis is God's blessing of "the great sea monsters and every living creature that moves" in chapter 1:21–22 (NRSV). As expressed in Genesis 1 in regards to creation (vv. 21–22) and later humankind (vv. 27–29; 5:1b–2), there exists a pattern within the blessing passages, of God (1) creating, (2) blessing, and declaring (3) fruitfulness:

TABLE 2
GENESIS 1:21–22[17]

Recipient	Created	Blessed	Fruitfulness
Every living creature (1:21–22)	"So God *created* the great sea monsters and every living creature that moves, of every kind, with which the waters swarm and every winged bird of every kind. And God saw that it was good" (1:21).	"God *blessed* them, saying . . ." (1:22a)	"Be *fruitful* and *multiply* and *fill the waters in the seas*, and let birds *multiply on the earth*" (1:22b).

Within this combination of the act of creation, the act of blessing and the declaration of fruitfulness, there is an important element of God's character and the nature of blessing that is expressed.

First, it is inherent within the creation act (Gen 1:21) that God not only imparts life but also simultaneously blesses creation with the ability to reproduce. Therefore God's seemingly repetitive act of blessing creation and his additional command to "be fruitful and multiply" (1:22) begs our attention. In light of this apparent reiteration of blessing, the question must be asked: What is the distinction between the creation act, the blessing of God, and God's speaking forth of fertility? While a contemporary interpretation of this Genesis 1:21–22 passage would suggest a linear sequencing of these events, the ancient Hebrew worldview held by the original author(s) leads to a more holistic approach. As Laurence Turner explains, within Hebrew literature "repetition serves . . . to reinforce the important";[18] thus although not an exact replication of each other, the three acts of God can be seen as overlapping in purpose and thus interrelated. This interdependence is observed by Westermann who explains: "Gen[esis] 1:22 shows . . . the blessing that confers the power

17. NRSV; italics in this table are added.

18. Turner, *Genesis*, 15.

of fertility is inseparable from creation where the creator is the one who blesses and the created living being has the power to reproduce itself because of the blessing."[19] He continues that "blessing implies creation and is effective as the work of the creator. To speak of life and its dynamism is to speak of the effective action of the creator."[20] As such, God's creation of the animals and his blessing upon them are in some ways an expression of each other. Through the creation act itself the blessing of God is expressed.

Another noteworthy aspect of the blessing of Genesis 1:21–22 is that blessing is communicated through the spoken word of God. Just as light/dark (Gen 1:3–4), day/night (1:5), the "dome of heaven" (1:6–8 NRSV), land/sea (1:9–13), plants (1:11–13), stars (1:14–19), fish/birds (1:20–22), and land animals (1:24–31) were spoken into life, so the blessings of God are imparted through speech. Hermann Gunkel remarks that all of creation "comes into being through God's word" as it is the very will of God which creates all things.[21] God has just to proclaim the existence of something and it is. Likewise, just as the pronouncement of creation led to its existence, so God's declaration of blessing made it come to pass. It is important to note again the supernatural nature of God's blessing upon creation which "once uttered . . . carries its own life-giving power and cannot be revoked by man."[22] The blessing of God as it is spoken to creation and later to humankind guarantees its complete fulfillment within the life of the recipient.

In regards to the spoken nature of God's blessing upon creation, the fact that for the first time God is speaking to an audience other than himself is also significant. Goldingay aptly notes: "For the first time God speaks in the imperative, overtly speaking to someone. Apparently the animal world is able to hear God speak and respond to it, as the cosmos and the plant world cannot."[23] This communication between God and his creation, especially as expressed later within God's communion with Adam and Eve, highlights the personal nature of God's relationship with his creation. While this interaction with creation in Genesis 1:21–22 is

19. Westermann, *Genesis 1–11*, 140.

20. Ibid.

21. Gunkel, *Genesis*, 106.

22. Wenham, *Genesis*, 24.

23. Goldingay, *Old Testament Theology*, 55.

not elaborated upon, it does lay a foundation for the relational nature of the patriarchal blessings to come.

In addition to this verbal proclamation of divine blessing, the fruitfulness with which God blesses creation is also very significant to the nature of blessing. God's command to creation "to be fruitful and multiply" (Gen 1:22b NRSV) as discussed previously not only incorporates the ability for the blessed to have offspring but also the ability of the future generations to reproduce. Gerhard von Rad explains that "these [first] living creatures are the recipients of a life-giving divine power by virtue of which they themselves are capable of passing on the life they have received by means of their own procreation."[24] It is this ability to give life and multiply greatly which is the essence of God's blessing upon creation.

Furthermore, this ability to produce life and to pass on that capacity to one's offspring reaches beyond the immediate divine blessing given at the time. More specifically, as the animals in Genesis 1:21–22 passed on God's blessing to their offspring they in fact themselves became vehicles of God's blessing. God's blessing upon creation was not a onetime event but instead introduced an ongoing fulfillment that was passed from generation to generation.[25] The outplaying of blessing as expressed in Genesis 1:21–22 is an ongoing and continual transference of blessing from one party to another. This characteristic of divine blessings is later echoed in the patriarchal history of chapters 12–50. In such, God's blessing upon Abraham and his offspring is also essentially passed from father to son and from each patriarch to the surrounding nations.

Blessing of Humankind

In God's blessing upon humankind (Gen 1:27–29; 5:1b–2), the pattern of "creating" and "blessing" continues. However, it is within these divine blessings upon Adam and Eve and their offspring that God also introduces not only the blessing of fruitfulness (1:28b), but also that of dominion over creatures (1:28c) and all plant life (1:29). Thus, the blessings of God to humankind are threefold:

1.	Fruitfulness; multiplication; filling the earth	Gen 1:28b
2.	Dominion over creatures of the sea, air and land	Gen 1:28b
3.	Resources (plant life)	Gen 1:29

24. Von Rad, *Genesis*, 54.

25. Turner, *Genesis*, 23.

A distinction between God's blessing upon creation (1:21–22) and that of humankind (1:27–29; 5:1b–2) is God's gift of dominion over all creatures. Wenham states that "God's purpose in creating man was that he should rule over the animal world (Gen 1:26) . . . Because man is created in God's image, he is king over nature. He rules the world on God's behalf."[26] He continues that "unbridled exploitation" of nature is by no means implied in this command, but instead humankind is called to act as God's representative "therefore treating them in the same way as God who created them."[27] But there is a strong sense in the Genesis 1:28–29 that God's blessing of humankind "subduing" the earth and having "dominion" over the animals (1:28c NRSV) set humanity apart from the rest of creation. The implication extends that as human beings are set above creation they are also in some ways closer to God on the universe's hierarchal structure.

This implied connection with God expressed in the Genesis 1:28–29 blessing is emphasized more concretely in the author(s) declaration that humankind has been made "in the likeness of God" (Gen 5:1b). Possibly the most ambiguous terms in Genesis 1–11—the "image" (*tselem*) and "likeness" (*dĕmut*) of God—have been interpreted in numerous ways throughout recent centuries. Thus as God stated, "Let us make humankind in our image, according to our likeness" (1:27 NRSV), a variety of definitions have been proposed. Although some scholars have attempted to distinguish the terms "image" and "likeness,"[28] it is more likely that they were commonly used interchangeably by the original Hebrew author(s).

TABLE 3
GENESIS 1:27–29; 5:1B–2[29]

Humankind	Genesis 1:27–29	5:1b–2
Created	"So God *created* humankind in his image, in the image of God he *created* them; male and female he *created* them" (27).	"When God *created* humankind, he made them in the likeness of God. Male and female he *created* them . . ." (1b–2a).
Blessed	"God *blessed* them and God said to them . . ." (28a).	". . . and *blessed* them . . ." (2b).

26. Wenham, *Genesis*, 33.

27. Ibid.

28. Wenham, *Genesis*, 30.

29. NRSV; italics in this table are added.

Named		"... and *named* them 'Humankind' when they were *created*" (2c).
Fruitfulness	"Be *fruitful* and *multiply* and *fill the earth ...*" (28b).	
Dominion over animals	"... and *subdue it*; and *have dominion over* the fish of the sea and over the birds of the air and over every living thing that moves upon the earth" (28c).	
Resources	"God said, "See, I have given you every plant yielding seed that is upon the face of all the earth and every tree with seed in its fruit; you shall have them for *food*. And to every beast of the earth and to every bird of the air and to everything that creeps on the earth, everything that has the breath of life, I have given every green plant for *food*" (29).	

Wenham presents some of the more established explanations of the terms: (1) image refers to "the mental and spiritual faculties that man shares with his creator"; (2) image refers to "a physical resemblance"; (3) being made in the image of God places man as God's "representative on earth"; and finally, (4) being in God's image enables man to relate to God.[30] Although it is impossible to determine without doubt which definition is most accurate, the continued theme of relationship with God is notably present or implied within each option. It is the God-human relationship and the distinction of God making humankind into "God's image" that separates humankind from the rest of creation.

The naming of humankind by God (Gen 5:2c) additionally expresses another element of the Creator's relationship with human beings. When God spoke forth creation and blessings, God's action of naming humankind imparted a sense of divine destiny and distinctiveness. Although God's naming of human beings does also indicate God's sovereignty, it likewise "gives identity and an assurance of definitive existence."[31] In ancient thought, names were not merely coincidental but were "an obvious expression of the thing itself: things [were] called what they [were]."[32] In the case of human beings, God, through the uttering of their names in

30. Wenham, *Genesis*, 29–30.

31. Goldingay, *Old Testament Theology*, 55.

32. Gunkel, *Genesis*, 108.

fact imparted upon them their identity and determined their relationship with one another, with all of creation, and with himself.

As God named humankind, who was under his authority, so man named the creatures under his authority.[33] As Genesis 2:19 records, God himself "brought [every animal of the field and every bird of the air] to the man to see what he would call them." It is consistent in the narrative text, as Umberto Cassuto argues, that the naming of the animals is indicative of man's authority over them.[34]

TABLE 4
GENESIS 9:1–7[35]

Noah/Sons	Genesis 9:1–7
Blessed	"God *blessed* Noah and his sons and said to them . . ." (1a).
Fruitfulness	"Be *fruitful* and *multiply* and *fill the earth*" (1b). "And you, be *fruitful* and *multiply, abound on the earth* and *multiply in it*" (7).
Dominion over animals	"The fear and dread of you shall rest on every animal of the earth and on every bird of the air, on everything that creeps on the ground and on all the fish of the sea; *into your hand they are delivered*" (2).
Resources	"Every moving thing that lives shall be *food* for you; and just as I gave you the green plants, I give you everything" (3).
Curse	"Only, you shall not eat flesh with its life, that is, its blood. For your own lifeblood I will surely require a reckoning: from every animal I will require it and from human beings, each one for the blood of another, I will require a reckoning for human life. Whoever sheds the blood of a human, by a human shall that person's blood be shed; for in his own image God *made* humankind" (4–6).

Blessing of Noah and Family

The blessing of Noah and his sons comes climactically after the destruction of the entire earth through the flood. The question of whether or not the blessing of God upon humankind can be undone was answered in the reinstatement of God's blessing after the flood through the person and family of Noah. In such, the blessing of God upon Noah (Gen 9:1–7) mirrored the previous divine blessings upon humankind as God blessed Noah and his sons with (1) fruitfulness (vv. 1b, 7), (2) dominion (v. 1),

33. Cassuto, *Commentary* 1, 92.

34. Ibid.

35. NRSV; italics in this table are added.

and (3) resources (v. 2). The reinstatement of the same blessings given to humankind in Genesis 1:27–29 emphasizes God's obvious desire after the flood to reestablish his relationship of blessing with humankind once again.[36]

A major difference, however, between the original blessing of God upon humankind (Gen 1:27–29; 5:1–2) and that given to Noah and his sons (9:1–7) was God's pronouncement that God was entering into a covenant relationship with Noah and his descendents. God's declarations that he "will establish [his] covenant with [Noah]" (6:18) and later that "I am establishing my covenant with you" (9:11) stand out as the first mention of what later is going to become (in Gen 12–50) a major theme in Israel's history. It is interesting to note that God's action of establishing a covenant with Noah, his sons, and every creature on earth (9:8–17) was preceded by God's blessing on Noah and his sons to "be fruitful and multiply and fill the earth (9:1, 7). This sequence of events suggests that divine blessing was not restricted to a covenant relationship with God. If anything, this literary order implies that the covenantal relationship that ensued between creation and God was in fact a part of the overall blessing of God. Although the blessing of God upon humankind (1:27–29; 5:1–2) and creation (1:21–22) already implied a relationship with the creator, the establishment of the covenant now cemented this union.

It is important at this moment to pause to explain the nuances of the covenant treaty and its consequential impact upon the Creator-humankind relationship. In ancient times, the act of "cutting" a covenant (*bĕrit*) initiated the establishment of a legal and binding treaty between two individuals or parties (god/man; man/man; man/group; group/group). Unlike the covenants of marriage of our contemporary age which can so easily be broken, the ancient covenant was considered permanent and practically unbreakable unless one party desired to receive the curses pronounced for breaking the covenant treaty. Covenants were additionally deemed viable through the partaking of covenant rituals. Some of the rituals that are recorded within the Old Testament include:

1. A holy meal	Gen 31:54; Exod 24:9–11
2. Circumcision (as a sign of the covenant)	Gen 17:10–11
3. Sprinkling of blood and salt	Exod 24:3–8
4. Exchange of clothes and belongings	1 Sam 18:1–4

36. Goldingay, *Old Testament Theology*, 179.

5. Cutting of animals	Gen 15:8–21; Jer 34:18
6. Verbal oaths	Gen 26:26–31
7. Blessing and curses	Gen 12:2–3

Through the participation of both parties in these covenant rituals, the covenant was officially established and the consequences of breaking the covenant were formally put into place.

In light of the nuances of the covenant treaty, the covenant initiated by God in Genesis 9 requires a second look. Unlike some of the later covenants between God and man (Gen 17:10–11), the covenant of Genesis 9:7–17 stands out as entirely one-sided in both its initiation and responsibilities.[37] Goldingay observes:

> Here at the beginning the commitment is wholly God's. God "establishes" it without human cooperation . . . God simply "gives" the covenant (Gen. 9:12; cf. Gen. 17:2). Noah and the other recipients of God's pledge contribute absolutely nothing to the covenant relationship. They do not even have to believe in it. It will still be a reality. Out of God's own being comes the one-sided pledge that there will be no more world-denying catastrophes. It is a covenant that will stand forever (Gen. 9:16).[38]

It is this one-sidedness within the covenant that further displays the persistent desire of God to preserve humanity despite its evident shortcomings. Westermann relates that

> the unconditional approval that God gives to his creation is the basis of the history of nature and of humanity. It is the basis of all life which can be shaken neither by natural catastrophes of any sort . . . nor by the transgressions, corruption or revolt of human beings. God's assurance remains firm "as long as the earth lasts."[39]

In the covenant between God and Noah there was a foreshadowing of the relationship between God and humankind to come. This foreshadowing of a future divine-human relationship is not only a reference to the patriarchal histories of chapters 12–50 but it is also an indication of the reconciliation of God and the world that will come through Christ. Within these passages God proved without a doubt that the preservation

37. Goldingay, *Old Testament Theology*, 182.

38. Ibid.

39. Westermann, *Genesis 1–11*, 473.

of the world was of great value to him and that regardless of the sins of his creation he would always attempt to reestablish his relationship with them.

As God initiated this covenant relationship, he made particular binding promises not only to Noah and his descendants, but also to every animal that came out of the ark. God stated: "I establish my covenant with you, that never again shall all flesh be cut off by the waters of a flood and that never again shall there be a flood to destroy the earth" (Gen 9:11 NRSV). God then declared the "sign of the covenant" (9:12), or the eternal proof of the establishment of this covenant, as being the "bow in the clouds" (9:13) which God would in turn see and thus remember his covenant (9:14–15). Through establishing this covenant with Noah, his offspring, and all the animals, God promised to preserve all of creation regardless of future actions of disobedience or neglect. Ross notes that God would "definitely judge sin, but he would also make a covenant of peace with the survivors" and as such his "covenant of peace would reign over the new era."[40] It is this "covenant of peace" that was now marked permanently in creation through the "sign of the covenant."

This "sign of the covenant" as created by God symbolized not only the establishment of the covenant but also the peaceful laying down of arms of God. Von Rad notes in his commentary on Genesis that the Hebrew term used in verse 13 for "bow" (*qesheth*) is actually the same term used for "bow of war."[41] Goldingay elaborates on this image of a warrior's bow and explains how the "bow" being unsheathed represents God's laying down of arms in regards to creation.[42] This powerful allusion to the warrior King undercuts any interpretation of the [rain]bow as simply being a "bright and comforting reminder that the race shall endure."[43] Instead it served to majestically counteract the very real devastation of creation with an equally powerful symbol of a warrior establishing peace after war. Once again, the wrongdoing and reprimand of humankind as expressed in Genesis 6–9 was counterbalanced by the gracious forgiveness of God.

40. Ross, *Creation and Blessing*, 207.

41. Von Rad, *Genesis*, 130.

42. Goldingay, *Old Testament Theology*, 182.

43. Speiser, "Genesis," 59.

The Flood and the Tower of Babel

Although the Genesis narrative does not present the flood[44] or the scattering of nations as a "curse," there is an unmistakable parallel between the expulsion of Adam and Eve (Gen 3:24), the flood (7:11–24), and later the Tower of Babel (11:8–9). Led by Westermann, various scholars have embraced the idea of a crime/punishment motif in order to explain the ensuing pattern of blessing and punishment in Genesis 1–11.[45] This ever-increasing crime and punishment pattern reached its climax with the story of the Tower of Babel (11:8–9). Repeatedly throughout the previous narratives, after the crimes of individuals and humanity, God restored life once again, first through the birth of Cain and Abel (4:1–2) and then with the preservation of Noah and his family (8–9). Thus, the arrogance of humankind, once more displayed through the building of the Tower of Babel, forces the reader to ask: What now? How can God redeem humanity yet again from another tragic proof of its sinfulness and disregard of God?

However, despite the overall negative portrayal of the Babel story, the narrative's actual placement in the Genesis text also suggests a positive fulfillment of God's blessing in its events. Sandwiched between the Table of the Nations in chapter 10 and the genealogy of Shem (Gen 11:10–32), Clines suggests that the Babel story is not only a judgment upon humankind but it is also a fulfillment of God's original blessing of fruitfulness. Clines explains:

> If the material of ch. 10 had followed the Babel story the whole Table of Nations would have to be read under the sign of the judgment; [however] where it stands it functions as the fulfillment of the divine command of 9:1, "Be fruitful and multiply and fill the earth" which looks back in its turn to 1:28.[46]

Clines continues that the conjointly positive chapter 10 and negative chapter 11 outcomes of the "dispersal of the nations"[47] affects the future of humankind after Babel. Clines states that "since Babel, mankind stands under both the blessing and the curse of God; the division of the peoples and their languages is both a token of the divine judgment and . . . of man's fulfillment of the divine command and so part of the divine

44. Rendtorff, "Genesis 8 21," 70.

45. Westermann, *Promises*, 55.

46. Clines, *Theme*, 68.

47. Ibid.

'blessing' (Gen. 9:1)."[48] Although this two dimensional view of the scattering of all peoples does have scriptural support, it is important to note that the credit of this positive fulfillment of the blessing should not go to humankind. Instead, it is simply once again an example of God's "secret increasing power of grace" upon human beings.[49] It is thus God, and not humanity, who brought the fulfillment of the blessing of fruitfulness through an otherwise tragic event.[50]

Perhaps the most significant impact of the Babel story was its preparatory nature for the Abrahamic narrative to come. A "final parable of human sin and God's response,"[51] the Babel narrative moves the reader from the universal to the particular. Bengt Sundkler explains that

> the catastrophe of Babel's tower marks the end of the first chapter in the history of mankind. Its original universal purpose and its cosmopolitan scope became drastically reduced. The perspective of salvation became foreshortened and narrowed into a way of substitution. The blessing had to be concentrated upon one people—a people chosen by God for His very own.[52]

Although there is no explanation for God's change of focus from all the nations to one individual (Abraham), it is clear that God deemed the switch necessary to preserve his covenantal relationship and blessing with mankind. The "hopeless flight of mankind [as seen] without the intervention of God"[53] at the end of Genesis 11:9 prepared the way climactically for the new chapter of God's blessing upon and through the patriarchs.

GENESIS 12:1–3 ABRAHAMIC BLESSING

With the beginning of chapter 12, the Genesis text makes a dramatic turn from the primeval history of chapters 1–11 to the patriarchal world of chapters 12–50. In addition, the universal focus of the first section

48. Ibid., 68–69.

49. Von Rad, *Genesis*, 23.

50. This union of negative and positive outcomes is also evident in the coupling of the expulsion of Adam and Eve (Gen 3:24) and the immediate blessing of life upon them through the birth of Cain and Abel (4:1–2). The flood narrative (7:11–24) is also coupled with the salvation of Noah and his family and new life upon the earth (8–9).

51. Whybray, *Introduction*, 35.

52. Sundkler, *World*, 13–14.

53. Wenham, *Genesis*, ii.

is suddenly interrupted by the introduction of an unknown individual from the line of Shem: Abraham, son of Terah. The narrative that ensues introduces the reader to the new idea of God's blessing given to one person, one family, and one people group. To explore this universal blessing through Abraham, in the following section I discuss the person and choosing of Abraham in addition to the nuances of the Genesis 12:1–3 promise.

Person of Abraham

The introduction to the person of Abraham in Genesis 11:26 and following stands out for its absence of specific details about Abraham. The reader of Genesis 11–12 is given only a basic summary of Abraham's history to consider; the audience is informed that Abraham was from the line of Shem, son of Noah (Gen 11:10); was the son of Terah (11:26); the brother of Nahor and Haran (11:26); was the husband of Sarah,[54] who was barren (11:28–30); and was originally from Ur of the Chaldeans, but was now living in Hārān (11:31). Additional information is given regarding Abraham's relatives: Abraham's brother Haran had a son, Lot (11:31); Haran died in Ur (11:28); and Terah died in Hārān (11:32); and Lot accompanied his grandfather to Hārān (11:31). But, the information given remains general and distant.

Despite the lack of details in Genesis regarding Abraham's past, biblical scholars have used archeological evidence and ancient literary archives to surmise most of what we know about Abraham. Originally said to be from a group of nomadic tribes called the "Apiru," Abraham appears to have been a member of a group of traveling merchants who moved throughout Babylonia during the late third and early second millennium BC.[55] Although some scholars point to the term "Hebrew," which later was connected with Abraham and his descendants[56] as generating from the clan name "Apiru,"[57] it was most likely not a "national designation, but rather a frequent designation . . . for a lower class of society."[58] Von

54. For reasons of consistency the use of Sarai's name "Sarah" will be used throughout this book to refer to Abraham's wife both before and after her name change in Gen 17:15.

55. Albright, "From the Patriarchs," 7–15.

56. Gen 14:13; 39:14, 17; 40:15; 41:12; 43:32.

57. Albright, "From the Patriarchs," 7–15.

58. Von Rad, *Genesis*, 174.

Rad explains that in "the Old Testament the expression is used by non-Israelites or Israelites for foreigners."[59] Thus, Abraham entered into the narratives of Genesis as a nomadic foreigner following God into the land of Canaan.

Although there is no indication in the Genesis 11:26–32 text as to Abraham's religious history, there are later scriptural hints that indicate he had an idolatrous past. Joshua 24:2–3 is probably the most straightforward in its interpretation of Abraham's history: "Long ago your forefathers, including Terah the father of Abraham and Nahor, lived beyond the River and worshipped other gods. But I took your father Abraham from the land beyond the River and led him throughout Canaan." This mention of Abraham "worship[ing] other gods" is further enforced by Abraham's continued use of some of the common religious forms of surrounding religions although he now followed Yahweh. David Burnett writes:

> The conversion of Abram from his traditional religion to that of worshipping Yahweh did not mean a distinct break with his culture. In the majority of his ways Abram still lived according to the customs of his people. He set up shrines in a similar way to those erected by the people of Canaan. He established "sacred places" at Shechem (Gen. 12:6), Bethel (Gen. 12:8), Hebron (Gen. 13:18) and Beersheba (Gen. 21:33).[60]

Despite this adherence to the religious forms of his time, Abraham made a clean break from his idolatrous past upon deciding to obey God in Genesis 12:4–9. The covenant relationship of Genesis 12:1–3 appears to dissolve any previous religious affiliations as worshiping idols was no longer mentioned in connection with Abraham in the biblical text.

Choosing of Abraham

Although Abraham was chosen by God in Genesis 11:26 and following, the text gives no indication as to why God would single out Abraham from all the peoples of the world. For a person who later rose to religious acclaim within the Jewish community, it is curious that no redeeming characteristic is mentioned, that no note of special talents is recorded, and particularly that no indication of Abraham's previous relationship with God is told. A clear contrast to this literary silence can be seen in

59. Ibid.

60. Burnett, *God's Mission*, 57.

God's choosing of Noah in Genesis 6:8–9. In this narrative, the author(s) notably describe Noah as finding "favor in the eyes of the Lord" (Gen 6:8). Noah is moreover described as "walk[ing] with God" of being "a righteous man, blameless in his generation" (6:9 NRSV). Thus, while there is still no indication as to whether these qualities determined Noah's election, there exists imbedded in the narrative a possible rationale for God's choice. This additional commentary, however, is not evident in the Abrahamic narrative. Abraham, unlike Noah, is simply presented as a man without distinction or mark. It is thus that Abraham begins his entrance into literary fame as an unknown with no recorded personal achievements, no remarkable character traits, and no glorious religious past.

Nevertheless, despite the lack of information in Genesis as to why the person of Abraham was chosen, there is little doubt as to what he was chosen for. In direct contrast with the scattering of the nations in Genesis 11:1–9, Genesis 11:26–32 ushers in a new era in which one single family is chosen to be a blessing to "all the families of the earth."[61] Johannes Verkuyl explains that in God's subsequent choosing of Abraham and later Israel, God by no means losses sight of the nations. Instead, the "people of Abraham," although separated from the nations for a time, enable God to "achiev[e] his world-embracing goals. In choosing Israel as segment of all humanity, God never took his eye off the other nations; Israel was the *pars pro toto*, a minority called to serve the majority."[62] It is for the purpose of blessing and preserving the nations that God chose Abraham and his descendants; not to bless a specific individual or nation but to bless all the nations of the world. Abraham was thus set apart "not only to be an example of blessing, but [to be] a channel, means and cause of blessing."[63]

Genesis 12:1–3

The divine call of Abraham as recorded in Genesis 12:1–3, departs from the pattern of blessing displayed in the primeval history of chapters

61. Kidner, *Genesis*, 13.

62. Verkuyl, *Contemporary Missiology*, 91–92.

63. Van Engen, *Growth*, 142. Also see Blauw, *Missionary Nature*, 19; Calvin, *Genesis*; De Ridder, *Discipling*, 26, 32, 153; Driver, *Book of Genesis*, 145; Glasser and McGavran, *Contemporary Theologies*; Peters, *Biblical Theology*, 89; Von Rad, *Genesis*, 155–56.

1–11. Although the blessing of fruitfulness[64] and blessing in general[65] are picked up again in later chapters, 12:1–3 stands in marked contrast to the blessings that went before. Not only did God command Abraham to follow him (v. 1), but for the first time there was the promise of nationhood (v. 2a), blessing (vv. 2b–3b) and blessing the nations (v. 12:3c). I explore every section individually as each of these blessings/promises is repeated throughout the Genesis text.

TABLE 5
GENESIS 12:1–3[66]

Recipient	God's Command /Commentary	Land/Nation	Blessing	Blessing to Nations
Abraham 12:1–3	"Now the Lord said to Abram, "Go from your country and your kindred and your father's house to the land that I will show you" (12:1).	"I will make of you a great nation . . ." (2a).	"and I will bless you, and make your name great, so that you will be a blessing. I will bless those who bless you, and the one who curses you I will curse" (2b–3b).	". . . and in you all the families of the earth shall be blessed" (3c).

Abraham's Call

The first facet of the Genesis 12:1–3 text is Abraham's call by God to "go from your country and your kindred and your father's house to the land that I will show you" (Gen 12:1). Just as the introductory sentence of the primeval history begins with God—"In the beginning when God created the heavens and the earth . . ." (1:1 NRSV)—so the beginning of patriarchal history also begins with God. The opening sentence of Genesis 12:1, "Now the LORD said to Abram . . ." (12:1a NRSV), indicates that God is both the instigator and first subject of these events "and thus the subject of the entire subsequent sacred history."[67] Von Rad writes:

64. See Gen 13:16; 15:4b–5; 16:10b; 17:2b, 4b, 5b–6, 16b, 16d, 19a, 20b; 18:18a; 22:17b–c; 24:60b; 26:4a, 24c; 28:3b, 14a; 35:11; 46:3; 47:27b; 48:16b; 49:22.

65. See Gen 14:19–20a; 17:16a, 16c, 20a; 22:17a; 24:1b, 34a, 60a; 25:11a; 26:3a, 12–13, 24b; 28:3a, 4a; 32:29b; 35:9b; 48:15–16a; 49:23–26.

66. NRSV.

67. Von Rad, *Genesis*, 154.

> God is everywhere the real narrative subject, so to speak, of the saga—or, rather, its inner subject; men are never important for their own sakes, but always as objects of the divine activity, as those who both affirm and deny God and his command.[68]

It is therefore within the opening passages of the patriarchal history that the reader once again hears the voice of God and is reminded of God's undeniable sovereignty and influence upon the present and future of his creation.

In addition, as with God's call to Noah (Gen 7:1), Abraham is called into action. In an increasingly narrowing circle of belonging, God called Abraham to leave his (1) homeland, (2) kindred, and (3) father's household (12:1). Von Rad explains that Abraham was called to "radically [abandon] all natural roots," systematically dismissing his general connection with the "land," his clan, his distance relatives, until finally his own immediate family is highlighted.[69] The author suggests, however, that the ever narrowing of terms as expressed in the text demonstrates "that God knows the difficulties of these separations."[70] Gunkel expands upon this understanding of separation and suggests that God's command to Abraham was indeed "the most difficult test of faith." Gunkel notes that "the ancient lives at home in the secure protection of large and small units . . . Abroad, he is free as a bird. Expulsion is like death."[71] The author surmises that God's call to Abraham was not simply a command but instead was God's first test requiring monumental obedience.

A sheer departure from this understanding of great faith can be seen in Westermann's analysis of the Genesis 12:1 command. Westermann argues that from the perspective of nomadic Abraham and his contemporaries, God's call would be seen "as the offer of a saving hand," not as a devastating tearing away from family and land.[72] The first audience, he continues, would see the situation as "the instruction of the God of the fathers in a crisis situation, ordering the group to set out for another territory."[73] They would understand, he comments further, that "it was aimed solely at rescuing the group from or preserving it in the

68. Ibid., 35.

69. Ibid., 154.

70. Ibid.

71. Gunkel, *Genesis*, 163.

72. Westermann, *Genesis 12–36*, 148.

73. Ibid.

crisis."[74] Westermann holds that the interpretation that Abraham found it painful to leave his homeland and family was introduced later by the author of the Jehovistic history book (J)[75] during an age when Israel had a homeland and sedentary lifestyle. The patriarchs themselves, Westermann argues, would not have had this sedentary perspective of the later redactors. Although there is potential truth within the author's argument, the Genesis text itself appears to provide little support for this theory. Although Westermann would argue that the text was fashioned by J and thus couldn't support an alternate explanation, the absence of a "crisis situation" before Abraham's call also seems to bring doubt upon the argument. Nevertheless, whether or not Abraham found God's calling to be his salvation or a troubling separation, Abraham's act of faith cannot be denied as he obeyed God's call "to the land that [God] will show [him]" (Gen 12:1).

The faith that Abraham exhibited in following God to a land yet untold foreshadows the great faith that continued to intermittently surface throughout his lifetime. In the context of the Genesis 12 narrative, R. W. L. Moberly notes that Abraham's obedience to God immediately extends into worship as the "first two things he does in the land of Canaan are to build altars to YHWH, thus indicating his responsive reverence to God's leading (12:7–8)." The author also notes that "the second time [Abram] builds an altar, it is also said that he 'called on the name of YHWH,' that is, he prayed."[76] Although the intermediary actions of Abraham and his family are unknown, the narrator structured the text in such a way as to point to the immediate obedience of Abraham, and Abraham's continued worship of and prayer to God. The structure of the opening passages of Genesis 12 presents Abraham as a man of great obedience, humility, and faith before God.

Promise of Nationhood

The second element of the Genesis 12:1–3 passage is God's declaration to Abraham that he will "make of [him] a great nation" (v. 2a NRSV). This

74. Ibid.

75. Westermann is referencing the theory first presented by Julius Wellhausen (*Prolegomena*, 6–9) that the Pentateuch was in fact a composite of four distinct sources: the Jehovistic history book (J), the Elohistic document (E), the Priestly Code (P), and Deuteronomy (D); all differentiated by their diverse authorship and date of composition.

76. Moberly, *Genesis*, 22–23.

promise of nationhood is repeated throughout the Genesis 12–50 narratives and is continued in the sequential book of Exodus. It is this early mention of the future nation of Israel which has historically identified Abraham as a type for Israel. Moberly notes that "although Abraham is an individual figure, he is also often a representative or embodiment of Israel as a people."[77] It is this representation of Israel through the character of Abraham that gives the Abrahamic narratives multiple levels of significance. For example, as Abraham is described as following God's call to the promised land (12:1) so the nation of Israel is also "being led on a special road whose plan and goal lay completely in Yahweh's hand."[78] The mention of the future nation of Israel within the Genesis text indicates that the original author(s) probably did not restrict their narratives to past events but instead included allusions to the continuing identity of the nation of Israel.[79] It is therefore this double identity of Abraham that gives greater importance to the narrative text as it served as a constant reminder to the Hebrew audience of what God had done and what God was doing at the time.

The particular promise of God to Abraham that he would make him a "great nation" (Gen 12:2) pledges a "blessing of abundant offspring in wondrous measure."[80] As Abraham's wife Sarah was still barren (11:30), this promise of nationhood would have indeed been a divine blessing. Wenham denotes the meaning of the term "nation" (*goy*) as used in Genesis 12:2. He states that

> a "nation" is a political unit with a common land, language and government . . . A large population, a large territory and a spiritual character make a nation great . . . Thus this very first word to Abram encapsulates the full range of divine promises subsequently made to him.[81]

God's promise to Abraham that he would "make of [him] a great nation" (12:2 NRSV) had personal significance for Abraham in providing a child in his old age as well as national significance for the future nation of Israel and its "greatness."

77. Moberly, *Genesis*, 22.

78. Von Rad, *Genesis*, 154.

79. Ibid.

80. Cassuto, *Commentary*, 313.

81. Wenham, *Genesis*, 275.

God's command to Abraham to follow God to the land (*erets*) God would show him (Gen 12:1) and God's promise of nationhood (*goy*) (12:2) are closely linked to the later patriarchal promises of God to Abraham (12:7; 13:14–16, 17–18; 15:7–8, 17–21; 17:8), Isaac (26:2–5; 28:4), and Jacob (28:12–14; 35:12, 14).

God's promise to give the land (Canaan) to Abraham and his descendants, however, was not fulfilled during their lifetimes but was an enduring promise that continued throughout Israel's history until it reached fulfillment in the book of Joshua. The only land that Abraham indeed owned at the end of his lifetime was a Hittite field and cave facing Mamre (Hebron) where he buried his wife Sarah upon her death (Gen 23). Furthermore, the book of Genesis ends with the placement of the family of Israel in yet another foreign land, Egypt (45–50). Yet even in the closing chapters of Genesis the echoes of God's original promise to the patriarchs is recorded as Jacob remembers God's covenant to him in the land of Canaan: "I am going to make you fruitful and increase your numbers; I will make of you a company of peoples, and will give this land to your offspring after you for a perpetual holding" (48:4 NRSV).

TABLE 6
PROMISE OF LAND IN GENESIS[82]

Recipient	Land/Nation
Abraham 12:1–4	"I will make of you a great nation . . ." (2a).
12:7	"To your offspring I will give this land" (7b).
13:14–16	"for all the land that you see I will give to you and to your offspring forever" (15).
13:17–18	". . . for I will give it to you" (17b).
15:7–8	". . . to give you this land to possess" (7b).
15:17–21	"To your descendants I give this land, from the river of Egypt to the great river, the river Euphrates, the land of the Kenites, the Kenizzites, the Kadmonites, the Hittites, the Perizzites, the Rephaim, the Amorites, the Canaanites, the Girgashites and the Jebusites" (18b–21).
17:8	"And I will give to you, and to your offspring after you, the land where you are now an alien, all the land of Canaan, for a perpetual holding; and I will be their God" (8).

82. Scriptures quoted in this table are from the NRSV.

Isaac 26:2–3a	"The Lord appeared to Isaac and said, "Do not go down to Egypt; settle in the land that I shall show you" (2).
26:3b–4a	". . . for to you and to your descendants I will give all these lands . . ." (3b).
26:4b–5	". . . and will give to your offspring all these lands . . ." (4b).
28:4b	". . . so that you may take possession of the land where you now live as an alien—land that God gave to Abraham" (4b).
Jacob 28:12–14	". . . the land on which you lie I will give to you and to your offspring" (13b).
35:12, 14	"The land that I gave to Abraham and Isaac I will give to you, and I will give the land to your offspring after you" (12).

BLESSING OF ABRAHAM

The promises of God in Genesis 12:1–3 to Abraham are expressed as subordinate to and incorporated in the overarching blessing of God. The repetition of the blessing motif through the fourfold promises of "nationhood, a great name, divine protection and mediatorship of divine blessing"[83] suggests that the promises are in fact a part of the wider blessing of God upon Abraham. W. Zimmerli identifies the primary theme in Genesis 12:1–3 as blessing not promise. He writes that "[Genesis 12:1–3] indeed sounds the note of land and posterity as elements of promise, but it clearly places them in the shadow of the pledge of blessing (unmistakable in the fivefold use of the root *brk*)."[84] Consistent with God's blessing of creation (Gen 1:21–22), humanity (1:27–29; 5:1b–2) and Noah and his family (9:1–7), God's blessing was the overarching action of God that included his promises of fruitfulness and prosperity.

The term "blessing" (*brk*) within this context, as in Genesis 1–11, refers "to God's characteristically generous and abundant giving of all good to his creatures and his continual renewal of the abundance of created life."[85] But, blessing in the context of God's blessing upon humankind is not to be simply known as a vehicle of abundant provision, it is, more importantly, a relational agreement. To "be blessed by God is not only to know God's good gifts but to know God himself in his generous

83. Wenham, *Genesis*, 274.

84. Zimmerli, "Promise," 92.

85. Bauckham, *Bible and Mission*, 34–35.

giving."[86] Those who receive the abundant provision of God also gain a deeper knowledge of God in the process. In addition, those blessed also enter into an ongoing relationship with their benefactor. As Westermann notes, "Blessing is realized in the succession of generations."[87] In such, the blessings of God poured upon his people guaranteed them that God's continual presence and help would be with them throughout the generations. The blessing of God upon Abraham in Genesis 12:1–3 not only opened Abraham's eyes to God, but marked the beginning of his relationship with the Creator.

Of the particular promises of God incorporated into the Genesis 12:1–3 blessing, God's promise to Abraham to "make [his] name great" (v. 2b) clearly points to the wider purpose of God's selection of Abraham. J. Gerald Janzen notes the direct parallel between the Babel story of Genesis 11:1–9 and God's promises to make Abraham's name great (12:2b) and to make him a great nation (12:2a). He highlights that the desire of the people of Babel for a "name" (11:4) mirrors the promise that Abraham will receive a "name" and "that 'great' (Heb *gdl*) echoes the tower (*mgdl*, literally 'great structure') in 11:4, 5."[88] Janzen also explains that

> there is a vivid contrast between God's opposition to human attempts to make a name for themselves and God's intention to give Abram a great name. This contrast matches the contrast between fearful human attempts to safeguard their unity in one place by building a walled city, "lest we be scattered abroad upon the face of the whole earth" (erets), and Abram's willingness to follow God's call to leave his own place and people and go to a land (erets) he does not yet see. The separation from familiar place and faces, which the people in 11:4 see as filled with danger, is a separation that to Abram is filled with promise.[89]

In addition to the literary parallels between the two passages there is also a theological significance in their alignment. More than God simply giving men the greatness they once desired,[90] the Abrahamic blessing of Genesis 12:1–3 "is designed to contend with and to overcome its opposite: God's curse."[91] More specifically, the universal curse given during the

86. Bauckham, *Bible and Mission*, 35.

87. Westermann, *Blessing in the Bible*, 30.

88. Janzen, *Abraham*, 15.

89. Ibid., 15–16.

90. Von Rad, *Genesis*, 155.

91. Bauckham, *Bible and Mission*, 34–35.

Babel story—"the Lord scattered them over the face of the whole earth" (Gen 11:9)—is followed by and counteracted by the blessing of God upon Abraham: "and in you all the families of the earth shall be blessed" (12:3c NRSV).[92] The blessing of Abraham then must be seen in the light of its universal significance. As discussed previously, God's choosing of Abraham did not display his particularistic preferences but instead marked his universal desire to bless all the nations of the world through Abraham.[93]

Another important characteristic of the blessing of Genesis 12:1–3 is its foreshadowing of the covenant relationship between God and Abraham. Although Genesis 15 is often marked as the first reference to this covenantal relationship, there are elements within the Genesis 12:1–3 passage that suggest the establishment of a preliminary covenant between God and Abraham. First, God's command to Abraham to leave his land, clan, and family and follow God (Gen 12:1) suggests transference of loyalty and allegiance from Abraham's family to God. If not an official transfer of commitment, Abraham is asked to join an exclusive relationship between the divine Creator requiring obedience from him and offering divine protection in return, "I will bless those who bless you, and the one who curses you I will curse" (12:3a–b NRSV).

In addition this particular phrase, "I will bless those who bless you, and the one who curses you I will curse" (Gen 12:3a–b NRSV), refers to the fact that "Yahweh thus stands on the side of his people and protects them while intervening against their enemies."[94] The phrase is repeated with slight variation in Genesis 27:29 when Isaac blesses Jacob ("Cursed be everyone who curses you, and blessed be everyone who blesses you!")[95] and Numbers 24:9 when the spirit of God comes upon Balaam and Balaam blesses Israel: "Blessed is everyone who blesses you, and cursed is everyone who curses you." In all three cases, the divine and supernatural protection of God is included as a vital component within the blessings of Abraham (Gen 12:1–3), Jacob (27:29), and Israel (Num 24:9). The presence of blessings and curses is also a common element within the covenant ritual of later chapters.[96] Therefore, although Genesis 12:1–3 does not use the term "covenant" (*berit*), the implications of the

92. Also see Wright, *Mission of God*, 202–3; Rendtorff, *Old Testament*, 134.

93. Also see Alexander, "Abraham," 13.

94. Westermann, *Genesis 12–36*, 150.

95. NRSV.

96. Van Engen, *Growth*, 123.

text itself present an echo of the covenantal relationship to come as God is described as Abraham's benefactor, source of blessing, and protector.

Blessing of the Nations

One of the unique elements within the Genesis 12:1–3 blessing is God's inclusion that he would make Abraham's name great "so that you [Abram] will be a blessing" (v. 2c NRSV). Christopher Wright argues that the literary structure of verses 1–3 identifies two imperatives of God to Abraham: "Go" (v. 1) and "be a blessing" (v. 2c):

> And YHWH said to Abram,
>
> *Get yourself up and go*[97]
>
> From the land, and from your kindred, and from your father's house, to the land that I will show you.
>
> And I will make you into a great nation;
>
> and I will bless you;
>
> and I will make your name great.
>
> *And be a blessing.*
>
> And I will bless those who bless you;
>
> whereas the one who belittles you, I will curse;
>
> and in you will be blessed all kinship groups on the earth.
>
> And Abram went just as YHWH said to him.[98]

As highlighted by Wright, the Hebrew version of "so that you will be a blessing" (Gen 12:2c) contains an imperative, and, as many scholars are now suggesting, can be translated "Be a blessing!" (12:2c).[99] If this is the case, "Abram is not simply being informed that he will become a blessing, but is commanded to be a blessing."[100] Nevertheless, it is important to note that even with the divine command to "be a blessing" it is only God who had the power to enable Abraham to be a blessing to those around him.

This interpretation of the imperative of Genesis 12:2c implies a cause and effect relationship between the commands of God and the

97. Italics added.

98. Wright, *Mission*, 194.

99. Turner, *Genesis*, 64.

100. Ibid.

response of Abraham. Turner, an advocate for the contemporary imperative translation, explains that

> if the force of the imperative is retained then the following Hebrew clauses should be rendered as consequences of that imperative: "Be a blessing, so that I may bless those . . ." In other words, the promises of 12:3 depend upon Abram being a blessing. Just as clearly, the promises of 12:2a (great nation, blessing and great name), depend upon Abram obeying God's command in 12:1, "Go!"[101]

This concept of fulfillment through the obedience of Abraham, however, is not supported by all. While not denying the imperative form of the verse, Goldingay argues that "it would be misleading to emphasize that obedience to YHWH's charge is a precondition of receiving God's blessing."[102] The author continues that while trust is present within their relationship it is "clear that fulfilling God's charge is not a condition of the promise coming true."[103] Similarly, in the study of the imperative "Be a blessing" (Gen 12:2c), it is clear from the nature of the command that the power of fulfillment has to come from God himself and not Abraham. It is outside of Abraham's control whether or not he is a blessing on any level other than material to those around him; it is God who is responsible to bring blessing and prosperity through the person and offspring of Abraham.

The second reference to Abraham as a blessing to others comes in Genesis 12:3c: "and in you all the families of the earth shall be blessed" (NRSV). The English reference to "families of the earth" in verse 3 has been translated from the Hebrew term *mishpachah*. Although the term is sometimes translated "'families,' . . . that is too narrow in its common English meaning. *Mishpachah* is a wider kinship grouping. In Israelite tribal structure it was the clan, the subgroup within the tribe. It can sometimes imply whole peoples, considered as related by kinship (as in Amos 3:1–2)."[104] This wider meaning incorporated within the term "clan" indicates that "not every individual is promised blessing in Abram but

101. Ibid.

102. Goldingay, *Old Testament Theology*, 198. See also Westermann, *Blessing in the Bible*, 52–53.

103. Goldingay, *Old Testament Theology*, 198–99.

104. Wright, *Mission*, 200.

every major group in the world will be blessed."[105] This is evident within the previous specifications of God's blessing upon Abraham during his lifetime: "I will bless those who bless you, and the one who curses you I will curse" (Gen 12:3a–b NRSV). Although God did promise that Abraham will be the vehicle of blessing to the primary groups of the earth, those individuals who opposed Abraham and his descendants were not guaranteed the blessing of God.[106]

Within the Genesis 12:3 promise, no other section has been as dissected and discussed with such widely differing results as 12:3c. Various scholars have attempted to understand the relationship between Abraham and the nations in this verse and have thus translated the verb "to bless" (*brk*) in a variety of ways: as (1) a reflexive ("they will bless themselves"); (2) a receptive ("they will find blessing"); and as (3) a passive ("they will be blessed").[107] The three main translations advocated by scholars are thus as follows:

1. ". . . and that by you all the families of the earth may bless themselves."[108] Janzen bases his translation on the reflexive use of the verb and explains: "To bless oneself 'by' Abraham is to use Abraham's name when asking a blessing from God, as in saying 'O God, make us like Abram and his descendants.'"[109] Other scholars who support the reflexive translation of the verb include F. Delitzsch, A. Dillmann, H. Gunkel, H. Holzinger, G. Von Rad, J. Skinner, C. Westermann, and E. A Speiser.

2. ". . . through you all the families of the earth will find blessing."[110] In this case, the families of the earth are not presented as passive recipients or aggressive pursuers of blessing. Instead, they are portrayed as being in the "middle" as described by T. Desmond Alexander. This receptive translation of the Genesis 12:3c text is supported by Alexander, O. Procksch, C. A. Keller, J. Schreiner, H. W. Wolff, and Schmidt.

3. ". . . in you all the families of the earth will be blessed." This passive translation of the text emphasizes the future tense and implies that

105. Wenham, *Genesis*, 278.

106. Ibid.

107. Alexander, "Abraham," 13.

108. Janzen, *Abraham*, 15.

109. Ibid.

110. Alexander, "Abraham," 13.

the future families of the earth will be blessed through Abraham and/or his descendants. This interpretation finds support from scholars such as E. König, Jacob, A. Cassuto, and W. H. Gispen.

Nevertheless, it is important to note that despite the critical support given to each varying translation, neither option can be supported with unswerving certainty. Instead, the lack of data within the Genesis text itself preserves the uncertainty as to which translation of Genesis 12:3 is correct.

Although the correct interpretation of Genesis 12:3c cannot be proven, each of the proposed translations share one important factor in common: their universal focus. Regardless of whether or not the passive, receptive, or reflexive verb is used, each translation distinctly points to the fact that God's blessing upon Abraham was not meant for him alone. Westermann remarks that regardless of which version is used, Genesis 12:3 says that "God's action proclaimed in the promise to Abraham is not limited to him and his posterity, but reaches its goal only when it includes all the families of the earth."[111] Wright also notes that

> [Genesis 12:1–3] is the climax of God's promise to Abraham. It is also a pivotal text not only in the book of Genesis but indeed in the whole Bible. So important is it in Genesis that it occurs five times altogether, with minor variations of phraseology (Gen. 12:3; 18:18; 22:18; 26:4–5; 28:14). Clearly, therefore, it is not just an afterthought tacked on to the end of God's promise to Abraham but a key element of it. Blessing for the nations is the bottom line, textually and theologically, of God's promise to Abraham."[112]

It is within the Abrahamic blessing of Genesis 12:1–3 that God changes the entire future of human history. Placed directly after the tragic failings of humanity at Babel, the promise of God to Abraham—"in [Abram] all the families of the earth shall be blessed" (12:3c NRSV)—marks the beginning of God's salvation plan in which Abraham is to be the mediator of God's blessing.[113] Thus, as Wright originally highlighted, the promise of God that Abraham would bring blessing to the nations is not a side note added without thought, but is instead a foundational truth

111. Westermann, *Genesis 12–36*, 152.

112. Wright, *Mission*, 194.

113. Von Rad, *Genesis*, 156.

upon which God established his universal salvation plan which reached its greatest fulfillment through Christ.

This universal focus of Genesis 12:1–3 is often expressed in terms of universalism versus particularism. The term "universalism" in reference to the Old Testament means that the Scriptures have "the whole world in view" and have "validity for the whole world."[114] A particularistic perspective on the other hand, implies that within the Old Testament, Abraham and the people of Israel were the only ones in God's view and thus God cared for their well-being alone. However, as argued previously in regards to Genesis 12:1–3, although "particularistic in method" God's choosing of Abraham is "universalistic in promise, design and effect."[115] This truth, as George Peters enforces, "needs to be seen clearly and grasped firmly, or else the God of the Old Testament Himself becomes a particularist . . . [and as] a particularist He would cease to be Elohim the God of creation and the God of the nations."[116] Charles Van Engen affirms the universal purposes within the Old Testament:

> Yahweh's universal intention is a conviction which underlies all of the Church's missionary theology . . . The first and last word of any Old Testament theology of Israel must take into account that Israel very uniquely understood her God as the sovereign not only of Israel, but of all nations. All God's covenants are to be understood as assuming YHWH's lordship over all peoples.[117]

The calling of Abraham in Genesis 12:1–3 thus becomes a turning point within the greater narrative of Genesis; moving the reader from the universal focus of God in Genesis 1–11 to the universal focus of God in Genesis 12–50 as it is held within the narrative of a particular people group.

This understanding of the universal focus of Genesis 12:1–3 is confirmed in the New Testament as Paul related God's salvation plan foretold in Genesis to the Gentiles. In his letter to the Galatians, Paul stated:

> Just as Abraham "believed God, and it was reckoned to him as righteousness," so, you see, those who believe are the descendants of Abraham. And the Scripture, foreseeing that God would justify the Gentiles by faith, declared the gospel beforehand to

114. Blauw, *Missionary Nature*, 17.

115. Peters, *Biblical Theology*, 89.

116. Ibid.

117. Van Engen, *Growth*, 136.

> Abraham, saying, "All the Gentiles shall be blessed in you." For this reason, those who believe are blessed with Abraham who believed. (Gal 3:6–9 NRSV)

As Paul related to the Galatians, the Old Testament Scripture itself records God's desire for all peoples to be reconciled to him. The apostle noted that as believers in Christ, one becomes a part of the family of Abraham and thus becomes a recipient of the blessings of God given to Abraham and his descendants. It is evident from both Paul's interpretation of Genesis 12:3 and the Genesis text itself that "Abraham has an important role in God's redemptive plan for all mankind."[118] The introduction of Abraham did not signal the termination of God's concern for the nations but instead marked the beginning of God's sacred protection of his blessing that "stretches from Abraham to the Messiah."[119]

GENESIS 12–50: ABRAHAMIC BLESSING TO THE NATIONS

The Abrahamic blessing to the nations in Genesis 12:3c is a continued theme throughout the Book of Genesis. Not only is the blessing to the nations repeated to each patriarch—Abraham, Isaac, Jacob—but it is also partly fulfilled during the lifetimes of the patriarchs. The following section highlights the development of the Abrahamic blessing concept in Genesis and the extension of the Abrahamic blessing to the patriarchs and to the nations in Genesis 12–50.

Abrahamic Blessing

Even though the phrase "blessing of Abraham" is only mentioned once in the book of Genesis (28:4), the concept of the Abrahamic blessing is evident throughout the text. In the case of Isaac's pronouncement of the "blessing of Abraham" upon Jacob when given the firstborn's blessing (Gen 28:4), it is evident from the context that "Abraham is the real recipient of the blessing . . . [and] Jacob is its heir."[120] This understanding of individuals as "heirs" to the blessing of Abraham is emphasized by God himself. In speaking to Isaac, God says:

> Do not go down to Egypt; settle in the land that I shall show you. Reside in this land as an alien, and I will be with you, and

118. De Ridder, *Discipling*, 22.

119. Sundkler, *World*, 17.

120. Westermann, *Genesis 12–36*, 448.

> will bless you; for to you and to your descendants I will give all these lands, and I will fulfill the oath that I swore to your father Abraham. I will make your offspring as numerous as the stars of heaven, and will give to your offspring all these lands; and all the nations of the earth shall gain blessing for themselves through your offspring, because Abraham obeyed my voice and kept my charge, my commandments, my statutes, and my laws. (Gen 26:2–5 NRSV, italics added)

It is clear that while God renewed his initial promises to Isaac, the blessings given were a continuation of the original blessings and covenantal oaths given to Abraham. This concept is repeated once again in Genesis 26:24–25 when God reappeared to Isaac and stated: "I am the God of your father Abraham; do not be afraid, for I am with you and will bless you and make your offspring numerous for my servant Abraham's sake" (Gen 26:24–25 NRSV). This continued reference to God's original blessings given to Abraham (12:1–3ff.) establishes the concept that the Abrahamic blessing is foundational to all the blessings that follow. Furthermore, the new benefactors of the renewed Abrahamic blessing joined as heirs of the promise and thus heirs of Abraham.[121]

An additional distinction of the Abrahamic blessing is its relationship with the covenant treaties which God established with the patriarchs. Often seen as a by-product of God's covenant with the patriarchs, the blessing of God is in fact the umbrella under which the covenant falls. More specifically, God's blessing preceded humankind's sin thus covenant was first introduced in Genesis 9:9–17 as God's response to this sin. Furthermore, covenant was later reintroduced in Genesis 15:1–21 as God's response to human doubt. The covenantal relationship of God with Abraham established in Genesis 15:1–21 and Genesis 17 is therefore evidence of God's continued blessing upon Abraham, not the first example of this blessing. Ronald Clements states that "the original basis of the oracle [in Genesis 15] would seem to have been a divine assurance that Abraham's inheritance would pass to his direct descendants, and not to those who were regarded as born from a slave wife."[122] Genesis 15:7–21 "does not present the concluding of a covenant between God and Abraham . . . but rather God's assurance or promise to Abraham solemnized by a rite."[123] God's first invitation to a covenantal relationship in Genesis

121. Also see Gal 3:6–9.

122. Clements, *Abraham and David*, 19.

123. Westermann, *Genesis: An Introduction*, 205.

15:7–21 does not in any way change the former blessings of God given to Abraham in Genesis 12:1–3 but instead it establishes a ritual agreement which declares that the blessings will come to pass.

This firm confirmation of God's blessing through the covenant ritual also brings God's greatest gift to Abraham and his descendants, an intimate covenantal relationship with himself.[124] Although Abraham is the only patriarch to be invited into a covenantal relationship by God (Gen 15:1–21; 17:1–14, 19–27), the Abrahamic covenant is both affirmed and given to Isaac (26:2–6, 23–25) and Jacob (28:12–19; 39:9–15; 46:2–4). While not establishing new covenants with God, Isaac and Jacob clearly joined and remained within the same covenantal relationship of Abraham. It was within this covenant relationship that God promised Abraham and his descendants: "I will be with you" (26:3 NRSV) and that "I . . . will keep you wherever you go . . . for I will not leave you until I have done what I have promised you" (28:15 NRSV). It is through the patriarchs' covenantal treaty with God that they receive the greatest blessing of all: a personal relationship with their Creator.

Abrahamic Blessing Extended to the Patriarchs

The promise of Genesis 12:1–3 stands as a thematic foundation for all the patriarchal stories that follow. Within the wider patriarchal narrative "we find that the theme of God's promise to Abraham of descendants, land and blessing is of central importance in Genesis 12–25."[125] Renewed for every patriarch, "God's promise to Abraham in verses 1–3 extends through the patriarchal stories like a red thread."[126] However, the benefits of the extension of the Abrahamic blessing to the patriarchs are not theirs alone. Instead, they are threefold as God's blessing fell upon the patriarchs, was preserved for the nation of Israel, and was then released to the nations.

The significance of this extension upon the concept of blessing is profound. In contrast to the possibility of immediate fulfillment, God's blessing as given to Abraham was not fulfilled at once but instead unfolded as it was renewed with each generation. Within the book of Genesis, the promise of blessing extended from its initial proclamation in Genesis 12:1–3 to its partial fulfillment through the coming of Israel to

124. Clines, *Theme*, 32.

125. Moberly, *Old Testament*, 140.

126. Von Rad, *Genesis*, 160–61.

the Promised Land in the book of Joshua. Westermann remarks upon this future-focused characteristic of God's blessing. He explains:

> The cycle of Abraham stories does not begin with Abraham receiving God's blessing and then this blessing coming to pass in what befalls Abraham. Rather, Abraham at the outset receives the command to go forth, and the blessing that is connected with this is not simply there, but it is seen in prospect, so that it comes to pass in the history that begins with Abraham and continues not just throughout his lifetime but on after his death.[127]

Westermann expands his observations by noting that God's blessing upon the patriarchs is thus "incorporated into history" as it did not invite immediate fulfillment but instead extended throughout the ages.[128] In light of this understanding of divine blessing, the role of the patriarchs as "bearers of Israel's hope"[129] and bearers of the world's hope is enforced. The patriarchs were not allowed to revel in the blessing of God alone but instead the very delay of the complete fulfillment of the blessings during their lifetimes points to the fact that the blessings have a longer lifespan. Therefore, the promised blessings of God upon Abraham and his offspring were clearly pronounced as promises held for future generations.

Within the history of the patriarchs, the Abrahamic blessing is seen to be renewed again and again among Abraham's descendants. As first expressed to Abraham in Genesis 12:1–3, God blessed Abraham and his descendants with land (v. 1), blessing (vv. 2–3), greatness (v. 2), abundant offspring (v. 2), protection (v. 3), and the promise of being a blessing to the nations (v. 3).[130] This blessing to Abraham was enforced throughout his lifetime and extended to his offspring: Isaac, Jacob, and Joseph (see table 7). With each extension of the Abrahamic blessing to Abraham's offspring, small variations of expression did exist. However, the motifs of fruitfulness, blessing, promised land, covenantal relationship, and blessing to the nations were consistent within the patriarchal blessings. It is interesting to note the parallel between the blessings of Genesis 1–11 (blessing, fruitfulness, dominion and resources) and those of Genesis 12–50. Although Abraham and his offspring did receive additional blessings

127. Westermann, *Blessing in the Bible*, 52.

128. Ibid.

129. Childs, *Introduction*, 151.

130. See appendix C for a detailed account of the extension of the Abrahamic blessing to Abraham, Isaac, and Jacob.

from God as expressed in Genesis 12–25, Abraham served functionally as a continuation of a line of universal blessing which began in Genesis.

TABLE 7
PATRIARCHAL BLESSING IN GENESIS

Recipient	Land	Blessing	Fruitfulness	Blessing to Nations	Dominion/ Greatness	Covenantal Relationship/ Protection
Abraham	12:2a; 12:7; 13:15; 13:17; 15:7; 15:18–21; 17:8	12:2b–3b; 14:18–20; 15:1; 17:16–19; 22:17; 24:1	12:2; 13:16; 15:4–5; 17:2; 17:4–6; 17:16, 19; 20; 22:17	12:3c; 18:18; 22:18	12:2; 18:18; 22:17	12:3; 15:17–21; 17:2–14
Isaac	26:2, 3; 26:4	25:11; 26:3; 26:12–13 26:24	26:4a; 26:14	26:4	26:14	17:19–22; 26:3
Jacob	28:4; 28:13, 15; 35:12	28:3; 28:4a; 32:29; 35:9	28:3b; 28:14; 35:11; 46:3; 47:27	28:14	35:11; 46:3	28:15; 46:4
Joseph		48:15–16; 49:23–26	48:16; 49:22			

Although the patriarchs were probably not "preoccupied with blessing" as some suggest,[131] it was a very important element in their lives. In accordance with the customs of the time, fathers blessed their sons (Gen 27:28–29, 39; 28:1–4; 49:1–28; 48:13–20), superiors blessed inferior (14:17–20), blessings were used in parting (24:60) and sometimes even as prizes won in combat.[132] During patriarchal times, people believed that blessings contained a nearly magical, primitive power that was released through the spoken word. When given from one human being to another, as from a father to a son, only one blessing could be given which in turn could not be annulled or changed.

The fervent belief in the power of blessing held by the patriarchs can be seen in Esau's severe despair upon losing the blessing of the firstborn to his brother Jacob (Gen 27). As Isaac explained Jacob's deceit to Esau, Esau expressed his sheer agony at hearing the loss of his blessing:

131. Brueggemann, *Genesis*, 227.

132. Westermann, *Blessing in the Bible*, 54–55.

> When Esau heard his father's words, he cried out with an exceedingly great and bitter cry, and said to his father, "Bless me, me also, father!" But he [Isaac] said, "Your brother came deceitfully, and he has taken away your blessing." . . . Then he [Esau] said, "Have you not reserved a blessing for me?" Isaac answered Esau, "I have already made him your lord, and I have given him all his brothers as servants, and with grain and wine I have sustained him. What then can I do for you, my son?" Esau said to his father, "Have you only one blessing, father? Bless me, me also, father!" And Esau lifted up his voice and wept. (Gen 27:34–38 NRSV)

Although the supernatural power of blessing is a foreign concept in contemporary Western society, the holistic provisions of blessing were not lost on the patriarchs. Esau's intense sorrow, expressed upon hearing about the theft of his blessing, and his entreaty to his father to bless him as well, displays in no uncertain terms an example of the people's firm belief in the power of spoken blessings.

Therefore, in light of this traditional understanding of the power of blessing, God's blessings given to the patriarchs take on greater significance. As the Abrahamic blessing was renewed with each patriarch, the divine blessings were understood as "manifestation[s] of a power-filled word" which would certainly come to pass.[133] The declaration of the blessings by God spurred the patriarchs to great acts of obedience (Gen 12:4; 22:18), worship (12:7; 13:18; 17:3; 26:25; 28:16–20; 35:14), belief (15:6), and to the pronouncement of vows to the Lord (28:16–20). It is evident from their reverent responses that they believed the word of the Lord and held God's words as irrevocable promises that would become reality.

This firm belief is apparent in Genesis 32:9–12 when Jacob heard of Esau's approach toward his family with two hundred men. It was then that Jacob reminded God of his irreversible blessing upon his life:

> And Jacob said, "O God of my father Abraham and God of my father Isaac, O Lord who said to me, 'Return to your country and to your kindred, and I will do you good,' I am not worthy of the least of all the steadfast love and all the faithfulness that you have shown to your servant, for with only my staff I crossed this Jordan; and now I have become two companies. Deliver me, please, from the hand of my brother, from the hand of Esau,

133. Ibid., 51.

> for I am afraid of him; he may come and kill us all, the mothers with the children. Yet you have said, 'I will surely do you good, and make your offspring as the sand of the sea, which cannot be counted because of their number.'" (Gen 32:9–12 NRSV, italics added)

In the midst of the possible annihilation of his family, Jacob turned to God and fervently reminded God of the divine promise that he had received that could not be broken (Gen 28:12–14). Jacob cried out to God declaring the dangerous situation he was in and proclaimed, "For I am afraid of him; he may come and kill us all, the mothers with the children. *Yet you have said*" (32:11b–12 NRSV, italics added). For in the midst of his fear, Jacob knew that God's words could not be undone. God had foretold and promised Jacob and the patriarchs his blessings; therefore they knew the blessing would come to fruition.

An additional factor in the outplaying of the Abrahamic blessing was the fact that not all received God's covenantal blessing. The passing over of Ishmael (Gen 17) and Esau (Gen 27) stand out in particular; the first was the firstborn son of Abraham and the second the rightful heir of Isaac. George W. Coats notes in regard to Ishmael's dismissal that "it is somewhat surprising that Ishmael receives circumcision, the sign of the covenant and is heir to a similar promise. The promise of the covenant nonetheless passes over Ishmael, the firstborn and resides in Isaac."[134] Although at Abraham's insistence God did bless Ishmael, Isaac was still declared the child of the promise and thus became the recipient of God's greater covenantal blessings (17:20–22). This counterbalance between the two brothers resides within the Genesis text in the parallel narratives of Isaac and Ishmael and Jacob and Esau. Walter Brueggemann remarks upon the narrative of Jacob and Esau and states:

> The narrative becomes aware that somebody is destined to lesser blessing. One son cannot have the full blessing, for there is only one such blessing . . . The whole family knows that without the power of the blessing, life has no fresh possibility handed with only pragmatic forms of power, mechanistic ways of speech and futures only they can shape.[135]

Although the author adds that "nobody wants a life without the special words and gestures that bind that life to a precious past and a

134. Coats, *Genesis*, 31.

135. Brueggemann, *Genesis*, 228.

promised future,"[136] the actualization of these words was evident within the life of Esau. In spite of these distinctions, both Ishmael and Esau were remarkably blessed by God despite their eventual position outside of the official Abrahamic line of descent.

Abrahamic Blessing Extended to the Nations

Although the Abrahamic blessing was extended and passed to each patriarch, the blessing of God also fell upon the peoples surrounding Abraham and his descendants. This "overspill of blessing beyond the Abrahamic family"[137] can be seen not only in the establishment of covenantal relationships between the patriarchs and their neighbors, but also in the unwitting extension of God's blessing upon unprepared recipients. While the spoken declaration of God that he would bless the nations through Abraham is repeated five times through Genesis (Gen 12:1–4; 18:17–18; 22:15–18; 26:2–5; 28:12–14), it was the partial fulfillment of these words during the lifetime of the patriarchs that generate the most interest. Chosen to be "bearers of a blessing . . . for the sake of all,"[138] Genesis records that Abraham, Isaac, Jacob and Joseph each participated, albeit sometimes unknowingly, in God's blessing to the nations.[139]

136. Ibid.

137. Clines, *Theme*, 78–79.

138. Newbigin, *Open Secret*, 32.

139. See appendix D.

3

Old Testament: Unfolding of God's Blessing

Throughout the Old Testament the theme of the Abrahamic blessing appears again and again throughout the Torah, the Prophets, and the Writings. The concept of Israel as a "light to the nations" (Isa 42:6; 49:6), for example, is particularly significant in the outplaying of this missional motif. In addition, the understanding that God has set Israel apart as a "priestly kingdom and a holy nation" (Exod 19:6 NRSV) is likewise central to the development of God releasing his blessing through Israel. In both of these representations, God places his chosen people as a beacon and witness to the pagan nations around them. Israel is not only God's "treasured possession out of all the peoples" (19:5), but is also identified as a priestly vehicle through which all peoples may access God. Additionally, societal and religious laws were made protecting the rights of the foreigner in Israel's midst (20:10; 22:21; Lev 18:26; 20:2; 25:40; Num 15:14–16; Deut 10:18–19; 26:5–11; 1 Kgs 8:41–43; 2 Chr 6:32ff.) and the very temple of the Lord was dedicated as a "house of prayer for all the nations" (Isa 56:7; see also 2 Chr 6:32–33; Mic 4:1–2; Jer 7:11).

Alongside the examples of Israel's calling to bless the nations there is also a simultaneous resistance upon Israel's part to interact with the surrounding pagan nations. As Michael A. Harbin notes in *The Promise and the Blessing*, "The nation of Israel did not accomplish its intended goal, which was to represent the true God to the nations, that is, being a kingdom of priests."[1] This was due in part to the great sinfulness of some of the nations around Israel which God in turn commanded the people to avoid (e.g., Exod 32; 1 Sam 15; 28:18; 1 Kgs 11:7–10; 20:42).

1. Harbin, *Promise*, 448.

However, disobedience of God's command and a sense of ethnocentricity and prejudice were also factors of this avoidance, as seen in the book of Jonah. Regardless of Israel's mixed response to their God-given role, God decidedly used his people throughout the Old Testament as a witness of God's presence, an example of God's interaction, and a vehicle of God's loving-kindness.

One of the means via which Israel served as a blessing was through its witness of God's presence. Brueggemann writes "that [the] power of blessing concentrated in Israel is no property for Israel" but it was meant to "be transmitted to and for the others who have, since their embrace of the curse, been deficient in the power to choose a prosperous future."[2] Israel's "ministry among" was one of the ways through which the nations received God's holistic blessing. Although rarely actively recruiting or converting foreigners to Yahwehism,[3] Abraham and his kin served as living testimonies of God's goodness and blessing. Their witness was in fact twofold as they were (1) living examples of God's blessing and greatness and were (2) "visibly available with the life-force of a viable future of shalom."[4] Walter Kaiser describes this process as "centripetal" mission as "the burden rested on the unreached to take the initiative to become converts to the faith."[5] As seen in the lives of the Abraham and his immediate descendants, "God's blessing on their lives was a testimony to God's existence and power (Gen. 26:28, 39:2)"[6] which the other nations were in turn drawn to. By simply living in covenantal relationship with God, Israel became a "light to the nations" shining forth the character of God and making available the blessings of God.

In addition, Israel served as a model to the nations of how God "works in the world as a whole, in deliverance, in obligation, in blessing and in danger."[7] When God released the Hebrews from captivity in Egypt for example, God told Moses, "I have raised you up for this very purpose, that I might show you my power and that *my name might be proclaimed in all the earth*" (Exod 9:16, italics added). Later, as God led the people of Israel across the Red Sea the author records that God "did *this so that all*

2. Brueggemann, "Ministry Among," 24.
3. Ibid., 25.
4. Ibid.
5. Kaiser, *Mission*, 83.
6. Bowling, "Be a Blessing," 11.
7. Goldingay, *Israel's Faith*, 294.

the peoples of the earth might know that the hand of the Lord is powerful and so that [Israel] might always fear the Lord your God" (Josh 4:24, italics added). The reputation of the miracles of God in fact did spread far and wide among the nations, so much so that Rahab of Jericho exclaimed the following to Joshua's spies forty years after the fact:

> I know that the Lord has given this land to you and that a great fear of you has fallen on us, so that all who live in this country are melting in fear because of you. We have heard how the Lord dried up the water of the Red Sea for you when you came out of Egypt, and what you did to Sihon and Og . . . whom you completely destroyed. When we heard of it, our hearts melted and everyone's courage failed because of you, for the Lord your God is God in heaven above and on the earth below. (Josh 2:8–11, italics added)

This demonstration of God's power and his miraculous works in Israel served as a witness to the nations. Additionally, this testimony drew select non-Israelites into covenantal relationship with Israel, incorporating them into the blessings of God.

Although Israel's witness of God's presence and saving works indirectly extended God's blessing, it is the interaction between God's people and the nations that allowed God's blessing to be abundantly poured out. This took place via two principal means: (1) non-Israelites joining in covenantal relationship with Israel, and (2) God's blessing on Israel spilling over upon foreign individuals and people groups. With the first approach, the "absorption of outsiders into [Israel]. . . was a method which brought [non-Israelites] into a potentially redemptive relationship with God."[8] Thus, purchased slaves, men and woman who joined Israel, and foreign leaders who made covenants with God's people could enter into God's blessing via the covenant ritual.[9] Additionally, the blessing of God appeared to repeatedly fall upon non-Israelites who were in contact with Abraham and his descendents through Scripture. The book of Genesis in particular describes the transferable nature of the divine blessing as Canaan (Gen 14), Abimelech (20:17), Laban (30:27), Potiphar (39:2–6), the prison guard (39:21–23), the Egyptian Pharaoh (41:39–40; 47:7–10) and the nation of Egypt (41:13–26) all benefit from the tangible blessings of God via his chosen people. Through this conscious and sometimes

8. Bowling, "Be a Blessing," 11.

9. Ibid., 10–11.

unconscious transference of God's blessing to the nations, the promise of God given to Abraham in Genesis 12:3 began its implementation within the Old Testament.

ABRAHAMIC BLESSING THROUGH THE ABRAHAMIC LINE

The "state of blessedness"[10] in which Abraham and his progeny existed reached past themselves and impacted the nations around them. Sometimes through the establishment of covenantal relationship and other times through the supernatural power of God, the Abrahamic blessing began its fulfillment within the narratives of the patriarchs. Observable examples of this realization include Joseph's blessing of Egypt during the famine (Gen 41:53–57; 47:13–26) and Jacob's blessing of the Egyptian Pharaoh (47:7–10).

Joseph in Egypt

Within the patriarchal narratives, the person of Joseph stands out alongside Abraham as the living fulfillment of the Abrahamic blessing. Upon his entrance into Egypt, Joseph repeatedly is said to have brought blessing to each master under which he served.[11] When Joseph entered Potiphar's household, for example, it is recorded that God "blessed the Egyptian's house for Joseph's sake; the blessing of the Lord was on all that he [Potiphar] had, in house and field" (Gen 39:5 NRSV). Likewise, when in the Egyptian prison, the author writes that "the Lord was with Joseph and showed him steadfast love; he gave him favor in the sight of the chief jailer . . . The chief jailer paid no heed to anything that was in Joseph's care, because the Lord was with him; and whatever he did, the Lord made it prosper" (39:21, 23 NRSV). While the first two examples have received much attention in biblical commentaries, it is the third example—Joseph's blessing of Egypt and the surrounding nations during the famine (41:53–57; 47:13–26)—that has the most profound and universal impact.

As with the original intention of the Genesis 12:3 blessing to the nations, God's conveyance of blessing through Joseph impacted people groups outside the Hebrews' covenantal relationship with Yahweh. Andrew Bowling writes:

10. Westermann, *Blessing in the Bible*, 33.

11. Bowling, "Be a Blessing," 13.

> Speaking in terms of the Covenant duty to be a blessing, Joseph can be viewed as an archetypal example of the individual who brings Covenant blessing to the world. Thus, he becomes an archetypal example of Old Testament mission at work . . . No doubt, much of this blessing was simply the exercise of Joseph's God-given abilities. Other blessing, however, could have come from God's supernatural work through Joseph. But, however it happened, God used Joseph as a channel for blessing gentiles. And there is no reason not to see this blessing as obedience to God's command for the elect nation to be a blessing to the world."[12]

By living out the Abrahamic blessing, Joseph figuratively and literally blessed the foreign individuals and nations around him. Whether as Bowling suggests, Joseph was obeying the divine imperative to "be a blessing" or acting on the passive interpretation, "you will be a blessing," the bounty of God clearly followed Joseph into every community he entered impacting everyone in his path.

However, despite the clear result, the motivation by which God blessed Potiphar's household, the royal prison, and the Egyptian Pharaoh is not as evident. In the case of Potiphar's household, the author mentions that God blessed Potiphar for "Joseph's sake" (Gen 39:5) which in the English translation could be interpreted as meaning "for the benefit of Joseph." In the original Hebrew translation, however, *galal* is most often translated as "on the account of" or "because of" which in turn broadens the possible interpretations of the English translation. Thus, with the expanded translation the blessing given to the Egyptians can be seen as coming to them simply because of Joseph's presence in their midst. As Genesis 12:3 suggests, then, and as the following patriarchal narratives reaffirm, the Abrahamic blessing can in fact overflow to the non-Yahwists simply because of the physical presence of Abraham or one of his descendants.

Within Genesis 41:53–57 and 47:13–26, the impact of Joseph's presence comes into play as the blessing of God falls not only upon foreign individuals, but upon whole nations and people groups. Westermann describes God's role within this episode:

> God's action extends far beyond the personal fate of the innocent prisoner, Joseph; the interpretation of the dreams leads to the preservation of a whole people from severe famine. God can "preserve the life of a whole people" through the institution

12. Bowling, "Be a Blessing," 13.

> of the kingship, and he endows Joseph with the ability to carry it through. God's assistance to Joseph first had its effect on his Egyptian master; now it is at work on the Pharaoh and his kingdom. God's blessing is universal.[13]

Here the author suggests that the primary concern of God is not Joseph alone but Joseph, his family, the Egyptian Pharaoh, the nation of Egypt, and the peoples surrounding Egypt. While preserving Joseph and his family through the famine, God was simultaneously saving the whole region from desolation. In addition, the great prosperity and well-being that God conveyed through Joseph to Pharaoh and his people[14] suggests that God was not only concerned with the survival of all nations but their level of prosperity and well-being. As expressed in primeval literature, God desires all people, including Egypt in this case, to be blessed, fruitful, and to have authority in the land (Gen 1:27–29).

Through Joseph's statesmanship a multitude of blessings were poured out upon Egypt including an abundance of food during widespread famine, increased property ownership for the royal family, and ultimate salvation for Egypt from destruction and death. John Skinner writes of Genesis 47:13–27:

> Joseph is here represented as taking advantage of the great famine to revolutionize the system of land-tenure in Egypt for the benefit of the crown. In one year the famishing people have exhausted their money and parted with their live-stock, in exchange for bread; in the next they forfeit their lands and their personal freedom. Thus by a bold stroke of statesmanship private property in land (except in the case of the priests) is abolished throughout Egypt, and the entire population reduced to the position of serfs, paying a land-tax of 20 per cent per annum to the king.[15]

While Skinner's summary of the events comes from a distinctly socioeconomic perspective, the financial and agricultural blessings gained through Joseph's administrative skills cannot be overlooked. The "stockpiling of grain" outlined by Joseph indicates "a well-thought-out policy"[16] which in turn introduced another avenue through which blessing could be administered. Within the book of Genesis up until this point, there

13. Westermann, *Genesis: An Introduction*, 252.

14. Westermann, *Genesis 37–50*, 328.

15. Skinner, *Critical*, 498–99.

16. Westermann, *Genesis 37–50*, 98.

is little indication of a set systematic structure through which blessing flows. However, as in the case of Joseph and the Egyptians, the use of economic policy as a vehicle of blessing from God was introduced as a viable and effective method.[17]

An interesting twist in the Genesis 41–47 narrative is that although God brought blessing to Egypt through Joseph, God in turn used Egypt to bless Joseph and his family. Westermann states the situation plainly when he writes, "The monarchy and its potential is taken up into God's plan to save the lives of many."[18] This interconnection between the two parties was further established through the fact that it was to Pharaoh that God spoke through a dream and through Joseph that it was interpreted. Although to the modern reader this concept may seem foreign, within the ancient Near East the understanding of a supernatural connection between royalty and the divine was widespread. The king was known to be "the distributor of divine blessing" and although Joseph served as the interpreter, God's message was clearly addressed to Pharaoh, not to Joseph.

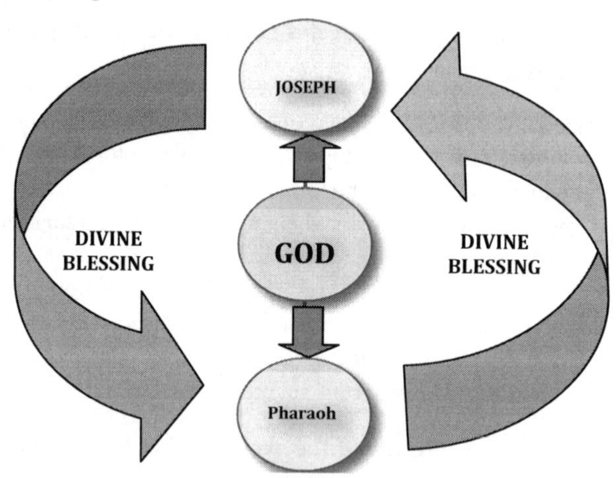

FIGURE 3
GOD'S CIRCULAR BLESSING

Therefore, within the Joseph narrative we see a circular effect wherein the blessings of God were given to Joseph via the Egyptian pharaoh and to the pharaoh via Joseph. This interaction between God and the Pharaoh indicates once again the universal nature and purposes of

17. Ibid.

18. Ibid., 251.

God who, while working through Abraham's descendants, is also open to working through those outside of the covenant relationship.

Jacob's Blessing of Pharaoh

While the blessing of the Egyptian nation through Joseph is intertwined throughout the narrative, Jacob's pronouncement of blessing upon Pharaoh in Genesis 47:4–10 is an example of a verbal "blessing." As biblical scholars have historically approached this text there have been three main responses: (1) ignoring the text; (2) interpreting the Hebrew term *brk* as a greeting; and (3) translating the term *brk* as an act of "blessing" within the greeting. Gunkel, in his commentary on Genesis,[19] chooses the first option, skipping over the Genesis 47:7–10 text altogether, ending his comments at 47:6 and starting again at 47:12. Likewise, von Rad, while translating *brk* as "blessed," fails to mention anything regarding Jacob's double-blessing upon the Egyptian Pharaoh.[20] S. R. Driver comes closer to discussing the text; however, while translating *brk* in Genesis 47:7, 10 as "blessed," he explains the term to mean "saluted with wishes for his welfare"[21] which seems to straddle both a greeting and a blessing. Historically, there appears to be no reason as to why these authors fail to address the Genesis 47:7–10 text however this neglect does appear to exemplify the general absence of the theme of blessing in Genesis commentaries and academic texts.

The second position, understanding *brk* as a greeting, comes closer to discussing the original meaning of the text. Speiser translates the 47:7–10 passage: "Then Joseph brought his father Jacob and presented him to Pharaoh. Jacob *paid respects to* Pharaoh . . . [10] Then Jacob *took his leave from* Pharaoh and left his presence."[22] Similarly, Nahum M. Sarna translates the literal "and he blessed" to "Jacob *greeted* Pharaoh" (Gen 47:7) and "Then Jacob *bade Pharaoh farewell*" (Gen 47:10).[23] While not entirely missing the mark, interpreting the Hebrew term *brk* simply as a commonplace greeting or farewell overlooks the full meaning of the word. Claus Westermann explaining the multileveled nature of the term writes:

19. Gunkel, *Genesis*, 441–42.

20. Von Rad, *Genesis: A Commentary*, 406–8.

21. Driver, *Book of Genesis*, 371.

22. Speiser, "Genesis," 348–49, italics added.

23. Sarna, *Genesis*, 320, italics added.

> It can, to be sure, mean a simple greeting (e.g., 1 Sam. 13:10; 2 Kgs. 4:29); but the meaning "bless" always resonates. In certain circumstances, determined on each occasion by the context, the meaning "blessing" prevails . . . The meaning of the blessing must emerge from the context. As part of the audience it is of course also a greeting; but in this particular situation it has the force of a blessing.[24]

Therefore, while Jacob's declaration of blessing upon Pharaoh could have doubled with his greeting, the significance of the act of blessing in the event cannot be dismissed.

The third interpretation of the Genesis 47:7–10 text is reading the event as both a greeting and a blessing. Robert Alter comments:

> The Hebrew verb here [v. 7] also has the simple meaning of "to greet," but it seems likely that in this context it straddles both senses. Jacob of course accords Pharaoh the deferential greeting owed to a monarch, but it would be entirely in keeping with his own highly developed sense of his patriarchal role that he—a mere Semitic herdsman chief addressing the head of the mighty Egyptian empire—should pronounce a blessing on Pharaoh.[25]

The combination of a greeting and a blessing is therefore both possible and likely within the text. However, the fact that an elderly nomadic herdsman was blessing the mighty Pharaoh of Egypt is at first puzzling. At the source of the blessing is God himself; it is clear that it was God who blessed Pharaoh not Jacob, the displaced shepherd. This enforces the fact that even the poorest foreign shepherd once blessed by God has "something to give or bestow by blessing."[26] Before God "the Pharaoh and the old man are as one-human"[27] thus Jacob's covenant relationship with God allows God's blessing to pass to one in a higher position politically, socially and economically. As with Abraham, God's blessing was conveyed to Pharaoh through the most humble of vessels, indicating that the source of power was God himself not mankind.

The ancient Near Eastern understanding of the power of the spoken word adds to the interpretation of the narrative. When the author wrote that Jacob "blessed" Pharaoh, he was writing to an audience that

24. Westermann, *Genesis 37–50*, 170.

25. Alter, *Genesis*, 280.

26. Westermann, *Genesis 37–50*, 170.

27. Ibid., 172.

understood the supernatural happenings surrounding verbal pronouncements. As James Montgomery Boice writes, "To understand this story we need to remember the importance the Hebrews put on words, especially words spoken on formal occasions. A word was not a light thing, as we think it is. A word spoken was a deed done."[28] The author continues that:

> Words spoken on formal occasions could be expected to have consequences. We cannot imagine that Jacob would have blessed Pharaoh with any lesser thought than that he was conveying on him the favor of almighty God, the God of his fathers Abraham and Isaac. Jacob was giving testimony to the name and nature of the only true God, whom he worshiped, and he was expecting that true God to bless Pharaoh.[29]

The intentionality of Jacob's blessing upon Pharaoh corresponds well with the seriousness with which blessings are pronounced throughout the book of Genesis (1:21–22, 27–29; 2:3; 5:1–2; 9:1–7; 12:1–7; 18:17–18; 22:15–18; 26:2–6; 28:1–4, 12–14). Not once is an act of blessing treated lightly or given simply as a formality. Words spoken in a blessing were always believed to come to pass and have the support of the divine; with conscious and meaningful pronouncement Jacob spoke the words of blessing upon Pharaoh, not once but twice.

As Jacob blessed Pharaoh with the blessing of God, the partial fulfillment of the Abrahamic promise of blessing to the nations is seen. Westermann explains:

> He [Jacob] wants to bless his children and their children before he dies. But the king of Egypt is also included in the dying man's blessing. There is a remote point of contact here with the promise of blessing made to Abraham that extends to "all the families of the earth" (Gen. 12:1–3). Not only in the Yahwist's patriarchal story, but also in the priestly account, the blessing given to each of the successive patriarchs is not restricted to the ancestors of Israel and the people of Israel . . . It reaches far beyond the patriarchs and is directed to the whole of the human race.[30]

The universal nature of God's blessing given to Abraham was witnessed as Jacob reached out and blessed the Pharaoh of Egypt. The significance of this action is not only seen in the fact that Pharaoh was

28. Boice, *Genesis*, 1121.

29. Ibid.

30. Westermann, *Genesis 37–50*, 171.

outside of the covenant people, but also in the fact that he as the ruler of the people was seen as the representative of all of Egypt. As mentioned previously, the king was the vehicle through which all blessings flowed.[31] Therefore, in blessing Pharaoh, the leader of the nation of Egypt, Jacob was not only blessing Pharaoh and his household but also all the people over which he ruled. Moreover, no longer was Joseph the conduit of God's blessing to Pharaoh as in Genesis 41–47 but now Pharaoh himself had received the blessing of God Most High directly. This increased connection to God via Jacob's blessing foreshadowed the intimate relationship between God and all people which was yet to come through Christ as promised in Genesis 12:3.

ABRAHAMIC BLESSING THROUGH THE PROPHETS

While the unfolding fulfillment of the Abrahamic blessing is especially evident in the book of Genesis, the motif of blessing to the nations continues throughout the Law, Prophets, and Wisdom literature of the Old Testament. In the prophetic texts for example, the promise of an age of peace, prosperity, and blessing was prophesized for Israel and the surrounding nations (Mic 4:3–4; Isa 11). The total fulfillment of this promise is identified in the Messiah, "the mediator of blessing" who will bring "in an era of blessing and peace."[32] However, as in the book of Genesis, smaller fulfillments of this promise are scattered throughout the narratives of the prophets. Two such stories which exemplify the fulfillment of the Abrahamic blessing in the Prophetic texts include Elijah's interaction with the Widow at Zarephath (1 Kgs 17:8–16) and Elisha's healing of Naaman the Syrian (2 Kgs 5:1–27).

Elijah and the Widow at Zarephath

When the story of the Widow of Zarephath begins in 1 Kings 17:8, Elijah the Tishbite had just returned from hiding by the Wadi Cherith from King Ahab. The sin and disobedience of King Ahad had led to God's declaration that neither dew nor rain would fall upon the land except by Elijah's word (1 Kgs 17:1). Thus, the whole land was experiencing an increasingly severe drought and even the wadi from which Elijah had drawn water had now dried up. It was at this point that God spoke once more to

31. Ibid., 47.

32. Westermann, *Blessing in the Bible*, 34.

Elijah commanding him to go to Zarephath, a little town in Sidon, where he would find a widow directed by God to feed him (17:8–9). Already, upon this brief introduction, the readers of the original text would have noticed that something unusual was going to take place. In the midst of God's punishment of Ahab for marrying Jezebel (daughter of King Ethball of the Sidonians) and for worshipping false idols, God had commanded Elijah to go to the region of Sidon, the birthplace of Jezebel and the center of Baal worship. Furthermore, God had already declared that he had ordained one of the women of Zarephath, a non-Israelite, to feed Elijah (17:9), the holy prophet of God. Needless to say, in the introduction alone, the stage had been set for the controversial story that follows.

Thirteen kilometers south of Sidon along the Mediterranean coast, Zarephath falls within the territory of Sidon and was politically outside the borders of Israel.[33] It was this little town that Elijah entered and approached a poor widow collecting sticks to prepare her last meal for herself and her family. The fact that the woman was "a Phoenician [and] presumably a worshiper of Baal"[34] would not have been lost upon the original audience, nor would the fact that she was a widow and thus in one of the lowest positions of society. In ancient Near Eastern cultures, "widows [were] typically associated with the neediest elements of society, the orphans and the poor"[35] primarily because they were unable to support themselves and their families financially and were thus dependent upon the generosity of others.[36] The devastating famine during the time of Elijah would have been a disaster that the widow of Zarephath would have had little power to overcome. However, as in the case of Hagar (Gen 16:13–14), God indicated that he saw this foreign widow and moreover chose her to be a vehicle of salvation for Elijah and a recipient of God's supernatural blessing.

As God's representative to the Israelites, Elijah was known to speak and act according to God's will and command. Therefore, when God directed the prophet into enemy territory, Elijah followed by faith, obeying God's every command. Gene Rice, in his commentary on 1 Kings, notes that "Elijah was not only a spokesperson of the word, he was himself a living word, proclaiming through his name and life-style his wholehearted

33. Cogan, *I Kings*, 432.

34. Seow, *1 and 2 Kings*, 128.

35. Ibid.

36. Cogan, *I Kings*, 427.

and exclusive devotion to God."[37] The author adds that Elijah "so cultivated God's presence that he brought it near to others (1 Kgs. 17:18) and was capable of acting as an instrument of divine power (1 Kgs. 17:22)."[38] Thus, although the widow greeted Elijah respectfully with an oath in the name of Yahweh (1 Kgs 17:12),[39] it was clear that the prophet was now interacting with people who were not in a covenantal relationship with his God. As prophets were often called to bring judgment upon foreign kings and nations, the salvific purposes of this particular visit were not that common. As one considers Elijah's role as representative and mouthpiece of the true and living God, the prophet's communication with the widow becomes all the more important, for Elijah's presence indicated the presence of God and Elijah's actions and desires those of God. Therefore, within this narrative God, through Elijah, is revealing his heart for the nations.

As discussed previously, at the core of God's blessing was a life power which enabled individuals and communities to be fruitful and prosper in all elements of their lives. In contrast to this state of blessedness, within the story of the Zarephath widow there are two areas mentioned in which life itself was almost extinguished. First, upon his initial encounter of the widow, the prophet Elijah found out that she was preparing to eat her last meal after which she and her family would most likely die (1 Kgs 17:12). Later, as the story unfolds, the widow's son died suddenly (17:17), which in turn was the complete elimination of life altogether. In this second incident not only did the widow's son die but through his death the widow was also sentenced to death. A son within the ancient Near East was the breadwinner and security in old age for a widow,[40] thus without her son, the widow once again returned to poverty and imminent death. Needless to say, in both cases life itself was threatened and the absence of God's blessing was clearly felt. Elijah's response to both scenarios was indicative of the type of life-giving assistance that he was giving her.

The first miracle that Elijah performed for the widow was the gift of a meal pot and oil pitcher that never ran dry. In great obedience to Elijah's request for food and water, the widow took a step of faith in the midst of her plight to share her final meal with the unknown prophet. When she

37. Rice, *I Kings*, 145.

38. Ibid.

39. Walsh, *1 Kings*, 229.

40. Goldingay, *Israel's Faith*, 456.

initially hesitated, God spoke through Elijah as he proclaimed: "For thus says the Lord the God of Israel: The jar of meal will not be emptied and the jug of oil will not fail until the day that the Lord sends rain on the earth" (1 Kgs 17:14). In following Elijah's instructions, the words of the Lord immediately came to pass as the widow's diminished ingredients became abundant and she never lacked food again (17:15–16). The magnitude of the miracle for the widow and her family cannot be underestimated. God's abundant provision for them saved them from sure death, renewing their lives daily. Echoes of the blessing of God upon creation in the book of Genesis are evident as God restored fruitfulness (Gen 1:22, 28) and the abundance of food upon the widow and her household (1:28–29).

An interesting element of this particular faith narrative is the repeated circular pattern of blessing that extends between Elijah and the Sidonian widow. As in the Joseph narrative, a circular relationship is evident in the 1 Kings story as God blessed his chosen representative, Elijah, who in turn blessed the foreigner, who in turn blessed him.[41] Particularly evident in the opening narrative (1 Kgs 17:8–16), the interdependence of this process reinforces within the narrative the universal perspective of God whose love and concern abounds to all his creation. Additionally, God's omnipotence outside of the boundaries of Israel was revealed,[42] identifying God not only as the God of Israel but as the God of all nations. Thus, the sovereignty of God over nature and humanity, the heavens and the earth and Israel and the nations is imprinted in the narrative itself and reinforced with the circular distribution of blessing where God did not distinguish between Yahwist and heathen.

Throughout the story, the author(s) additionally present a positive image of the foreign widow in which her great faith in God is presented as a model for Israel. Simon J. DeVries writes that the widow's faith is itself a gift from God that was granted to her during her plight. He notes:

> The marvel is that God gave her faith sufficient to believe his assurance and his prophecy—but the God who can direct ravens to bring food in a desolate wadi can surely create faith in this widow's heart. To the miracle of faith Yahweh adds the miracle of a never-empty jar of meal and a never-failing cruse of oil.[43]

41. Fritz, *I and II Kings*, 183.

42. Cogan, *I Kings*, 432.

43. DeVries, *I Kings*, 218.

Although the exact source of the widow's faith cannot be determined, it is evident that the widow did show tremendous trust in God as she risked her family members' lives on the basis of a stranger's promise. The seriousness of her situation is presented very clearly in the text and it can be deduced that the widow and her family had long felt the pangs of hunger and desperation at the point that she first met Elijah. However, despite her dire situation, Elijah challenged the widow's faith asking her to give the little that she had away.[44] The widow rose to the challenge and invited the prophet into her house and in doing so simultaneously invited in the blessing of God. The widow was greatly rewarded for her faith and the blessing that she needed most was bestowed upon her, illustrating that "in contrast to the manipulative sexual rites of Canaanite religion, the word of God, when accepted in faith, is able to supply one's needs even under the most adverse conditions."[45] The widow of Zarephath was thus presented as a model of faith in the narrative as she accepted the word of the Lord by faith without even knowing the True and Living God.

In the second miracle, Elijah restored the widow's son to life, once again bringing the blessing of God upon the widow and her household. As mentioned previously, the death of a son was considered one of the worst possible scenarios for a widow within ancient Near Eastern cultures. Within the narrative, the widow had not only lost her son and her husband, but had just recently faced the possible death of her entire household. Coming from a holistic worldview, the widow would have considered the recent series of events, in particular the death of her son, as God's punishment on her for "some secret sin she had committed."[46] Tragedy in the midst of God's blessing appears to have confused both the widow and the prophet as Elijah diligently "intercedes on the boy's behalf."[47] Elijah called out to God and asked, "O Lord my God, have you brought tragedy also upon this widow I am staying with, by causing her son to die?" (1 Kgs 17:20). Stretching out his body upon the boy three times the prophet then called out to God, "O Lord my God, let this boy's life return to him" (17:21). God heard Elijah's prayer (17:22) and returned life to the boy. The widow's response to this life-giving miracle was not "profuse expressions of gratitude" but "instead . . . a profound profession

44. Ibid., 217.

45. Rice, *I Kings*, 143.

46. Ibid., 145–46.

47. Seow, *1 and 2 Kings*, 129.

of faith in Elijah and the word he bears."[48] After witnessing the miraculous blessings of God, the widow acknowledged that "Elisha's deity, the God of Israel, is truly the Lord of life, for even one who has already died could be brought to life again by that deity's power."[49] Thus, the blessing of God not only brought abundant life back to the widow and her household but also led the widow to a powerful revelation that Yahweh was both living and active in the world.

Elisha and Naaman the Syrian

The narrative of the prophet Elisha's healing of Naaman the Syrian in 2 Kings 5:1–27 is another example of the partial fulfillment of the Abrahamic blessing to the nations in Hebrew Scripture. The story opens with reference to the long-standing struggle between Israel and the nearby kingdom of Syria (2 Kgs 5:2) both of whom "fought chiefly over possession of the disputed territories in northern Transjordan."[50] Again, as in the story of Elijah and the widow of Zarephath, the foreign nation involved was not only idolatrous but a long-standing enemy of Israel. However, the universal involvement and sovereignty of God is identified in both Syria and Israel. Naaman, for example, the Syrian soldier afflicted with leprosy, is noted as having received victory in battle from God, Israel's God (5:1).[51] It is thus with this strange conflict of interests that the narrative begins, introducing the kingdom of Aram, one of Israel's long-term enemies, within reach of the blessings of Yahweh, Israel's God.

While the blessings of God promised to the Sidonian widow were first introduced by Elijah the mighty prophet of Yahweh, Naaman first heard of the power of God via a young Israelite girl living in captivity. Below even the status of a widow, the young captive child was about as insignificant as you could be within the social strata of Syria. Yet, it was through her witness to her mistress, Naaman's wife, that her master first sought permission to find Elisha the prophet of God in Israel. Where

48. Walsh, *1 Kings*, 232.

49. Seow, *1 and 2 Kings*, 129.

50. Dentan, *First and Second Books*, 80–81.

51. In Seow's commentary on 1 and 2 Kings, the author notes that "in Israelite theology no foreign army can be victorious over Israel unless it is by the will of the Lord" (193). He continues that the inclusion of this fact is consistent with the understanding that any defeat of Israel was the will of God and would in the end bring about the greatest good for Israel as can be seen with the eventual conversion of the prominent Gentile military commander in 1 Kgs 5:15–18 (193). Also see Kaiser, *Mission*, 43.

the young girl developed her theologically advanced understanding that God could heal Gentiles is not recorded, but it is markedly evident in the text.[52] Thus, the young girl expressed in faith that Naaman would be cured of leprosy "if only [her] master would see the prophet who is in Samaria" (2 Kgs 5:3). "The Hebrew term introducing the girl's exclamation—*ylta*, 'I would that'—(which occurs only here and in Psalm 119:5) is analogous to *yrca*, 'blessed is.'"[53] Thus the "happiness" and "blessedness" to come is foreshadowed even in this opening text. The blessings of God are once again introduced by a most unlikely source indicating more than ever that it is through the power and discretion of God that divine blessings come, not the strength of humankind.

The 2 Kings 5 narrative also provides a convicting message regarding the lack of faith in Israel. Beginning and ending the Naaman narrative with striking contrasts, the author(s) blatantly compares the faith of the Israelite slave girl with that of the king of Israel (2 Kgs 5:2–8) and the Syrian military officer with that of Gehazi the servant of Elisha (5:15–27). In both cases it is the least likely individual—the young captive and non-Yahwist general—who exhibit extreme faith and obedience to Yahweh. In noting the stark contrast in the opening sequence, Choon-Leong Seow writes, "Ironically, the king of Israel does not seem to know what the captive slave girl in Damascus knows: that there is a prophet in Samaria who could perform the miracle. He sees only the impossibility of the case; she sees its possibility."[54] Likewise, the disparity is further established as Naaman the Syrian professed faith in God (5:15–18) and Gehazi disobeyed the word of the Lord spoken through Elisha (5:21–27); for "the Gentile Naaman was restored, while the Israelite Gehazi was cursed."[55] The glaring contrasts in the text are later referenced by Jesus who noted again to the Galilean crowd that just as in the days of Elijah and Elisha a prophet was still not accepted among his own people (Luke 4:24–27). Within these contrasts, the universality of God once again is addressed as the story illustrates that faith is not the property of one gender, one social group, or one nation. Instead, true faith can be found outside of Israel's borders among the Israelites in captivity and among the non-Israelites that God calls to himself.

52. Kaiser, *Mission*, 44.

53. Hobbs, *II Kings*, 57.

54. Seow, *1 and 2 Kings*, 193.

55. Ibid., 197. Also see Cogan, *I Kings*, 67; and Cohn, *2 Kings*, 42.

As with the Sidonian widow, Naaman received the restoration of his life through an act of faith. The promise of God to Abraham in Genesis 12:3 again became apparent in this story as Elisha blessed Naaman with a renewed body and thus new life. Although the skin disease which afflicted Naaman was most likely not Hansen's disease (or leprosy as it is known today), it carried "with it a social stigma and [was] associated with death."[56] Therefore the complete healing that Naaman received via Elisha (2 Kgs 5:14) would have enabled him to return fully to his military duties and once again be accepted wholly back into society. The incredible restoration of life to this diseased warrior was an overwhelming experience for him and evidence of the amazing impact of God's touch upon one's life. The author(s) mentions that Naaman's flesh "was restored and became clean like that of a young boy" (5:14) echoing the reference to the faithful young Israelite girl who led him to Elisha (5:2–3) and the future faithfulness of this formally pagan soldier.

As a result of God's restoration of Naaman's body, the Aramean officer acknowledged Yahweh as the one and only living God. Upon his healing, Naaman proclaimed, "Now I know that there is no God in all the world except in Israel" (2 Kgs 5:15). In order to fulfill his oath to "never again make burnt offerings and sacrifices to any other god but the Lord" (5:17), Naaman asked for soil to take with him to Syria upon which he will worship God. Although perhaps exhibiting an "unsophisticated" theology[57] in the removal of soil from Israel, Naaman showed his dedication to worshipping Yahweh outside the borders of Israel through a traditional method of the time.[58] Naaman in fact became a proselyte of Yahweh[59] denying all other gods and embracing monotheism.[60] As such God's words to Isaiah come to mind: "The Sovereign Lord declares—he who gathers the exiles of Israel: 'I will gather still others to them besides those already gathered'" (Isa 56:8).

Referenced in Jesus' speech to the Nazarenes (Luke 4:24–27), both the story of the Sidonian widow and Naaman the Syrian reveal that

56. Seow, *1 and 2 Kings*, 193.

57. Ibid., 195.

58. Fritz, *I and II Kings*, 260–61.

59. Cogan and Tadmor, *II Kings*, 67.

60. Fritz, *I and II Kings*, 260.

"God's universal love reaches beyond the boundaries of nationality, ethnicity and even religious affiliation."[61] Kaiser writes:

> Only one explanation will satisfy all the data: the divine revelation wanted us to see that Yahweh was truly calling all the families of the earth—even one's enemies—to the same Savior and salvation. Nothing could force God to bestow his gifts of grace or mercy, not even those of royalty or position. But then, neither could ethnicity detract from his plan to spread his grace far and wide.[62]

As such it is not surprising that Jesus would later allude to these narratives "to justify the inclusivity of his ministry (Luke 4:27). [For] just as Elijah ministered to the Phoenician widow of Zarephath and just as Elisha ministered to Naaman the Aramean, so, too, Jesus proclaimed good news to the outcasts of Jewish society as well as to some Gentiles."[63] Acknowledging the "universalism embedded in the narrative,"[64] Jesus also revealed the heart of God the father as he reached out with blessing to the nations surrounding Israel. The blessing of God through Israel proved to be a shadow of the divine blessing that would later come to all peoples of the world through Christ Jesus the Messiah.

61. Seow, *1 and 2 Kings*, 130.

62. Kaiser, *Mission*, 50.

63. Seow, *1 and 2 Kings*, 197.

64. Hobbs, *II Kings*, 69.

4

New Testament: Fulfillment of God's Blessing

In the New Testament the Abrahamic blessing sees its greatest fulfillment in the life and ministry of Jesus Christ. However, the theme of divine blessing which ran so strongly throughout the Old Testament appears to surface only sporadically within the New Testament. While the climatic fulfillment of the Abrahamic promise is in Christ, the detailed theology and explanation of the ritual of blessing is noticeably absent. Westermann explains this absence as evidence of how well the concept of blessing was already known in both Hebrew Scripture and Israelite culture. He writes that in the New Testament "blessing is spoken of without reflection as something that is known and that undeniably belongs there. No question is raised as to its meaning, and it is not regarded as a problem to be investigated."[1] Ulrich Bergmann adds that the mindset from which the apostles wrote the New Testament eliminated the need to teach any of the new believers about divine blessing. Bergmann notes:

> The reason for the concept of blessing not being stressed in the New Testament lies in the fact that it was well known from the Old Testament, and a majority of New Testament Scriptures were written in the expectation of an immediate return of the Lord. Not so in the Christian Church of the West.[2]

Therefore, the absence of a detailed explanation of the blessing act in the New Testament by no means undermines the fulfillment of the Abrahamic blessing motif through Christ and his church. On the contrary, as the idea of God's blessing was already ingrained in the theological

1. Westermann, *Blessing in the Bible*, 24.
2. Bergmann, "Old Testament," 179.

mindset of the Israelites, further explanation was not necessary. Instead, as made evident by the Apostle Paul's letter to the Galatians, the Messiah was naturally identified as the fulfillment of this promise. However, the shift from the Old Testament concept of blessing to the New Testament's concept was not entirely void of change.

One of the major differences between the Old and New Testament's interpretation of the Abrahamic blessing was the transliteration of the concept. Whereas in the Old Testament the concept of God's blessing was communicated through the Hebrew term *brk*, the New Testament translated "blessing" with the Greek term *eulogia*. With the changeover of terms, the inherent meaning of the concept of blessing also shifted slightly. The term used in Greek for the verb "to bless"—*eulogeo*—literally means "to speak well of" which is translated as (1) "to praise, to celebrate with praises," (2) "to invoke blessings upon a person," (3) "to consecrate a thing with solemn prayers, to ask God's blessing on a thing," and (4) "to cause to prosper, to make happy, to bestow blessings on."[3] In addition, the Greek verb *makarizo* is also translated in English as "to bless," here signifying "to pronounce happy, blessed."[4]

While at first glance the terms *eulogeo* and *makarizo* appear to embody the heart of the Hebrew *brk*, the New Testament concept of blessing is significantly different from the ritualistic rural practices of the nomadic Hebrews of the Old Testament. In both Greek terms, the ritualistic background of the concept is replaced with a more modern interpretation focusing primarily on praise, benediction, and happiness. While marks of all three of these elements of blessing are present in the Old Testament, the New Testament version is decidedly more refined and urbanized than its primitive counterpart. John Koenig notes that while there are references to blessing in the New Testament "it is the language of thanksgiving that predominates in our canonical Gospels and epistles."[5] In addition to the focus on praise, the New Testament also routinely adopts the invocation of blessing as a means of ritual benediction or dismissal of a group[6] which is more than a subtle shift from the serious invocation of blessing from one individual to the next in the Old Testament. Finally, blessing is sometimes equated with "the condition of happiness resulting from

3. *Vine's Complete Expository Dictionary*, s.v. "Bless, Blessed, Blessing."

4. Ibid.

5. Koenig, *Rediscovering*, 68.

6. Comfort and Elwell, *Tyndale Bible Dictionary*, 227.

being favored," as in Luke 1:42, 45, with the roots of both Greek terms being used interchangeably.[7] With the different foci in the New Testament on blessing, it is important to note that the evolution of the concept did not occur spontaneously but over many centuries. The introduction of the Greek language alone did not lead to the change, but rather a natural progression that the Israelites experienced as they moved from their nomadic upbringing to the logic-filled world of the Greek Empire.

Despite the differing emphases of blessing in the Old and New Testaments, the understanding that Christ was the fulfillment of the Abrahamic blessing was uncontested by the apostles and the early church. In fact as seen in Galatians 3:8–9, Acts 3:25–26, and Ephesians 1:3, the concept of blessing in the New Testament "has been modified to mean more or less specifically God's saving deeds in Christ."[8] The fact that "the Messiah was the fulfillment of God's covenant with Abraham, the 'seed' through which all the families of the earth would be blessed"[9] was recorded both explicitly and implicitly within the New Testament writings. Duane L. Christensen notes that both the actions of Christ and the sequence of events as recorded by the Gospel writers reveal "a consciousness that the promise made first to Abraham was being fulfilled."[10] Thus, with the coming of Christ, the apostles realized that they were eyewitness to the fulfillment of the promised "Abrahamic blessing" to the nations. Moreover, not only was God's blessing brought to the nations through Christ's teaching and words but the apostles themselves joined Christ in reaching the nations for God.

ABRAHAMIC BLESSING THROUGH JESUS

In the book of Isaiah, the prophet foretold a time when one would come who would bear "the sin of many" (Isa 53:12) and be "pierced for our transgressions . . . [and] crushed for our iniquities" (53:5). However, this suffering servant of God (52:13) would also introduce an "everlasting covenant" (55:3) and the nations would be drawn to Israel because of the "Holy One of Israel" (55:5). These prophecies of Isaiah and countless others spoke of the coming of Christ, his suffering on the cross for humanity's sins, and his eternal covenant that would be available to all

7. Urbrock, "Blessing and Curses," 756.
8. Westermann, *Blessing in the Bible*, 24.
9. Harbin, *Promise*, 469.
10. Christensen, "Nations," 1047.

who believe. Thus when Jesus read the words of the prophet Isaiah aloud at the commencement of his ministry (Luke 4:18–19), his Galilean audience would have heard echoes of the prophecies of old in his voice. Jesus proclaimed to them:

> The Spirit of the Sovereign Lord is on me, because the Lord has anointed me to preach good news to the poor. He has sent me to bind up the brokenhearted, to proclaim freedom for the captives and release from darkness for the prisoners, to proclaim the year of the Lord's favor. (Isa 61:1–2)[11]

If the implied connotation of his choice of passage wasn't clear enough, Jesus explained to the filled synagogue that "today this Scripture is fulfilled in your hearing" (Luke 4:21). The response in the synagogue was unanimous; they were pleased and the narrator notes that "all spoke well of him and were amazed at the gracious words that came from his lips" (4:22). However, Jesus' teaching did not end there; as doubts began to arise in the crowd about how Joseph's son could make these statements (4:22), Jesus reminded his audience of other prophets who were not accepted by their own people (4:23–24).

The two prophets that Jesus referenced were Elijah the Tishbite and his successor Elisha: two of Israel's most honored and respected servants of God. Jesus not only noted that they were not accepted as prophets in Israel but additionally highlighted two occasions where both prophets left the people of Israel and ministered among the Gentiles of the land (Luke 4:24–27). Jesus explained to the Nazarenes:

> I tell you the truth . . . no prophet is accepted in his hometown. I assure you that there were many widows in Israel in Elijah's time, when the sky was shut for three and a half years and there was a severe famine throughout the land. Yet Elijah was not sent to any of them, but to a widow in Zarephath in the region of Sidon. And there were many in Israel with leprosy in the time of Elisha the prophet, yet not one of them was cleansed—only Naaman the Syrian. (Luke 4:24–27)

The audience's response to Jesus' words was volatile and wherein minutes earlier the crowds were singing his praises (Luke 4:22), they were now "furious . . . and took him to the brow of the hill . . . in order to throw him down the cliff" (4:28–29). This dramatic shift of attitude among

11. Jesus also referenced Isa 61:1–2 in his answer to John the Baptist who asked him if he was the promised Messiah (Luke 7:18–23).

the people indicates their comprehension of Jesus' message of warning to them via his reference to the prophets' ministry among the Gentiles. Alfred Plummer notes that Jesus' audience "see[s] the point of His illustrations; He has been comparing them to those Jews who were judged less worthy of Divine benefits than the heathen. It is this that infuriates them, just as it infuriated the Jews at Jerusalem to be told by S. Paul that the heathen would receive the blessings which they despised."[12] Thus as Jesus "sounds a warning of God's rejection of [Israel]" he simultaneously "hints that the benefits of the gospel will be given to the Gentiles"[13] passing "over a rebellious Israel and giv[ing] his blessings to Gentiles."[14]

The theological framework of Jesus' ministry was established even in the opening of his sermon. Jesus' words to the Nazarene synagogue not only emphasized his connection with the prophets who had gone before him but also foreshadowed the progressive focus of his own future ministry.[15] Reminding his audience that "the sovereign God is free to act beyond the borders of Israel, even through Gentile worshipers of foreign gods,"[16] Jesus laid the foundation for the future inclusion of Gentiles into the family of God. This anticipation of the Gentile mission[17] led to the further fulfillment of Isaiah's prophecy that God's house "will be called a house of prayer for all nations" (Isa 56:7). It likewise confirmed Jesus' role as a vehicle of God's glorious blessing to the nations as first proclaimed to Abraham.

LIFE AND MINISTRY OF JESUS

With the coming of God's promised Messiah, the blessing of God gained flesh and walked among God's people through the person of Jesus Christ. While in the Old Testament God's blessing was poured upon individuals and nations from afar, in Jesus Christ God's blessing was brought up close and personal. Westermann notes the radical modification as he states: "In the New Testament the decisive change was that the blessing

12. Plummer, *Critical and Exegetical Commentary*, 129.

13. Ellis, *Gospel of Luke*, 96.

14. Ibid., 98.

15. Seow notes the strong parallels between the life and ministry of the prophet Elijah and Jesus Christ. He explains that Elijah's ministry is a model for that of Christ; however surpassing Elijah on every level, Jesus' final testimony is his triumph over death. *1 and 2 Kings*, 130.

16. Ibid., 129.

17. Just, *Luke 1:1—9:50*, 195–96.

of Yahweh, the God of Israel, became blessing in Christ. Christ himself became the one who blesses, and all of God's bestowal of blessing became connected with God's work in Christ."[18] However, God's blessing through Jesus Christ cannot be limited solely to "God's saving activity in Christ" but instead retains within its very essence the life-giving power that was recorded so aptly in the Old Testament.[19] Thus, the divine blessing given through Christ in addition to bringing salvation led to the "growth, maturity, prosperity and the bearing of fruit" of Jesus' followers and the church to come.[20] In addition, the many healings, deliverances, and words of life given to those around him exemplified the life-giving nature of the blessing of God poured out through the actions and words of Christ.

As Simeon prophesized over the infant Jesus in Luke 2:32, Jesus was indeed God's "salvation" and would become "a light for revelation to the Gentiles." Jesus' own cross-cultural upbringing began his interaction and ministry both inside and outside the multicultural nation of Israel. The Gospel of Matthew records that due to the tyranny of King Herod, Jesus spent his early years outside of Israel in the nation of Egypt (Matt 2:15). Additionally, when Jesus and his family did return to Israel they settled in the outskirts of the nation living in "Galilee of the Gentiles" (4:15), a region heavily influenced by the outside world. However, this cross-cultural foundation was just the beginning of the fulfillment of Simeon's prophecy. Later in Jesus' ministry, his presence as a "light for revelation to the Gentiles" (Luke 2:32) was felt as he drew crowds from both Israel and the surrounding nations (3:8). Even in his visit to the Gentile regions of Tyre and Sidon (Matt 15:21),[21] Jesus continued to push boundaries in regards to the inclusion of Gentiles.

Despite the cross-cultural motifs that run through his life and ministry, Jesus himself made it very clear that his primary purpose was to minister to the nation of Israel, not to the surrounding Gentile nations (Matt 15:24). Occasionally, however, echoes of the church's ministry to come were present in Jesus life. In two such narratives, two individual Gentiles, a Centurion and a Canaanite woman, approached Jesus with serious needs. After listening to their pleas, Jesus answered their requests

18. Westermann, *Blessing in the Bible*, 64.

19. Ibid., 67.

20. Ibid., 100.

21. Christensen, "Nations," 1047. Jesus' ministry in Tyre and Sidon is interestingly parallel to that of Elijah before him who was led by God into the region of Sidon where he was used by God to bless the widow at Zarephath (1 Kgs 17).

and miraculously healed the Centurion's servant (8:5–10) and delivered the Canaanite woman's demon-possessed daughter (15:21–28). In both cases it is significant to note that Jesus emphasized the Gentiles' great faith and humility.[22] After Jesus' encounter with the Centurion, for example, Jesus praised his faith and warns his Israelite audience:

> I tell you the truth, I have not found anyone in Israel with such great faith. I say to you that many will come from the east and the west, and will take their places at the feast with Abraham, Isaac and Jacob in the kingdom of heaven. But the subjects of the kingdom will be thrown outside, into the darkness, where there will be weeping and gnashing of teeth. (Matt 8:10–12)

This message of Israel's needed repentance and the future inclusion of Gentiles is repeated throughout Jesus' teaching. In speaking of the kingdom of God, for example, Jesus often referred to the inclusion of Gentiles among the People of God: (1) the parable of the weeds (Matt 13:37–43), (2) the parable of the net (13:47–50), (3) the parable of the wedding banquet (22:2–13), (4) the parable of the sheep and the goats (25:31–46), and (5) the teaching of the narrow door (Luke 13:22–30). Thus, while not focusing chiefly on ministering to the Gentile populations, Jesus ushered in a time of great blessing for the nations. Moreover, in preparing his church for its Gentile ministry,[23] Jesus spoke of a time when Jew and Gentile would both be considered one under God and thus equally blessed by him.

Marking the point of God's greatest blessing to the nations, Jesus prepared his disciples to continue the outpouring of God's blessing to the world. Even during his ministry on earth Jesus called his disciples to be the "salt of the earth" and "light of the world" (Matt 5:13–14); in fact, Jesus exhorted them to be witnesses and instigators of change in the nations around them. Harbin elaborates in *The Promise and the Blessing* that

> bringing the Gentiles to the true God was one of the purposes of the Messiah and was part of the message of Jesus. He Himself claimed to be the Messiah and gave proof of it. He also told His disciples to take His message to the world—first to Jerusalem,

22. Achtemeier et al., *Introducing the New Testament*, 222.

23. Achtemeier et al. write on this subject identifying Jesus' transformation of the vision of the kingdom as "paving the way" for the early church's ministry to the Gentiles (*Introducing the New Testament*, 222).

then to Judea and Samaria and then to all the nations of the earth.[24]

This prophecy of worldwide mission within Acts 1:8 is notably preceded by the empowerment of Christ's disciples by the Holy Spirit. It is thus through the power of God himself that the church is enabled to be Christ's witnesses around the earth. And as witnesses of God's new covenant through Christ they therefore will proclaim and extend the blessings of God to all the nations as God declared to their ancestor Abraham.

ABRAHAMIC BLESSING THROUGH THE EARLY CHURCH

The continued fulfillment of the Abrahamic blessing to the nations can be seen throughout the letters and missionary journeys of the early apostles. Impacting both the ideological and missional framework of the early church, Jesus paved the way for God's blessing to be extended outside of Israel. As God led Gentiles to faith through Christ (Acts 8:4–40; 10:1–48), the mindset of the apostles grew into a deeper understanding of the commission Jesus had left them (see Acts 1:8). While having originally thought that converted Gentiles needed to adopt Jewish religious customs, the early church leaders grew in their awareness that only through faith in Christ was one saved, whether Gentile or Jew (Acts 11:18; 15:1–31). Thus, in accepting this new revelation, the apostles began to look at both the Old Testament writings and Jesus' teachings with new eyes (see Acts 2:14–39). Simultaneously, the missionary endeavors of the church began to extend further and further out into the surrounding nations, reaching a literary climax as Paul enters the capital of the world, Rome, in Acts 28:16–31. With both of these paradigm shifts, the words and deeds of the early church began to display the universal heart of God and the Abrahamic blessing was once more extended to the nations.

GENTILE MISSION OF THE EARLY CHURCH

The exegetical work of the Apostle Paul in particular was heavily influenced by Jesus' teachings and his own "missionary experiences of God's direct, redemptive dealings with Gentiles."[25] Moreover, Paul found the inclusion of the Gentiles into the kingdom of God "at the very heart of the Abrahamic covenant. In fact, as Romans 15:9–12 shows . . . Paul

24. Harbin, *Promise*, 448.

25. Longenecker, *Galatians*, 115.

found God's saving purpose toward Gentiles everywhere in the Old Testament."[26] Paul expressed his understanding of God's universal plan for the nations in a number of his missionary letters to the churches established outside of Israel's borders. In three of his letters in particular—Romans, Galatians and Ephesians—Paul elaborated upon the teachings of Christ and declared that through Christ the full blessings of God were in fact given to Gentile believers. Although each of these letters could be explored on numerous levels, the following study will be limited to examining Galatians 3:6–14, Romans 15:26–29, and Ephesians 1:3–14 and their connection to the fulfillment of the Abrahamic blessing.

The most well-known passage connecting the Abrahamic blessing and its fulfillment through Jesus Christ is Galatians 3:6–14. In speaking to the church in Galatia, Paul rebuked the local congregation for deceptively believing that salvation comes through the Law instead of through faith in Jesus Christ (Gal 3:1–5). In presenting his case, the apostle turned to Abraham who believed God and was thus deemed righteous before God (Gen 15:6; Gal 3:6). While the main purpose of Paul's discourse was to remind the new believers that it is through faith alone that one is saved, Paul revealed his missional theology in the midst of his argument. Paul declared to the Galatian church:

> Just as Abraham "believed God, and it was reckoned to him as righteousness," so, you see, those who believe are the descendants of Abraham. And the Scripture, foreseeing that God would justify the Gentiles by faith, declared the gospel beforehand to Abraham, saying, "All the Gentiles shall be blessed in you." For this reason, those who believe are blessed with Abraham who believed. (Gal 3:6–9 NRSV)

In this passage, Paul explained that through the act of faith in Christ, Gentiles were joined with their fellow Jewish believers as heirs of Abraham. As Abraham's heirs, Gentiles were additionally made heirs of the promise given to Abraham and thus received the blessings of God poured upon Abraham and his descendents.

Paul's interpretation of the Genesis 12:3 passage declared that both Gentile and Jewish believer alike were united together by being "in Christ."[27] Paul's argument was simple: "[Abraham] believed in God and

26. Ibid.

27. Ibid., 124.

was blessed; Christians believe and are blessed with Abraham."[28] Paul's conclusion was founded on the understanding that the redemptive work of Christ joined together that which was once separated. Austin P. Flannery in the *Documents of Vatican II* expounds on this theological understanding by identifying the revolutionary nature of the new covenant of Christ:

> Christ instituted this new covenant, namely the new covenant in his blood (cf. 1 Cor. 11:25); he called a race made up of Jews and Gentiles which would be one, not according to the flesh, but in the Spirit, and this race would be the new People of God. For those who believe in Christ, who are reborn, not from a corruptible seed, but from an incorruptible one through the word of the living God (cf. 1 Pet. 1:23), not from flesh, but from water and the Holy Spirit (cf. John 3:5–6), are finally established as "a chosen race, a royal priesthood, a holy nation . . . who in times past were not a people, but now are the People of God" (1 Pet. 2:9–10).[29]

This joining together of Jew and Gentile enabled the blessings of God first given to Abraham and his descendants to extend also to the recent members of the new covenant. As in the covenants of the Old Testament, individuals and nations who cut covenant with Israel would also enter into the blessings that had been given to the Hebrew nation by God. In Paul's discourse, he also noted that this extension of God's blessing to the Gentiles was not an afterthought but instead was planned by God from the beginning (Gal 3:8) revealing once again God's universal desire to bless all the peoples of the earth.

As Paul continued on his missionary journeys, he again noted the spiritual blessings which the Gentile believers had received through Christ. In the apostle's letter to the church in Rome, he wrote of the generosity of the congregations in Macedonia and Achaia who "were pleased to make a contribution for the poor among the saints in Jerusalem" (Rom 15:26). Paul noted in this transaction the reciprocation of blessings from the Gentile church to the believers in Israel (15:27). The circular benefit of blessings found in the Old Testament narratives of Joseph and Pharaoh (Gen 41–47) and Elijah and the Sidonian widow (1 Kgs 17:7–24) are brought to mind as Paul noted that in sharing the spiritual blessings of the Jewish believers, the Gentile believers returned the blessing in the

28. Ibid.

29. Flannery, *Documents*, 359.

form of material gifts (Rom 15:27). This "mutuality of blessing," which is later echoed in verse 29,[30] presents a case in which both the Jewish and Gentile church experience the "flow of blessing . . . at the spiritual level" and at the physical level.[31] Paul made a distinct statement in his narrative when he pointed out that the Gentiles were not only at the receiving end. of God's blessings, but were also used by God as vehicles of blessing to Israel.

In his letter to the Ephesians, Paul elaborated on the nature of the "spiritual blessings" (Rom 15:27; Eph 1:3) given through Christ to both Jewish and Gentile believers. Paul in fact included a list of spiritual blessings in Ephesians 1:5–14 stating them as follows:

- "[God] destined us for adoption as his children through Jesus Christ . . ." (Eph 1:5).
- "In him we have redemption through his blood, the forgiveness of our trespasses . . ." (Eph 1:7).
- "With all wisdom and insight he has made known to us the mystery of his will . . . as a plan for the fullness of time, to gather up all things in him, things in heaven and things on earth" (Eph 1:8–10).
- "In Christ we have also obtained an inheritance . . ." (Eph 1:11).
- "In him you also . . . were marked with the seal of the promised Holy Spirit; this is the pledge of our inheritance toward redemption as God's own people . . ." (Eph 1:13–14 NRSV).

This extensive inventory of spiritual blessings—including "election to holiness, instatement as God's sons and daughters, redemption and forgiveness, the gift of the Spirit and the hope of glory"[32]—is part of Paul's praise to God. Starting with the phrase "Praise be to the God and Father of our Lord Jesus Christ who has blessed us in the heavenly realms with every spiritual blessing" (Eph 1:3), Paul followed the traditional Jewish *berakhah* or "blessing." Most commonly found in Jewish synagogue worship, the *berakhah* declares the reasons for which God should be blessed.[33] While starting with the Hebrew term *drb*, "to bless," the act of the speaker blessing God is more an act of thanksgiving and praise than blessing as defined in Hebrew Scripture. However, the reciprocal

30. Moo, *Epistle*, 907.
31. Dunn, *Romans 9–16*, 876.
32. Bruce, *Epistles*, 253.
33. Ibid., 252–53.

interaction between the Divine and humans again emphasizes the cyclic nature of blessing which flows from one party to the next.

An additional factor to consider within this passage is Paul's emphasis on spiritual blessings versus material blessings. Though not dismissing the material, Paul was more concerned with the spiritual blessings that one attains through having a relationship with Christ than the blessings within the physical world. Within modern Western society the term "spiritual" is often connected to one's personal spirituality. However, as Andrew T. Lincoln notes, Paul's use of the term most likely refers to the work of the Holy Spirit and not an individual spiritual experience. Lincoln explains that the "fullness of divine blessing can be described as 'spiritual,' not because it belongs to a person's inner, hidden life . . . but because it is bound up with the Holy Spirit. This sense of 'spiritual,' as resulting from the presence and work of the Spirit."[34] Likewise, Paul's mention of blessing "in the heavenly realm" refers to "the realm to which Christ had been raised (Eph. 1:20) and to which his people, united to him by faith, were raised with him (Eph. 2:6)."[35] It is again through the work of the Holy Spirit that one can enter these heavenly realms while on earth and experience these spiritual blessings.[36]

In addition to Christ's influence on the theological teachings of the apostles, Jesus also impacted the missionary endeavors of the early church. In reaching out to the nations with the good news of Christ, the new believers found themselves to be the ambassadors of God's blessing to all people groups. Miraculous healings, deliverances, conversions, and the planting of churches all pointed to the role of the Holy Spirit working through the church to bless the nations. Flannery describes the role of the church after Pentecost as receiving "the mission of proclaiming and establishing among all peoples the kingdom of Christ and of God."[37] Thus, those nations "who [had] dropped out of the power of Yahweh's blessing"[38] were once again invited back into the blessing of God through faith in Jesus Christ.

34. Lincoln, *Ephesians*, 19–20.

35. Bruce, *Epistles*, 154.

36. Ibid.

37. Flannery, *Documents*, 353.

38. Brueggemann, "Ministry Among," 22.

5

Missional Analysis: Continuance of God's Blessing

In this chapter I interpret the data from my exegesis of the Abrahamic blessing motif in Scripture through the lenses of standard missiological categories.[1] As mentioned previously, the mission theology categories of agents of mission, motivational factors, message shared, methods of mission, and missional expansion are common categories of mission theology in addition to being natural categories which emerged out of my field research data. In this chapter I use these categories as a missional framework[2] to analyze the Abrahamic blessing motif in the patriarchal narratives in the book of Genesis, the narratives of the prophets Elijah and Elisha, the life and ministry of Jesus Christ, and the narrative of the early church.

AGENTS OF MISSION[3]

In this section, I identify the primary agents of God's blessing within the Abrahamic blessing motif. Specifically, I describe the characteristics of the individuals in both the Old and New Testaments who share God's blessing with the surrounding nations.

1. See table 1, Missional Categories, in chap. 2, "Methodology," for category definitions.

2. In order to avoid data manipulation, the subcategories listed in this chapter are unique to this particular data set and were not formulated to mirror other subheadings within this paper.

3. As the book of Genesis lists several key individuals in association with the Abrahamic blessing motif, in this section I have chosen to focus on the individuals' narratives rather than their shared general characteristics.

Abraham

Of primary importance in the Abrahamic blessing motif is the original recipient of the Abrahamic blessing, Abraham son of Terah. Called by God in Genesis 12:1, Abraham is commanded by God to leave his country and father's house and to go to the land that God will show him. This divine command was met with obedience, as the formally unknown Abraham "went, as the Lord had told him" (Gen 12:4). It is important to note that there is no indication within the Genesis narrative as to why Abraham the Hebrew was chosen by God or whether or not he worshipped God prior to his call. What is known, however, was that he was obedient to the call and continued to follow God both figuratively and literally during his lifetime.

The person of Abraham was also distinguished by the fact that God made a covenant with him. First established in their initial interaction in Genesis 12:1–9,[4] the covenant treaty was officially declared in Genesis 15 when the narrator proclaims: "on that day the Lord made a covenant with Abram" (Gen 15:18). The blessings associated with this covenant are also important as they present physical evidence of the covenant relationship between Abraham and God. Clearly visible to the neighboring peoples, God's physical blessings upon Abraham and his family was testament to the fact that the presence of the Lord was with them. For example, when Abimelech invited Abraham to cut a covenant with him in Genesis 21, the foreign king exclaimed to Abraham that he noticed that "God is with you in everything that you do" (21:22). This interconnection between the blessings of God and the presence of God is repeated in the Genesis narrative as both kings and relatives equate the physical blessing of God upon Abraham and his family as evidence of God's presence with them.[5]

Another significant characteristic of Abraham was his role as God's vehicle of blessing to the nations. As first spoken in Genesis 12:3, it was to be through Abraham and his seed that God would bless all the peoples of the world.[6] Repeatedly proclaimed upon Abraham,[7] God repeated this missional blessing to both Abraham's son Isaac (Gen 26:4) and his grand-

4. God also reiterated his covenantal blessing upon Abraham in Gen 13:14–18.

5. See Gen 26:12–16; 30:27; 39:3; 39:21–23; 41:37.

6. The introduction of Abraham therefore did not signal the termination of God's concern for the nations but instead marked the beginning of God's sacred protection of his blessing that "stretches from Abraham to the Messiah" (Sundkler, *World*, 17).

7. See Gen 12:3; 18:18; 26:4.

son Jacob (28:14). Thus, as God promised Abraham, the blessing to the nations through his family tree extended as God echoed the same promise to his descendents that "all the families of the earth shall be blessed in you and in your offspring" (28:14 NRSV).

A further distinguishing characteristic of Abraham was his alien status throughout his lifetime. Although God repeatedly promised Abraham from their first interaction that "the land that you see I will give to you and to your offspring forever,"[8] the fullness of this promise was not evident until the days of Joshua.[9] Abraham and his immediate descendents were instead nomads in the land, moving from region to region as they tended their flocks and herds. As strangers in the land, Abraham and his descendants interacted frequently with the non-Yahwist communities around them; Abraham and his family cut covenants with local rulers (Gen 21:22–34), partitioned to God on foreign leaders' behalf (20:17; 18:22–33), solved political conflicts (21:25–31), lived within foreign protectorates (12:10; 14:13; 20:1, 15; 21:34, 47:11–12), and on occasion sought vengeance on the surrounding communities through warfare (14:13–16; 34:1–29). The sons of Abraham in fact lived their entire lives as sojourners in the land as they waited for God's promise to come to pass.

Despite not witnessing the fulfillment of all that was promised during his lifetime, Abraham remained faithful to God in both word and deed. Abraham's constant faith is referenced by the Apostle Paul in Galatians 3:6 when he notes that Abraham "believed God and it was credited to him as righteousness."[10] Nevertheless, there were moments when Abraham did doubt the sovereignty of God as is evidenced in his repeated deception of King Abimelech and the Egyptian Pharaoh regarding his wife Sarah (Gen 12:11–20; 20:1–18) and his hesitancy in believing that he would inherit the land (15:7). But moments of great obedience and faithfulness mark his life.[11] A pinnacle event, for example, in Abraham's

8. See Gen 12:7; 13:14–16; 15:7–8, 17–21; 17:8.

9. Two exceptions to Abraham and his kin owning land include Abraham's purchase of the field of Ephron the Hittite in Machpelah in order to bury his wife Sarah (Gen 23), and Jacob's purchase of a plot of land from the sons of Hamor in Canaan (33:18–20).

10. Also see Rom 4:3 and Gen 15:6.

11. Examples of Abraham's faith are seen when Abraham chooses to follow God (Gen 12:1–4), when he believes God will provide an heir (15:4), and when he offers his son Isaac in obedience to God (22).

faith journey was his willingness to sacrifice his son Isaac (22). Prevented at the last minute from slaughtering his promised heir, an angel of the Lord proclaimed to Abraham that he would indeed be blessed by God: "Because you have done this, and have not withheld your son, your only son, I will indeed bless you, and I will make your offspring as numerous as the stars of heaven and as the sand that is on the seashore" (22:15–17). Although this divine proclamation of blessing had been given previously,[12] Abraham's demonstration of ultimate obedience to God appears to further cement the fulfillment of the blessings spoken over him and the covenantal relationship that he had with God.

Patriarchs

A continued vessel of God's blessing to the nations, the immediate descendents of Abraham were also called and blessed by God.[13] As the leader of his family, God's blessing upon the head of the clan, Abraham, implicitly caused all those underneath his leadership to also be blessed. With the introduction of each new patriarch, God clearly reestablished his covenantal promises with each of Abraham's descendents.[14] There were adaptations, however, in this passing down of the Abrahamic blessing to the official heir apparent as is seen in Genesis 27:25–29 when Jacob stole Esau's rightful blessing and in Genesis 49:22–26 when Joseph, the second-last born, was given a blessing above his brothers. Nevertheless, regardless of family politics, God did faithfully extend his original blessing from Abraham to each new patriarch and generation of Abraham's family.[15]

A contextual factor which also distinguishes Abraham's family from the future conduits of God's blessing in Scripture was its recent introduction to God. While the future people of Israel were swayed by the pagan worship of surrounding nations, Abraham's family showed evidence of having originally emerged from an idolatrous background. While each patriarch chose to follow God faithfully, instances such as Rachel stealing Laban's household idols (Gen 31:19) and Laban's use of a diviner (30:27)

12. Gen 12:1–4; 13:14–18; 15:1–21; 17:1–8.

13. As Kaiser notes, Abram was not given the missional blessing alone but instead "Israel was to be God's missionaries to the world" (*Mission*, 20).

14. See Gen 26:2–5, 24–25 (Isaac) and 28:12–20; 35:9–14; 46:1–3 (Jacob).

15. As Verkuyl explains, this choosing of Abraham's family by no means indicates that God has lost sight of the nations. Instead, Israel was selected as a "segment of all humanity . . . a minority to serve the majority" (*Contemporary Missiology*, 91–92).

indicate that the house of Terah may have worshipped other gods prior to God's calling of Abraham in Genesis 12:1–3. Additionally, God's identification as the God of Abraham, Isaac and Jacob[16] in the Genesis narrative illustrates that the patriarchs' knowledge of God only reached back to their ancestor Abraham. Despite this relatively new introduction to the God of Abraham, each patriarch accepted God as his God, following God faithfully and without deviation during his lifetime.

Evidence of the patriarchs' devotion to God was seen most fully in their faithful acts of worship. As Noah built an altar to the Lord after the flood (Gen 8:20), the patriarchs likewise worshipped their God through the building of sacrificial altars.[17] The sacrificing of animals upon these altars was equated with the act of worship as illustrated in Abraham's instructions to his servants: "Then Abraham said to his young men, 'Stay here with the donkey; the boy [Isaac] and I will go over there; *we will worship*, and then we will come back to you'" (22:5 NRSV, italics added). Thus, the building of stone altars and the patriarchs' act of calling upon "the name of the Lord" (13:4; 26:25) represented their loyal worship of the God of Abraham. Often located in areas where God had revealed himself to them,[18] the patriarchs exhibited an understanding and respect of sacred place. This is illustrated when Isaac, fleeing from his brother Esau, encountered God and his angels in a dream. Upon waking up, Isaac declared, "Surely the Lord is in this place and I did not know it! How awesome is this place! This is none other than the house of God, and this is the gate of heaven" (28:16–17 NRSV). It was thus in the midst of encountering God or in response to an interaction with God that worship took place.

Prophets

As previously mentioned, an exhaustive analysis of the agents of the Abrahamic blessing in the Old Testament is out of the scope of this present study. Thus, narratives from 1 and 2 Kings have been chosen as examples of the missional extension of God's blessing to the nations within the Hebrew Scriptures. Within these narratives, Elijah the Tishbite and his successor, Elisha son of Shaphat, played key roles as they offered God's

16. See Gen 24:12; 26:24; 28:13; 31:5, 13, 29, 42, 53; 32:9; 43:23; 46:1, 3; 49:25, 50:17.

17. See Gen 12:7, 8; 13:4, 18; 22:9; 26:25; 33:20; 35:7.

18. See Gen 12:7; 26:25; 35:7.

blessing to a Sidonian widow in Zarephath (1 Kgs 17:8–16) and a Syrian army commander suffering from leprosy (2 Kgs 5:1–27).[19] Both prophets in Israel,[20] Elijah and Elisha were called by God to be his mouthpiece to political leaders and the people of Israel.[21]

In addition to acting as vessels of God's word to the people, both Elijah and Elisha were characterized by their faithful obedience to God. The narrative of Elijah, for example, is filled with God's direct commands to the prophet and Elijah's immediate obedience: "Then the word of the Lord came to Elijah: 'Leave here . . .' So [Elijah] did what the Lord had told him" (1 Kgs 17:2–5). Likewise in the narrative of Elisha, when the prophet Elijah anointed Elisha son of Shapha to succeed him as prophet, the young farmer immediately responded. Moreover, he proceeded to slaughter his oxen and burn his plowing equipment[22] which all indicates the strength of Elisha's commitment as he had burned his livelihood, never to return to his old life or his old profession. Through these actions, Elisha demonstrated a complete surrender and obedience to the will of God.

Elijah and Elisha both demonstrated an intimate relationship and connection with God. This was evident in Elijah's life when God protected and fed the prophet as he fled King Ahab (1 Kgs 17:2–4); God heard Elijah's prayer and raised the Sidonian widow's son from the dead (17:22); God revealed himself to Elijah (19:9–13); and finally when God took Elijah directly up to heaven in a chariot (2 Kgs 2:1–12). Receiving a double portion of Elijah's spirit (2:9–10), Elisha also displayed an intimate relationship with God, apparent in the many miracles that took place at the word of Elisha his prophet.[23] Furthermore, Elisha was described as having the word of the Lord with him (3:12) and was referenced as having the hand of the Lord come upon him as he spoke God's message (3:15).[24] All these examples indicate that both Elijah and Elisha

19. Both of these narratives demonstrate Brueggemann's argument "that [the] power of blessing concentrated in Israel is no property for Israel" but it was meant to be transmitted to the surrounding peoples who "since their embrace of the curse, [had] been deficient in the power to choose a prosperous future" ("Ministry Among," 24).

20. See 1 Kgs 17:1; 19:16 and 2 Kgs 5:8.

21. See 1 Kgs 17:1, 14, 16, 24; 19:16.

22. See 1 Kgs 19:19–21.

23. See 2 Kgs 2:19–25; 4:1–37.

24. Elijah is also recorded as having the power of the Lord come upon him when

were beloved servants of the Lord and as such had the authority to bless, heal, curse, and work miracles in the name of the Lord.

A final characteristic which Elijah in particular exhibited was his boldness and courage in proclaiming the word of the Lord in the midst of persecution. Called the "troubler of Israel" (1 Kgs 18:17 NRSV) and Ahab's "enemy" (21:20), Elijah spent a large portion of his ministry running and hiding from the idolatrous King Ahab and his pagan wife Jezebel (17:3). Despite this persistent persecution, Elijah displayed tremendous courage as was illustrated in his challenge to the priests of Baal (18:16–46) and his message of death to King Ahaziah of Samaria (2 Kgs 1:4). But Elijah also displayed moments of fear: he ran for his life from an angry Queen Jezebel and prayed to God that he might die (1 Kgs 19:4). Overall, however, Elijah's faithful obedience to God was most prominent in his life and allowed him to fulfill his mission on earth before God took him to heaven (2 Kgs 2:11).

Jesus Christ

The greatest fulfillment of the Abrahamic blessing, Jesus Christ of Nazareth represented a turning point in the blessing of God reaching all the nations of the earth. A direct descendent of Abraham,[25] Jesus' sacrifice on the cross enabled all peoples, both Jews and Gentiles, to receive the blessing given to Abraham by faith.[26] Whereas prior to the coming of the Messiah the blessing of God was extended sporadically to the surrounding nations, the coming of Christ opened up the floodgates of God's blessing as the good news of Christ Jesus was sent out over all the earth.[27] Jesus Christ became not only an agent of his Father's mission but the blessing incarnate. He was the ultimate fulfillment of God's promise to Abraham and the means by which God blessed all the nations of the earth to an extent never seen before.[28]

As an agent of mission, Jesus was more than a vessel of God, he was God. Despite this difference between the son of God and other human

he ran ahead of Ahab to Jezreel (1 Kgs 18:46).

25. See Matt 1:1–17.

26. See Gal 3:14.

27. See Acts 1:8.

28. While the New Testament tends to equate the Abrahamic blessing with Christ rather than material blessing, there is no indication within the New Testament that the previous physical expressions of God's blessings as expressed in the Old Testament no longer exist.

agents of God's mission, Jesus displayed many of the same characteristics as the vehicles of God's blessing from the past. For example, Jesus was obedient to God unto death (John 10:18), he suffered great persecution,[29] and he shared an intimate relationship with his Father. His personal relationship with God was particularly evident in the many miracles and signs and wonders that he did during his ministry in Israel and in his vibrant prayer life with his Father.[30] In addition, as with the patriarchs, Jesus was a member of Abraham's own family; he was a direct descendent of Abraham and as such was heir to God's promise in Genesis 12:1–3. It was with these parallel characteristics that Jesus joined those who had gone before him in becoming the greatest vehicle of God's blessing to the nations.

Early Church

The disciples who were invited by Christ to join him became the next agents of God's mission to the nations. The calling of the patriarchs in the Old Testament often took place as a private encounter with the divine, but Jesus frequently called his disciples in the midst of their daily tasks. Matthew, for example, was sitting in his tax collector's booth when Jesus walked by and asked him to follow him.[31] Likewise, Simon Peter and his brother Andrew[32] were washing their nets after an unsuccessful evening fishing on Lake Gennesaret when they encountered Jesus on the shore. In the same narrative, James and John, the sons of Zebedee, were repairing their nets in a boat when Jesus called out to them.[33] Although John 1:35–51 indicates that both Andrew and Simon Peter had encountered Jesus previously, their immediate acceptance to his invitation "follow me" is still significant. In fact, all the individuals who were commanded by Christ to follow him accepted "at once" (Matt 4:20) or "immediately"

29. Jesus' greatest persecution, his trial and crucifixion, is recorded in Matt 27, Mark 15, Luke 23, and John 19.

30. There are numerous references to Jesus' prayer life in the New Testament, including those found in the following passages: Matt 14:23; Mark 1:35; Luke 3:21; 6:12; 22:39; and John 17.

31. See Matt 9:9–13, Mark 2:14–17, and Luke 5:27–32.

32. Although God's use of clans and families is not as prominent in the New Testament, it is interesting to note that two sets of the disciples were brothers: Andrew and Simon Peter, and John and James the sons of Zebedee. Thus, in these instances God did use families to bless his people.

33. See Matt 4:18–22, Mark 1:16–20, Luke 5:1–11, and John 1:40–42.

(4:22); or as in the case of Matthew the tax collector, they simply "got up and followed [Jesus]" (9:9). The immediacy displayed in all the recorded narratives of calling in the gospels displays the confidence and obedience that the disciples had as they responded to Christ. As the patriarchs before them, they both heard and accepted God's will for their lives and their future and current roles in God's mission.

In following Christ, Jesus' disciples joined him in blessing their immediate community. Focused during his lifetime on the "lost sheep of Israel" (Matt 15:24), Jesus "gave [his disciples] authority to drive out evil spirits, and to heal every disease and sickness" (10:1). In sending the disciples out into the Israelite communities, Jesus further instructed them: "As you go preach this message: 'The kingdom of heaven is near.' Heal the sick, raise the dead, cleanse those who have leprosy, drive out demons. Freely you have received, freely give" (10:7–8). It is this passing on of the physical and spiritual blessings of God to others that points to the disciples' role in the continuation of the Abrahamic blessing motif. Although the New Testament understanding of the Abrahamic blessing centers primarily around the person of Christ, the essence of God's physical, spiritual, economic, social, and environmental blessing is still evident in the life and ministry of Christ and his followers. And while reconnection with God is established on a spiritual level through Jesus' sacrifice, the tangible blessings of God are also present as Jesus, and later his disciples, preached good news to the poor . . . bound up the brokenhearted . . . proclaimed freedom for the captives and release from darkness for the prisoners . . . and proclaimed the year of the Lord's favor (Isa 61:1–2)[34]—both literally and figuratively.

As the early church grew following Christ's ascension, more individuals were called and chosen to continue Christ's work on earth. Of these, the most notable instance was the calling of Saul of Tarsus on the road to Damascus (Acts 9:1–19). Traveling down to Damascus with the authority to imprison any believers who belonged to "the Way," Saul was stopped in his tracks as "a light from heaven flashed around him . . . and [he] heard a voice say to him, "Saul, Saul, why do you persecute me?" (v. 3–4). Jesus then commanded Saul to "get up and go into the city" (v. 5–6) where he would receive further instructions. In obedience, Saul was led

34. Jesus references Isa 61:1–2 when he speaks in the synagogue in Nazareth (Luke 4:14–21) noting to the crowd that "today this Scripture is fulfilled in your hearing" (v. 21). He also refers to Isaiah's messianic prophecy when asked if he is the messiah by John the Baptist.

to town where eventually he met a disciple of Christ called Ananias who through prayer healed him and filled him with the Holy Spirit (v. 17–19). The calling of Saul by Christ marks a major turning point in the work and ministry of the early church. Whereas the original disciples were called to minister to the lost sheep of Israel, Saul was ordained by God to be his "chosen instrument to carry my name before the Gentiles and their kings and before the people of Israel" (v. 15). Thus, with the calling of Saul, the official expansion of God's blessing to the Gentiles began.[35]

With the expansion of ministry to the Gentiles, the new believers, both Jews and Gentiles, began to be included in God's mission as conduits of his blessing. A few of the more significant Jewish converts that joined Paul in his early ministry included Timothy of Lystra (Acts 16:1); Aquila and Priscilla, recent residents of Corinth (18:1–3); and Apollos of Alexandria (18:24). In addition, it was also recorded that Paul had several Gentile traveling partners who joined him in his ministry: "Sopater son of Pyrrhus from Berea, Aristarchus and Secundus from Thessalonica, Gaius from Derbe . . . and Tychicus and Trophimus from the province of Asia" (20:4). This expansion of calling given to both Jewish and Gentile believers continued to increase throughout the early missionary journeys. When Paul eventually wrote his letter to the Roman church, for example, the apostle extended a multitude of greetings to the many Jewish and Gentile leaders of the church.[36] Moreover, Paul's eventual arrest in Jerusalem was provoked by the rumor of his entering the holy temple with one of his Gentile coworkers (21:29). Therefore, it was during the first decades of the church's expansion that Gentiles not only began to receive God's blessing through Christ, but they also became co-ministers alongside their Jewish counterparts in extending God's blessing to all peoples.

MOTIVATIONAL FACTORS

In the following section the motivational factors that lead individuals and groups to participate in the *missio Dei* in Scripture are presented. As interviews cannot be conducted with the Hebrew leaders of old, their

35. Although Christ's calling of Saul to Gentile ministry is a significant turning point, it is important to note that God had already started reaching out to the non-Israelite community through the ministry of Philip in Samaria (Acts 8:4–40).

36. See Rom 16.

motivations and motivators will be determined through an analysis of their personal stories as recorded in the Old and New Testaments.

Old Testament

In the Old Testament the primary motivator of mission is God.[37] In analyzing the patriarchs' motivation for participating in God's mission, the underlying motivation is obedience to God. An additional motivation for participation in the *missio Dei* within the Old Testament was compassion. A final motivational factor in the Old Testament was the desire to declare the supremacy of Yahweh.

God as Motivator

While it would be wonderful to equate all of Abraham's interactions with his foreign neighbors with his desire to share the blessing of God with all nations, the reality is that it is God who is behind the scenes on every level. God is the originator, instigator, and distributor of his blessing to all peoples. For example, the blessing proclaimed over Abraham in Genesis 12:1–3 originated in God's desire to bless all nations, not Abraham's. Moreover, the passing of the blessing to each patriarch was initiated and fulfilled by God himself.[38] In addition, God often acted as a distributor of his blessing, as evidenced in the overflow of the blessing to Laban (Gen 30:25), Potiphar (39), the Chief Jailer (39:19–23), and Pharaoh (41:25). In fact, throughout the Genesis narrative, the narrator continually notes that it is God who has led his people and orchestrated their every step. Joseph in Genesis 45:4–8 explained God's divine providence to his brothers as he noted:

> God sent me before you to preserve for you a remnant on earth, and to keep alive for you many survivors. So it was not you who sent me here, but God; he has made me a father to Pharaoh, and lord of all his house and ruler over all the land of Egypt. (Gen 45:7–8 NRSV)

Thus, as with the literal steps of the people of Israel, it is God who initiates and distributes his blessing to all peoples.

37. Bosch goes a step further and notes that in fact "if there is a missionary in the Old Testament it is God himself" (*Transforming Mission*, 19).

38. See Gen 12:3; 18:18; 26:4; 28:14.

During the time of the prophets, God continued to be the motivator and distributor of blessing to the nations. In 1 Kings 17, for example, it was at God's command that Elijah traveled to Zarephath to see the Sidonian widow. The series of interactions that followed were thus the result of God's initial directive to the prophet. Likewise it was God who proclaimed the miraculous blessing of food upon the widow and her son: "For this is what the Lord, the God of Israel, says: 'The jar of flour will not be used up and the jug of oil will not run dry until the day the Lord gives rain on the land'" (1 Kgs 17:14). God continued to pour his blessings upon the Sidonian family when the widow's son died and it was God himself who heard Elijah's prayer and brought the boy back to life (17:22). God was thus the common factor behind each revelation of his blessing within this narrative as he both enabled and distributed his blessing.

Obedience

In analyzing the patriarchs' motivation for participating in God's mission, the underlying motivation is obedience to God.[39] Particularly within the Abrahamic narrative, there is a repeated theme of immediate obedience to God's command: "The Lord said to Abram . . . So Abram went, as the Lord had told him" (Gen 12:1–4); "The Lord said to Abram . . . So Abram moved his tent . . ." (13:14–18); "God said to Abraham . . . every male among you shall be circumcised . . . and [Abraham] circumcised the flesh of their foreskins that very day, as God had said to him" (17:9–23). In God's greatest test, Abraham was instructed to offer his son Isaac as a burnt offering to God (22:1–2), and in obedience Abraham traveled to Moriah to follow God's command. God's response to Abraham's obedience was profound: "Because you have done this . . . I will indeed bless you . . . and by your offspring shall all the nations of the earth gain blessing for themselves, *because you have obeyed my voice*" (22:15–18 NRSV, italics added). It was this obedience to God that enabled God's blessing to continue through Abraham to both his immediate descendents and the surrounding nations. As God explained to Abraham's son Isaac:

39. Wright suggests that God's blessing was in fact "dependent upon Abraham's obedience to the first command [of going to Canaan] combined with God keeping his word" (*Mission*, 206). While Wright's comment that "no leaving, no blessing" is not clearly addressed in Scripture, Abraham was motivated primarily by his desire to obey the command of the Lord which in turn enabled the blessing of God to come through his family line.

> I will be with you, and will bless you; for to you and to your descendants I will give all these lands, and I will fulfill the oath that I swore to your father Abraham. I will make your offspring as numerous as the stars of heaven, and will give to your offspring all these lands; and all the nations of the earth shall gain blessing for themselves through your offspring, because Abraham obeyed my voice and kept my charge, my commandments, my statutes, and my laws. (Gen 26:3–5 NRSV, italics added)

It was thus because of the obedience of Abraham that the blessing of God was realized and passed on to the generations to come.[40]

Compassion

An additional motivation for participation in the *missio Dei* within the Old Testament was compassion. An example of this missional empathy can be found in Genesis 18 when Abraham pleaded with God on behalf of Sodom and Gomorrah.[41] Upon hearing that God was going to judge the cities, Abraham engaged in a conversation with God begging for ever-increasing mercy: "Will you indeed sweep away the righteous with the wicked? Suppose there are fifty righteous within the city . . . Suppose forty . . . Suppose thirty . . . Suppose twenty . . . Suppose ten . . . ?" (Gen 18:23–32). This interchange with God illustrates Abraham's great concern for his pagan neighbors as they await God's judgment. While his conversation did not avoid the cities' eventual destruction, Abraham's missional intervention introduced the possibility of God's mercy to the cities; his compassion in effect introduced God's compassion into the equation.

The narratives of Elijah and Elisha also note compassion to be a motivator for missional activity. In 1 Kings 17:17–24, Elijah responded to the death of the Sidonian widow's son with great despair declaring to God: "O Lord my God, have you brought tragedy also upon this widow

40. Bowling also points out that the Joseph narrative also illustrates "obedience to God's command for the elect nation to be a blessing to the world" ("Be a Blessing," 13).

41. Abraham also intercedes regarding God's blessing being distributed to his own family in Genesis 17. In the midst of God's proclamation of blessings upon Abraham and his household, Abraham interrupts God proclaiming: "O that Ishmael might live in your sight!" (Gen 17:18). God responds that no, it will be through Isaac that the covenant will be established. However, hearing Abraham's plea God adds, "As for Ishmael, I have heard you; I will bless him and make him fruitful and exceedingly numerous; he shall be the father of twelve princes, and I will make him a great nation. But my covenant I will establish with Isaac" (17:20–21 NRSV).

I am staying with, by causing her son to die?" (v. 20). Stretching himself upon the boy's dead body three times, Elijah shouted out to God crying: "O Lord my God, let this boy's life return to him!" (v. 21). Elijah's immediate intervention in the widow's distress highlights his own passionate desire to redeem the situation. God responded to Elijah's distress and hearing his cry returned the boy's life to him (v. 22). Through this tragic situation and Elijah's compassionate intervention, the blessing of God fell once again upon the widow and her family. Likewise, in the Naaman narrative, the commander of Aram's army was brought healing through the compassion of one individual, a young Israeli slave girl (2 Kgs 5:3). It was this young woman's suggestion that started Naaman on his journey to physical healing and spiritual redemption. Thus, in both narratives it was the loving-kindness of select individuals that extended the blessing of God to their surrounding communities.[42]

Declared God's Sovereignty

A final motivational factor in the Old Testament was the desire to declare the supremacy of Yahweh. In the 2 Kings passage, for example, the king of Israel lost hope when he heard of Naaman's request to be healed from leprosy. At this Elisha retorted back to the king: "Why have your torn your robes? Have the man come to me and he will know that there is a prophet in Israel" (2 Kgs 5:8). Whether it was Elisha's intent to make a new convert to Yahweh is unclear, however the subsequent healing of Naaman's skin condition led to his declaration: "Now I know that there is no God in all the world except in Israel" (5:15). Naaman's interaction with Elisha further led him to state his allegiance to Yahweh declaring that he would "never again make burnt offerings and sacrifices to any other god but the Lord" (5:17). While Naaman's conversion was perhaps an additional benefit, Elisha's interaction with him was motivated by a desire to prove to the king of Israel and the surrounding peoples that Yahweh was the one true sovereign all-powerful God.

New Testament

With the coming of the Christ, it was God who continued to motivate and lead his people into mission. While God was the primary motivator

42. The compassion of God toward the nations is also evident within these passages, as Bosch notes, "Yahweh's compassion reaches out to Israel and beyond . . . God is as concerned with the nations as with Israel" (*Transforming Mission*, 19).

of mission in the New Testament, the believers were also inspired by their passionate desire to share the good news of Christ with others.

God as Motivator

The guidance and leading of God's Spirit is apparent throughout the early development of the church in Jerusalem and Judea and continued until the church was established in Rome. In the book of Acts, the work of the Holy Spirit leading the church to mission started immediately with the pouring out of the Spirit during the feast of Pentecost (Acts 2). All the believers "were filled with the Holy Spirit and began to speak in other tongues as the Spirit enabled them" (Acts 2:4). The Pentecost crowds were shocked to hear their own languages spoken by the Galileans, and listening to Peter's testimony three thousand Jews decided to follow Christ that day (2:5–40). For as Jesus foretold in Acts 1:8, the coming of God's Spirit ushered in a new day of missional expansion for the kingdom of God. Furthermore, as Peter noted in his speech, the words of the prophet Joel (Acts 2:17–21; Joel 2:28–32) came to pass as the Spirit of God was poured out on young and old alike as *they* began to prophesy, see visions, and dream dreams. While God was the primary motivator of mission even at the initial Pentecost celebration, it was both God *separate from* and *within* the believers who motivated people to share the good news about Jesus Christ.

God's intimate connection with the work of his people continued throughout the book of Acts as he, often through his Spirit, prompted, led, and spoke through the believers. In a series of events in Samaria and Judea, God supernaturally orchestrated every stage of the missional expansion of his kingdom. Philip's encounter with the Ethiopian official, for example, was instigated by an angel's message from God (Acts 8:26), guided by the Spirit (8:29), and drawn to a close by a supernatural departure (8:39). Likewise, the gospel message extending to the Gentile Cornelius in Acts 10 was preceded by an angel visitation (10:3), prompted by a vision from God (10:10–16), directed by the Spirit (10:19), and finalized by a pouring out of the Spirit upon the Gentile audience (10:44–46). In both narratives, the clear director behind the events was God and it was this fact that led the Jerusalem leaders to finally accept the events and declare: "So then, God has granted even the Gentiles repentance unto life" (11:18). In this initial missional expansion outside of the Jewish community of believers, it was unmistakably God who motivated and led his people to participate in his plan for the nations.

Shared the Good News

While God was the primary motivator of mission in the New Testament, the believers were also inspired by their passionate desire to share the good news of Christ with others. In reviewing the public speeches of the apostles alone, this motivation of sharing the "good news" to Jew and Gentile is apparent. Moreover, there is a sense of urgency and passion that undergirds the apostles' message as is evident in Peter's speech to the Pentecost crowd as he urges them to "repent and be baptized, every one of you, in the name of Jesus Christ for the forgiveness of your sins" (Acts 2:38). The narrator notes toward the end of the passage that "with many other words [Peter] warned them; and he pleaded with them, "Save yourselves from this corrupt generation" (2:40). This urgent conviction to warn the hearers and convey the good news message continued throughout the missionary journeys as Stephen, Philip, Peter, Paul, and others "proclaimed the Christ" (8:5) and shared about "the forgiveness of sins" (13:38). Even as Paul's narrative in Acts draws to a close, the narrator leaves us with the image of Paul surrounded by Roman Jews from morning to night "explain[ing] to them the kingdom of God and try[ing] to convince them about Jesus from the Law of Moses and from the Prophets" (28:23). It was this fervent desire to proclaim Christ to the nations that drove the apostles to participate in God's mission in Jerusalem, Judea and Samaria, and the ends of the earth.

MESSAGE SHARED

There are numerous missional messages expressed in the Hebrew Scriptures and the New Testament in regards to the Abrahamic blessing motif. As the writing of the Old and New Testaments took place over hundreds of years, the message itself, while not changing completely, does reflect differences in the audience's cultural background, religious rituals, and covenantal agreement with God. Due to these variances, the missional messages shared in the Hebrew Scriptures and those expressed in the New Testament will be considered separately. In addition, as many significant messages are expressed in Scripture, only those closely related to the Abrahamic blessing motif will be explored.

Old Testament

The missional message regarding the blessing of the nations is repeated various times through God's covenantal promise to Abraham and his successors. Thus, the promise that "in [Abram] all the families of the earth shall be blessed" (Gen 12:3 NRSV) in many ways becomes incorporated into the purpose and destiny of God's chosen people even after the death of its first recipient Abraham. Regardless of whether or not its original recipients understood the full significance of this divine oath, upon its delivery the Hebrew people became incorporated into a promise bigger than themselves; for the promise whispered to one man living in Hārān would soon be proclaimed to the entire world through the coming of the Messiah. This unique foreshadowing of the coming of Jesus Christ provided in Genesis 12 connects this universal promise to God's larger plan for humanity. As such there is a clear sense that the blessing of the nations motif expressed in Scripture is God-ordained, God-inspired, and God-fulfilled.

The continued expression of the "blessing to the nations" motif is present both directly and indirectly in Genesis. For example, God uses a willing Joseph to save both his family and the surrounding nations during the seven years of famine (Gen 41:41—50:21). Yet, there are also examples when God's blessing is more organic and unconscious as when Jacob's blessing overflowed upon his father-in-law Laban and all his property without Jacob's knowledge (30:27). Again, this direct and indirect expression of God's blessing on the nations points to God as the source and God's people as the conscious or unconscious vehicles of his blessing.

The missional nature of this promise is further reinforced by God's own cross-cultural interactions with the peoples surrounding Abraham and his descendents. While God's focus was still primarily upon the Hebrews, the continual demonstration of God's mercy and judgment upon the nations was also evident. God was clearly not only the God of the Hebrews but also visibly has dominion over all the earth.[43] In the book of Genesis this is evident in God's appointment of Melchizedek as his high priest (Gen 14:18–20), his providence toward Hagar the Egyptian (16:7–14), his protection of Abimelech the king of Gerar (20:3–7) and

43. God's dominion over all his creation and the nations of the world is evident throughout the Hebrew Scriptures. As God declares to Israel, "Are not you Israelites the same to me as the Cushites? . . . Did I not bring Israel up from Egypt, the Philistines from Caphtor and the Arameans from Kir?" (Amos 9:7).

in a negative way his judgment upon Sodom and Gomorrah (19:1–29). Likewise, in 1 and 2 Kings, God's loving-kindness was shown through his miraculous interaction with the Sidonian widow (1 Kgs 17:13–24) and the leprous Aramian commander Naaman (2 Kgs 5:14). Through God's interaction with individuals outside his chosen people, the promise of God's blessing upon the nations came to fruition.

New Testament

Although the New Testament incorporates a variety of literary works, there is a consistent message expressed in regards to the fulfillment of the Abrahamic blessing through Christ. More than just making this connection, however, the New Testament writers move a step further to explain the role of believers within this Abrahamic promise. Therefore within the following section I will explore both the fulfillment of the Abrahamic blessing through Christ, the inheritance of believers and the proclamation of the good news to the nations.

Promise Fulfilled through Christ

Of greatest significance in the New Testament is the joyous realization that Christ is the fulfillment of the promise given to Abraham centuries before. The Apostle Paul alludes to this promise during his trial before King Agrippa as the reason why he was jailed: "And now it is because of my hope in what God has promised our fathers that I am on trial today. This is the promise our twelve tribes are hoping to see fulfilled as they earnestly serve God day and night" (Acts 26:6–7). He again mentioned this divine promise in his letter to the Roman churches as he described himself as "Paul, a servant of Christ Jesus, called to be an apostle and set apart for the gospel of God—the gospel he promised beforehand through his prophets in the Holy Scriptures regarding his Son" (Rom 1:2). Both of these references to the promise of Christ given to Israel's forefathers indicate the sovereignty and orchestration of God in the fulfillment of the promise. As Peter notes to the Pentecost crowd in Acts 2:23: "[Christ] was handed over to you by God's set purpose and foreknowledge." It was the plan of God that the promise given to Abraham and the prophets would be fulfilled through the coming of his son to earth. Far from being a coincidence, Jesus Christ was the long-awaited answer to the prophecies given to the people of Israel throughout the centuries.

This equation between the gospel of Christ and the promise is again repeated in Paul's letter to the churches in Galatia. The Apostle Paul noted that "the Scriptures foresaw that God would justify the Gentiles by faith, and announced the gospel in advance to Abraham: 'All nations will be blessed through you'" (Gal 3:8). As such, Paul indicated that the promise of redemption for all humanity was foretold to Abraham through the covenantal promise of Genesis 12:3. Furthermore, Paul equated the gospel [of Christ] with the promise that "all nations will be blessed through [Abraham]." More than just the end fulfillment of God's original promise, the coming of Christ also indicated the coming of something new. God crafted a new covenant between himself and humankind; a covenant that would be cut through having faith in Christ; a covenant that would release God's blessing upon all the nations of the earth and which fully included Gentiles.

Heirs through Christ

A parallel message intertwined with the fulfillment of the Abrahamic blessing was that believers in Christ were equal heirs of the promise. In Paul's letter to the Galatians he explained that "those who believe are children of Abraham" and therefore "those who have faith are blessed along with Abraham, the man of faith" (Gal 3:7–9). In the context of Paul's exposition, those with faith in Christ Jesus are grafted into Abraham's family and thus become recipients of God's promise of redemption through Christ. A new concept was thus introduced in the discourse as Paul answered the age-old question: "How will Abraham and his seed bless the nations?" Paul suggested that individuals could become one of Abraham's heirs through their union with Christ. It was through their expression of faith in Jesus Christ that the promises proclaimed upon Abraham could become their own.[44]

Paul also noted the extension of the Abrahamic promise to both Jews and Gentiles alike. In his discourse to the Galatians, Paul elaborated upon this concept:

> You are all sons of God through faith in Christ Jesus, for all of you who were baptized into Christ have clothed yourselves with Christ. There is neither Jew nor Greek, slave nor free, male nor female, for you are all one in Christ Jesus. If you belong to

44. See John 1:12–13.

> Christ, then you are Abraham's seed, and heirs according to the promise. (Gal 3:26–29)

This inclusion of the Gentile believers through Christ in the Abrahamic promise was reiterated again in the apostle's explanation of the purpose of Christ's coming. Paul stated that "[Christ] redeemed us in order that the blessing given to Abraham might come to the Gentiles through Christ Jesus, so that by faith we might receive the promise of the Spirit" (Gal 3:14).[45] Therefore, far from just including the Gentiles in the Abrahamic promise, Paul went one step further to suggest that the entire purpose of Christ's death and resurrection was to allow for the inclusion of the Gentile peoples into the kingdom of God.[46]

Proclamation to the Nations

The long-awaited fulfillment of the Abrahamic blessing through Christ changed the future direction of the people of God. Righteousness acquired through the law was eclipsed by righteousness acquired through faith in Christ.[47] It was therefore through faith in Jesus Christ that humankind would receive the Spirit of God and be reconciled once more to God. This good news about Jesus was at the heart of the early church's message both locally and abroad. However, before this gospel was preached, the church received its commission by Christ. In his last recorded speech in the Gospel of Matthew, Jesus charges his disciples with this evangelicalistic task. He stated:

> All authority in heaven and on earth has been given to me. Therefore go and make disciples of all nations, baptizing them in the name of the Father and of the Son and of the Holy Spirit, and teaching them to obey everything I have commanded you. And surely I am with you always to the very end of the age. (Matt 28:18–20)

This commission was again recorded in the Gospel of Luke as the author records Jesus' prophetic words to his disciples: "The Christ will suffer and rise from the dead on the third day, and repentance and forgiveness of sins will be preached in his name to all nations, beginning

45. Also see Rom 4:16–17.

46. This realization is also expressed by the Jerusalem church in Acts 10:34–35, 47; 11:15–18.

47. See Gal 3:2–3.

at Jerusalem. You are witnesses of these things" (Luke 24:46–48). Jesus concluded that "I am going to send you what my Father has promised; but stay in the city until you have been clothed with power from on high" (24:49). The believers were therefore instructed to share the good news about Jesus first in Jerusalem and then to the all the nations. However, as Luke's Gospel noted they were to remain in Jerusalem until their reception of the Holy Spirit.[48]

As foreseen by Christ, the Holy Spirit did come upon the believers during Pentecost and the disciples immediately began to proclaim the good news about Jesus Christ. From Peter's speech to the Pentecost crowd in Acts 2:14–39 onwards, the believers shared the gospel of Christ both inside Jerusalem and in the surrounding regions. The apostles were so successful in spreading the gospel that they were reproached of the Sanhedrin council who commanded them not to teach in Jesus' name (Acts 4:18; 5:28). However, even after the Sanhedrin had the apostles flogged, the narrator records that "day after day, in the temple courts and from house to house, [the disciples] never stopped teaching and proclaiming the good news that Jesus is the Christ" (5:41–42). During these early days of establishing the community of believers, it was this good news about Christ which was repeatedly highlighted by the believers.[49]

The good news itself was a declaration of the promise of God to the nations fulfilled through Christ. In Antioch of Pisidia, Paul detailed the particulars of the gospel message to his synagogue audience:

> We tell you the good news: What God promised our fathers he has fulfilled for us, their children, by raising up Jesus . . . Therefore, my brothers, I want you to know that through Jesus the forgiveness of sins is proclaimed to you. Through him everyone who believes is justified from everything you could not be justified from by the law of Moses. (Acts 13:32–39)

The gospel message was thus the glad tidings of the forgiveness of sins through Jesus Christ. Whereas the law of Moses was unable to justify all humankind's sins before God, through Jesus Christ all of humanity's sins could be forgiven. In Paul's letter to the Roman church, the apostle explained further that through Christ's sacrifice, humans were also deemed righteous before God. He declared, "But now a righteousness from God, apart from law, has been made known, to which the Law and

48. Also see Acts 1:8.

49. See Acts 8:35; 10:36; 14:7, 15, 21; 17:18.

the Prophets testify. This righteousness from God comes through faith in Jesus Christ to all who believe" (Rom 3:21–22). The need humankind has for this justification through faith is evident in Paul's closing remarks that "there is no difference . . . for all have sinned and fall short of the glory of God, and all are justified freely by his grace through the redemption that came by Christ Jesus" (3:22–24). The good news about Jesus was thus a message that all people, both Jew and Gentile, needed to hear in order to be considered righteous before God.

METHODS OF MISSION

In this section I explore the biblical methods used to extend the blessing of God to Israel and to the surrounding nations within both the Old and New Testaments.

Old Testament

In the Hebrew Scriptures God used a variety of methods through which he extended his divine blessing to the nations.[50] Within the Genesis text, these approaches fall into three categories: (1) those blessed or cursed through association with the patriarchs, (2) those blessed through establishing covenant treaties, and (3) those blessed independently by God.

Blessed/Cursed by Association

Of those blessed through their interaction with the patriarchs, Lot (Gen 19:16, 29), Laban (30:27) and Potiphar (39:1–6) stand out as examples of individuals who benefited from being in close proximity to the patriarchs. For example, in Genesis 19 when God's rescued Lot from Sodom scripture records that "*God remembered Abraham*, and sent Lot out of the midst of the overthrow" (v. 29 NRSV, italics added). Reflecting on this phrase, R. Kent Hughes notes that even Lot, the righteous remnant of Sodom, "was not saved on his own merits but through grace effected by

50. It is important to note that the fulfillment of God's mission to the nations in the Old Testament is unique to that of the New Testament. While biblical theologians such as Bosch define mission narrowly as "being sent by God to cross geographical, religious, and social frontiers in order to win others to faith in Yahweh" (*Transforming Mission*, 17) and thus claim that the Old Testament is void of mission, this conclusion is not accurate. Not only does God send individuals such as Joseph, Jonah, Elijah, Elisha, Daniel, and Isaiah to engage with heathen peoples, but the fulfillment of God's missional promise through Abraham is also repeatedly seen within the history of Israel.

Abraham's intercession."[51] However, whether or not it was actually Abraham's intercession (18:20–33) or simply Abraham's familial relationship with Lot that saved him is unclear. It is evident that Lot and his family were not saved by their own merit but instead it was through Abraham that they were saved.

Perhaps one of the most prominent stories of blessing via relationship occurs in Genesis 30 within the story of Jacob and his father-in-law Laban. After working for Laban for more than fourteen years, Jacob asked Laban to "send me away" in order that he may return to his "own home and country" (v. 25 NRSV). In Laban's response to Jacob he highlights an interesting fact: that he had received material blessings through his relationship and close proximity with his son-in-law Jacob. Laban replied to Jacob: "I have learned by divination that *the Lord has blessed me because of you*; name your wages, and I will give it" (v. 27–28 NRSV, italics added). This declaration of blessing through Jacob is an indication once again of the outward impact of the divine blessing that rested upon Abraham and his family. Wenham notes the clear connection between the divine promise of Genesis 12:3c that "all the families of the earth will be blessed through Abraham" and the declaration of Laban that he has been blessed through Abraham.[52] He writes that this story "is one of several incidents where outsiders admit that God's blessing very apparently rests on Abraham's family and those associated with them."[53] It is therefore through Laban's interaction and connection with Jacob that he received the benefits and material blessings which God has so abundantly poured upon Jacob, Abraham's heir.

Similarly, in the case of Joseph, it was Potiphar who was abundantly blessed by God due to the presence of Joseph within his household (Gen 39:1–6). The narrator records that while Joseph was in Potiphar's service, Potiphar prospered greatly as "the Lord blessed the Egyptian's house *for Joseph's sake*" (39:5 NRSV, italics added). The narrative expounds in Genesis 39:5–6 and states that

> from the time that he [Potiphar] made him [Joseph] overseer in his house and over all that he had, the Lord blessed the Egyptian's house for Joseph's sake; the blessing of the Lord was on all that he had, in house and field. So he left all that he had in

51. Hughes, *Genesis*, 276.

52. Wenham, *Genesis 16–50*, 255.

53. Ibid.

> Joseph's charge; and, with him there, he had no concern for anything but the food that he ate.[54]

Just as Lot and his family were rescued from Sodom because "God remembered Abraham" (Gen 19:29), so Potiphar was also recorded as receiving blessing "for Joseph's sake" (39:5). An obvious distinction however between the two stories is that in the case of Laban, Jacob was not only married into the family but additionally Laban was his mother's brother and thus a blood relative. This could explain how God's blessing upon the family of Abraham could logically fall upon Laban. On the other hand, in the case of Potiphar, the beneficiary of God's blessing was clearly a foreign Egyptian man. Moreover, the relationship between Potiphar and Joseph was one of master and servant. Both of these facts dismiss the possibility of God blessing Potiphar due to familial ties or a covenantal relationship with Joseph. Thus, although the text only records that Potiphar was blessed for the benefit of Joseph, the fact remains that God blessed an Egyptian and his whole household due to his connection with Joseph, an heir of the Abrahamic blessing.

This distribution of blessing was not the only consequence of the nations' interaction with Abraham and his descendents. Just as Genesis 12:3 relates that "I [God] will bless those who bless you" it also states "and whoever curses you I will curse." These words came to pass in the stories of Abraham and Isaac's deception of the Egyptian Pharaoh (Gen 12:17–20) and Abimelech the king of Gerar (20:1–18; 26:6–16). In all three cases, the foreigners were cursed independently by God for claiming the wives of Abraham and Isaac. The complexity of all the stories is established in the fact that Abraham (12:17–20; 20:1–18) and Isaac (26:6–16) deceived the kings of the land concerning their wives claiming that they were their sisters. Nevertheless, God cursed both men for their crimes, bringing "great plagues" upon the household of the Egyptian Pharaoh (12:17) and by closing the wombs of the house of Abimelech (20:18). Within the story of Abimelech, however, God himself came to Abimelech in a dream and acknowledged Abimelech's innocence explaining that "it was I [God] who kept you from sinning against me" (20:6 NRSV). Therefore just as Genesis 12:3 proclaimed, the overflow of God's blessings were not the only results of Abraham and his descendents' interactions with the

54. NRSV.

nations. Instead, the curses of God also spilled over upon the individuals who cursed the people of God.[55]

Blessed through the Covenant

The Abrahamic blessing of God in the Book of Genesis was also passed on through the establishment of covenantal relationships. Ironically, Abimelech King of Gerar, who was deceived by both Abraham and Isaac, sought to establish covenant treaties with both patriarchs. Even though in later years the nation of Israel did not always maintain amiable relations with non-Israelites, "during the patriarchal period we sense a very cordial relationship with the Gentiles."[56] Abraham, for example, not only settled among the nations as a resident alien but also married "two secondary wives, Hagar (Gen 16:1–4) and Keturah (Gen 25:1), from the local people."[57] Thus, when Abimelech approached both Abraham (21:22) and Isaac (26:26–31) to establish a covenant, it would have been an accepted and usual occurrence to receive such a request.

Abimelech's act of cutting a covenant with Abraham and Isaac not only provided him with personal security but it also gave him a powerful ally in the form of the patriarchs and their God.[58] Similarly within the context of Genesis, it is apparent that Abimelech, an unrelated neighbor of the patriarchs, invited Abraham and Isaac into covenant relationships for his own protection after seeing the power of their God. Having been on the side of one cursed by the patriarch's God (Gen 20:17–18), it was no surprise that Abimelech desired to be on the side of the patriarchs the next time around. In line with this understanding, Abimelech's foremost request to both Abraham and Isaac was that they bring no harm upon his family or his descendents: "swear to me here by God *that you will not deal falsely with me* or with my offspring or with my posterity" (21:23 NRSV, italics added); "let there be an oath between you and us, and let us make a covenant with you *so that you [Isaac] will do us no harm*" (26:29,

55. Although the word "curse" is not used in these passages, the severe punishments listed in the narratives suggest the foretold consequences of those who curse Abram and his descendents (Gen 12:3).

56. Senior and Stuhlmueller, *Biblical Foundations*, 90.

57. Ibid.

58. Philip Potter explains that "covenants in the Near East were a means by which relationships were entered into by unrelated persons or peoples on a basis of community of interests and purpose in order to maintain these interests and fulfill the purpose" (Berkhof and Potter, *Key Words*, 25).

italics added). This request made sense in light of the recent curses placed upon Abimelech that devastated his family. Thus, with an attitude of self-preservation Abimelech approached Abraham and Isaac to establish covenants.

A further insight into the rationale of Abimelech's desire to cut covenants comes as he professed his observation of God's blessing upon the patriarchs. In explaining his request to Abraham, Abimelech stated: "*God is with you in all that you do*; *now therefore* swear to me here by God that you will not deal falsely with me or with my offspring or with my posterity . . . and the two men made a covenant" (21:22–27, italics added). In the same way, Abimelech and his advisors explained to Isaac: "*We see plainly that the Lord has been with you*; *so we say*, let there be an oath between you and us, and let us make a covenant with you so that you will do us no harm, just was we have not touched you . . . *You are now the blessed of the Lord*" (26:28–29, italics added). Therefore as proclaimed in both statements, one of the major reasons that Abimelech sought after a covenant relationship with the patriarchs was the powerful evidence of God's blessing upon Abraham and his descendents. Not only was this blessing evident to Abimelech but his advisors and military leaders also saw the clear hand of God upon Abraham's family.

It is with this understanding of Abimelech's motivations that the transference of the blessing of God to Abimelech can be witnessed. As with later Pentateuchal covenants, the cutting of a covenant with God's chosen people placed one under the protection and blessing of their God. Richard De Ridder notes that

> the bond that held Israel together as a people was more than racial: Israel was bound to Yahweh by a covenant bond. For this reason it was always possible for individuals of other nations to be admitted as members of the particularistic covenant with Israel and join with Israel in the service required by her election.[59]

Although De Ridder is referring to the establishment of later covenants between non-Israelites and the nation of Israel, this inherent characteristic of the covenant relationship was still apparent in the earlier period of the patriarchs. For when Abimelech established his covenant treaties, he came under the covering of Abraham's covenant with God. Abimelech was thus protected from the wrath of God and additionally gained the blessing of Abraham as one who was in covenant with

59. De Ridder, *Discipling*, 47.

Abraham and his descendants. It is therefore through the stories of Abimelech that the blessing of God is seen to be transferred from Abraham's family to the nations through the covenant ritual.

Blessed Independently by God

The final mode in which the Abrahamic blessing was conveyed to the nations was through the independent workings of God. Although each method revealed God's compassion, the unconstrained intervention of God undeniably emphasized his love for the nations. One such example occurs in Genesis 41:53–57, when God saved not only Israel from starvation but all the nations of the region including Egypt.[60] This great mercy of God to the nations is evident in God's blessing upon Egypt and the surrounding nations in the midst of their seven years of famine. Although Egypt has been likened to "God's handmaid" serving to "preserve [Israel] as a distinct nation and to enrich her culturally,"[61] Egypt was not only blessed for the sake of Israel. Instead, while saving Israel, it is noteworthy that God also saved Egypt and the surrounding nations from annihilation. As Joseph was revealing the meaning of Pharaoh's dream to him (Gen 41:25–36), Joseph declared to Pharaoh that "God has revealed to Pharaoh what he is about to do" (v. 25) "*so that the land may not perish* through the famine" (v. 36).[62] It was God's desire that not only would Israel survive but all the peoples of the land would as well. Therefore while bringing salvation to Jacob's family God himself extended the blessing of Abraham upon the peoples of the land.

New Testament

The New Testament contains a variety of methods through which the blessing of Jesus Christ was spread to the nations.[63] As the early church was in its infancy at the time, these modes of missional expression were

60. Bosch acknowledging the great compassion of God writes that "from an early stage [in Scripture] . . . there has been the conviction that God's compassion embraces the nations also" (*Transforming Mission*, 18).

61. Peters, *Biblical Theology*, 108.

62. NRSV, italics added.

63. It is important to note at this point that the Abrahamic blessing was holistic in nature including both physical and spiritual blessings. Thus, the methods used to express this blessing to all people resulted in both visible changes in the physical world in addition to internal changes of the heart and mind.

often founded in traditional Judaism in addition to the teachings and life of Jesus Christ.

Prayer

Throughout the New Testament the act of prayer routinely preceded the missional work of the Holy Spirit. For example, the believers prayed prior to the selection of Matthias (Acts 1:24); prior to the infilling of the Holy Spirit and preaching the gospel boldly (4:31); prior to the Samaritans receiving the Holy Spirit (8:15); prior to the miraculous resurrection of Tabitha (9:40); prior to Peter's visit to the Gentile Cornelius (10:9); prior to Peter's release from prison (12:5, 12); and prior to the selection of Barnabas and Saul as missionaries (13:3).[64] In the book of Acts it is evident that the ritual of prayer itself did not hold power but instead was through the power of the Living God. Moreover, it is clear that God was directing his mission; guiding, warning, releasing, healing, selecting, and pouring his Spirit on all peoples. There was no visible formula for the prayer ritual; at times the believers prayed to God in expectation of God's intervention as in the case of Peter's imprisonment (12:5, 12), but at other times believers were just in the midst of prayer when God interceded. The account of Cornelius in Caesarea falls in the latter category as both Cornelius and Peter were praying to God during the regular hours of prayer when God gave them both visions[65] resulting in the first Gentiles accepting Christ and being filled with the Holy Spirit (10:44–48). The role of prayer in the book of Acts was therefore a dynamic process which connected the church to the will and direction of God and inadvertently led to the outpouring of God's blessing on all peoples through Christ.

More than just a method of missional expansion, the prayer life of the early church also connected the people with the leader of the mission, God. From the beginning of the narrator's account of the Jerusalem church, the believers are noted as people "devoted" to prayer (Acts 2:42), and "join[ing] together constantly in prayer, along with the women and Mary the mother of Jesus, and with his brothers" (1:14).[66] More than just a ritual practice, the believers' prayers to God were more like an open conversation than a one-way monologue. As believers communicated to

64. This list is not exhaustive but does provide several key examples where prayer preceded the missional work of God.

65. See Acts 10:3, 9–10.

66. Also see Acts 2:42; 3:1; 4:24, 31.

God, their God communicated back to them. An example of this mutual interchange can be found in the Apostle Paul's narrative of his conversion in Acts 22:1–21. Speaking to a crowd in Jerusalem outside of the Roman soldiers' barracks, Paul described his encounter with the Christ on the road to Damascus:

> About noon as I came near Damascus, suddenly a bright light from heaven flashed around me. I fell to the ground and heard a voice say to me, "Saul! Saul! Why do you persecute me?" "Who are you, Lord?" I asked. "I am Jesus of Nazareth, whom you are persecuting," he replied . . . "What shall I do, Lord?" I asked. "Get up," the Lord said, "and go into Damascus. There you will be told all that you have been assigned to do." (Acts 22:6–10)

Upon entering Damascus, Ananias prayed for Saul and he was able to see; speaking a prophetic word over Saul he further declared: "The God of our fathers has chosen you to know his will and to see the Righteous One *and to hear words from his mouth*. You will be his witness to all men of what you have seen and heard" (Acts 22:15, italics added). Paul continued by stating that when he returned to Jerusalem and was praying in the temple, the Lord again spoke to him, this time commanding him to leave Jerusalem quickly and to go far away to the Gentiles (Acts 17–21). This series of events, as narrated by Paul, illustrates the type of communication which was present between God and his disciples. While it is impossible to determine whether Paul's case was the norm among all the believers, it is evident that God did guide, warn and encourage his followers throughout the establishment of his church through his Holy Spirit.[67] Prayer was thus not a one-sided mode of communication to their Creator but instead it was an intimate relationship which linked the believers with the heart and will of their God.

Proclamation of Good News

The blessing of Christ was also given to both Jews and Gentiles through the proclamation of the gospel message. From the initial outpouring of the Holy Spirit during the feast of Pentecost, the believers began sharing the good news about Jesus Christ within Jerusalem (Acts 2:4–41). Even after the ever-increasing persecution from the Sanhedrin council, the believers continued boldly preaching the gospel message that Jesus

67. See Acts 1:8; 2:4; 4:8, 31; 6:3; 8:17, 29, 39; 9:17, 31; 10:19, 44; 11:24; 13:2, 4, 9, 52; 15:28; 16:6; 19:6; 20:22–23, 28; 21:4, 11; 28:25.

was the Christ (4:31). Thus, despite persecution and even death,[68] the believers felt compelled to preach the gospel message within Jerusalem and eventually to the surrounding nations.

This commitment to preaching the good news illustrates the great salvific value the believers placed upon individuals hearing the gospel of Christ. As Peter proclaimed before the Sanhedrin council: "Salvation is found in no one else, for there is no other name under heaven given to men by which we must be saved" (Acts 4:12). It was therefore through Christ alone that individuals could be forgiven of their sins (2:38), receive the Holy Spirit (2:38), and be reconciled with God (2 Cor 5:18–19). Moreover, it was through Christ that the promise given to Abraham would be realized. As Peter states:

> Indeed, all the prophets from Samuel on, as many as have spoken have foretold these days. And you are heirs of the prophets and of the covenant God made with your fathers. He said to Abraham, "Through your offspring all peoples on earth will be blessed." When God raised up his servant, he sent him first to you to bless you by turning each of you from your wicked ways. (Acts 3:24–26)

Christ was the realization of the blessing of God promised to Abraham for all the nations of the world. The disciples' proclamation of this message fulfilled the prophetic promise that all the peoples of earth would be blessed through Abraham's seed. It was through the hearing of this gospel message that the blessing would be released.

Physical and Spiritual Healings

The blessing of God in both the Old and New Testament was holistic in nature including the blessing of God upon both the physical and spiritual realm. In the New Testament this is evidenced in the physical healings, demonic deliverances, and signs and wonders that accompanied or preceded the gospel message. These miraculous events recorded in the book of Acts often confirmed the authenticity of Christ as the Messiah in addition to demonstrating the love and mercy of God. This is seen in the case of the crippled man begging outside of the gate Beautiful in Acts 3:1–8. Upon hearing the man beg for money, Peter and John replied that "silver or gold I do not have, but what I have I give you. In the name of Jesus

68. Stephen is noted in the book of Acts as the first martyr who even upon the threat of death preached the gospel of Christ (Acts 7:2–53).

Christ of Nazareth, walk" (v. 6).[69] Later on in the narrative Peter did share the gospel message with the gathered crowd, however, the initial impetus of the event was simply the healing of a man separate from any opportunity to share the gospel. Furthermore, the question must be asked, "What did Peter and John give the man?" Looking at the result, Peter and John gave the man the gift of physical healing through the power of Christ.[70] This formerly crippled beggar experienced the love of God in a physical as well as potentially spiritual way.

The miraculous events recorded in the book of Acts also led to the proclamation of the gospel message. Far from strategizing about evangelical methodology, the early church believers are recorded as prayerfully moving forward in obedience to Christ. Nevertheless, as the acts of the apostles are examined in retrospect, the connection is clearly visible between the demonstration of the power of God and the proclamation of Jesus Christ. For example, this connection is seen in Acts 2:1–41 when the believers were filled with the Holy Spirit and spoke in the tongues of the gathered Pentecost crowd. Due to this miraculous event, Peter was given a platform to speak to the crowd and share the gospel of Christ (v. 14–41). Likewise, during Paul's stay in Paphos the act of blinding the false prophet Bar-Jesus led to the conversion of the proconsul Sergius Paulus (13:4–12). Similarly, the earthquake and miraculous release of prisoners' chains in the Philippian jail led to Paul and Silas leading the jailer and his whole family to Christ (16:24–34). While the miraculous work of Christ did sometimes lead to persecution,[71] the connection between the miraculous and the proclamation of the gospel is evident throughout the book of Acts. The manifestation of the power of God did exist in and of itself but also as a means through which the gospel was spread to all peoples.

MISSIONAL EXPANSION

In this section I analyze the local and foreign acceptance and geographical expansion of the Abrahamic blessing in the Old and New Testaments.

69. Wenham notes the power of a proclaimed blessing stating that blessing "once uttered . . . carries its own life-giving power and cannot be revoked by man" (*Genesis 1–15*, 24).

70. As Westermann explains, "Not only does God's blessing affect the phases of life but it actually brings literal life" (*Blessing in the Bible*, 18); in this example the dead limbs of the crippled man are once again brought to life.

71. See Acts 16:16–24.

In the Old Testament I focus on the familial expansion of the Abrahamic blessing through the line of Abraham. In the New Testament I explore the societal and geographic expansion of the Abrahamic blessing through to the coming of Jesus Christ.

Old Testament

From the inception of the Abrahamic blessing in Genesis 12:1–3, God used the family of Abraham as the vehicle of his blessings to the nations. The centrality of Abraham and his kin to the blessing of the nations was established through the calling of Abraham in Genesis 12. God's use of the family of Abraham as a vehicle of his blessing is confirmed in Genesis 22:15–18 when Abraham offered his son Isaac in obedience as a sacrifice to God. Upon the demonstration of Abraham's obedience, God declared:

> I swear by myself . . . that because you have done this and have not withheld your son, your only son, I will surely bless you and make your descendants as numerous as the stars in the sky and as the sand on the seashore. Your descendants will take possession of the cities of their enemies, and through your offspring all nations on earth will be blessed, because you have obeyed me. (Gen 22:16–18, italics added)

The Hebrew term *zera* translated here as "descendants" or "offspring" refers to the seed of Abraham through which the blessing of God will be revealed. This promise of extending God's blessing through Abraham's offspring is reiterated to his descendents Isaac (Gen 26:4–5) and Jacob (28:14). The same Hebrew term *zera* is used in these later passages as God declares that through Isaac and Jacob's seed all the families on the earth will be blessed (26:4; 28:14). This transference of the Abrahamic blessing to Abraham's son and grandson foresees a later extension of God's blessing to all peoples through Christ (Gal 3:8) in addition to an outpouring of God's blessing upon each patriarch and the nations surrounding them during their lifetime.[72] Thus, God's blessing upon Abraham unfolded as it is extended through Abraham's family tree making the blessing both poured out in the present and yet still to come through the future Messiah.

72. The blessing of God upon each patriarch is evident throughout the book of Genesis (25:11; 26:2–5, 12–14, 24–25; 28:12–20; 32:23–31; 35:9–14; 48:15–16; 49:22–26).

New Testament

Within the New Testament the expansion of the blessing of God to the nations was enabled through the person of Jesus Christ. Jesus became the vehicle through which all the nations of the world are able to become heirs of the promise of Abraham (Gal 3:9, 26–29). The extension of God's blessing through Christ became the main focus of the disciples and early church as they sought to share the good news about Jesus with all peoples.

Societal Expansion

One of the most significant aspects of the proclamation of the gospel of Christ in the New Testament was the inclusion of the Samaritans and Gentiles in the kingdom of God. While Jesus commanded his disciples to "Go into all the world and preach the good news to all creation" (Mark 16:15), there was an assumption among the disciples that Jesus' words referred to the proclamation of Christ among the Jewish Diaspora. However, led by the Spirit of God, individuals started to cross societal barriers with the gospel of Christ; Philip sharing the gospel in Samaria (Acts 8:4–40), Peter among God-fearing Gentiles in Caesarea (10:23–48) and Paul among the Gentile nations of the known world (9:15; 13:2). This systematic extension of the gospel of the Jewish Messiah to the Gentile nations fulfilled the words spoken long ago to Abraham in which God declared that God would bless all peoples through him (Gen 12:3).

This missional transition required a major paradigm shift for the circumcised believers of the early church. For example, as Acts 10:9–20 indicates, it was only through the leading of the Holy Spirit that the Apostle Peter agreed to share Christ with the Gentile Cornelius. Peter expressed this paradigm shift as he walked into Cornelius' home in Caesarea declaring: "You are well aware that it is against our law for a Jew to associate with a Gentile or visit him. But God has shown me that I should not call any man impure or unclean" (Acts 10:28). The following narrative continues this revelation as the Holy Spirit came upon Peter's Gentile audience leading the apostle to announce: "Can anyone keep these people from being baptized with water? They have received the Holy Spirit just as we have" (10:47). Despite the initial astonishment of the Jewish believers (10:45), God had indeed extended his blessing to the Gentiles through Christ. When the Jewish believers in Jerusalem heard Peter's full testimony, "they had no further objections and praised God" (11:18). This extension of the gospel of Christ to the Gentiles through the leading of the Holy Spirit changed the face of evangelism from that point forward. The blessing of God through Christ was now fully accessible to all the peoples of the world; for all were one in Christ, both Jew and Gentile (Gal 3:28).

Geographic Expansion

Upon the ascension of Jesus Christ, the gospel of Christ was extended geographically from the center of Judaism to the center of the known world, Rome. Before his ascension, Christ commanded his followers to "go and make disciples of all nations" (Matt 28:19) declaring that they would be his "witnesses in Jerusalem, and in all Judea and Samaria, and to the ends of the earth" (Acts 1:8). This advancement of the gospel to new political regions and cultural groups was recorded in the book of Acts as the narrator follows the missionary journeys of Paul, Barnabas, Silas and Mark.

What began as the evangelism of Jerusalem proper (Acts 1–7:60) became a regional and global movement as the disciples expanded their witness to Samaria (Acts 8) and eventually to the surrounding nations (Acts 9–28). The eventual arrival of Paul in Rome marked the literary climax of the book of Acts as Christ's words in Acts 1:8 came to pass. However, the narrator did not end with words of completion, but instead words of continuation as Paul rebuked his half-hearted Jewish audience in Rome by stating: "Therefore I want you to know that God's salvation has been sent to the Gentiles, and they will listen!" (28:28). The narrator states that for the next two years Paul continued to preach boldly about the gospel of Christ and the kingdom of God (28:30–31). By ending the narrative with Paul still preaching Christ, the author leaves the audience with the message that the work of Christ was not yet complete and that the global extension of the blessing of God is only just beginning.

PART II

Abrahamic Blessing in Context

6

Introducing the Context: Papua New Guinea

BIRTHED IN THE FINAL season of Australian colonial rule in British New Guinea and at the beginning of the nation's independence, the CRC's involvement in PNG falls within a unique time period. At the peak of the CRC revival in the late 1970s and early 1980s, PNG was a new nation on the world stage, brimming with optimism and hope as it considered its newfound political freedom. This widespread optimism directly affected the expansion of the CRC revival movement as believers young and old felt empowered to spread the gospel in conjunction with and separate from the foreign mission organizations. The backdrop of colonialism also played a large role in the CRC revival as long-standing denominational separations in the nation both assisted and inhibited the spread of the gospel message. In this next section I present an overview of the colonization and subsequent independence of PNG in addition to highlighting the expansion of Christianity within the nation. I also note the effects of these historic events on the CRC revival movement.

Colonization of PNG

Approximately fifty thousand years ago, seafaring peoples from Southeast Asia first settled the island of PNG, where they remained largely disconnected from the outside world except for the occasional visit from local traders.[1] Reappearing in world history in the mid-sixteenth century, the "black islands" were briefly explored by Portuguese and Spanish adventurers and the southern and northern regions of the island named Pepuah and Nueva Guinea respectively. However, it wasn't until the early

1. Magonet, "Abraham," 1.

nineteenth century that the black islands captured the more permanent interest of the non-Melanesian world. In the century that followed, consecutive waves of Dutch, German, British, French, and Australian entrepreneurs, companies, and churches entered the region establishing "trading posts and cash-crop plantations and . . . mission stations" throughout the island region.[2] In the resource hungry West, the natural resources of PN—ranging from pearls and fish along the coast to copra and gold inland—attracted the attention of the European powers of the time.[3]

By 1824 the Dutch crown claimed the entire western half of the island, and in 1884 Germany and England followed suit claiming control of the northeast and southeastern regions. Each nation had differing interests in colonizing New Guinea; "The Germans aimed to further their trading and plantation interests. The British, concerned by the Dutch and German presence, wished to protect Australia, their most important colony in the South Pacific."[4] Over the next few decades PNG continued to change hands as Britain "handed their colony to the newly independent Commonwealth of Australia" in 1908 and Germany lost their PNG colonies in 1914 during World War I.[5] World War II also brought challenges to the island as American and Australian military forces fought some of their fiercest battles against the invading Japanese army in the jungles of Kokoda, Oro Province, and the eastern coastline. Implementing various social, educational, and political reforms after the war, the Australian government continued to control the territory for the following three decades.

One of the most prominent ways that the colonization of PNG influenced the CRC movement was the establishment of the "spheres of influence." Originally encouraged by the colonial government to avoid competition among church denominations, the concept of dividing the colony by "spheres of influence" was adopted in 1890 by the London Missionary Society and the Methodist and Anglican Churches.[6] The Catholic Church, also a great influence in the territory, was excluded from the discussion but allowed to continue working in their original mission stations. The spheres of influence agreement dictated that churches already

2. Turner, *Historical Dictionary*, 4.
3. Magonet, "Abraham," 6–9.
4. Turner, *Historical Dictionary*, 4.
5. Bartle, *Death*, 21.
6. Turner, *Historical Dictionary*, 6.

established in one area would hold the exclusive rights to minister in that region. Thus as new missionary organizations and churches entered the territory the fledgling groups were directed to establish their work only in the denominationally unclaimed lands. John Barker summarizes the comity division of PNG according to religious creed:

> In the Australian colony of Papua, the London Missionary Society shared the southern region with French Catholics and a small Seventh Day Adventist mission. The north coast was divided between the Methodists in the eastern islands and the Anglicans on the mainland. Australian Methodists and French Catholics arrived in the Bismark Archipelago in the 1870s. After the Germans assumed control over northwest New Guinea, Lutheran and Catholic missions began steadily to penetrate the interior. The four major Christian churches of Papua New Guinea-United (Congregationalist and Methodist), Catholic, Anglican and Lutheran) developed from these early missions and continue to represent different parts of the coastal regions.[7]

While resistance to this sectarian agreement increased and eventually officially "broke down under pressure from the Catholic Church [and] the Seventh-Day Adventists,"[8] the denominational separation continued to affect the nation long after its official conceptual demise.

Entering PNG in the 1950s, new religious organizations found their work largely restricted to urban centers and unevangelized highland regions. While the spheres of influence model had long since officially been discarded, it was still very much the living framework of the nation. Thus, as Baptist, Salvation Army, and Pentecostal Churches arrived in PNG after World War II,[9] the larger cities became their primary bases and attempts to establish churches outside of their territory were met with resistance. Despite concentrated efforts to eliminate denominational boundaries, the long-standing work of the early religious organizations remained permanently rooted to their original "sphere of influence."

The long-term effects of the sphere of influence model upon the PNG territory and the CRC revival crusade were multiple. As a result of the separatist paradigm, a fierce loyalty often existed between regional peoples and their local denomination. A region's inherent identity also was often equated directly with the denomination that originally

7. Barker, *Christianity in Oceania*, 3–4.

8. Turner, *Historical Dictionary*, 54–55.

9. Ibid., 55.

evangelized the area; for example, individuals from Oro Province considered themselves to be Anglican by birth and those from Central Province automatically belonged to the United Church.[10] This indigenous identity by church affiliation was prominent particularly throughout the coastal and island regions; the one exception to this rule was the highland area which was last to be evangelized and was more parochial in its religious affiliation.[11] The established churches also were highly protective of their influence over the provinces and systematically discouraged new churches from establishing themselves in their territories. This combination of denominational loyalty and territorial ownership made the work very challenging for denominations entering the country after World War II.

This same sphere-of-influence dilemma became one of the primary obstacles facing the CRC during the revival period as it established new churches in old denominational lands. As the CRC revival entered into already-claimed regions, such as Oro, Central and East New Britain Provinces, the Pentecostal evangelists were met with heavy resistance by the existing church bodies. While many of the villages were syncretistic and nominal in their Christian faith, they identified themselves strongly with the original denomination that pioneered their area. This identification and intense loyalty led many of the villagers to strongly oppose the CRC's revival efforts in the area. The revivalists were often met with physical persecution and verbal abuse and the new believers with social opposition and in some cases banishment from their families due to the heavily ingrained loyalty to their original denomination. However, winds of change were just around the corner as the Australian government came under global pressure to establish PNG as an independent nation.[12]

PNG Independence

The move toward independence started as early as 1960 and progressed in stages as PNG made steps toward full independence. Largely due to the support of Australian Prime Minister Gough Whitman, the transition moved rapidly forward and "in 1964 the Legislative Council was replaced

10. This denominational identification was a repeated theme throughout all my interviews in PNG as CRC leaders recalled both their own loyalty to their original denomination and the persecution that resulted as they pioneered new churches in already "claimed" areas of the nation.

11. Barker, *Christianity in Oceania*, 4.

12. Turner, *Historical Dictionary*, 12.

by a House of Assembly" followed by free elections in 1972.[13] The self-government of PNG was declared on December 1, 1973 with Australia handing "over all powers except those concerning foreign affairs, defense and the legal system."[14] Handed over to Prime Minister Michael Somare on September 16, 1975, the nation was finally able to declare full independence from colonial rule.

Although an amiable transition, there were mixed feelings and numerous fears about PNG independence. Prior to independence, Australians with economic interests in the nation felt threatened by the potential loss of their investments and feared that the more educated coastal peoples would gain control within the nation.[15] Questions were also raised about the nation's preparation to enter the global market and its ability to maintain the infrastructure formerly established by the Australian government. Margaret Mead, a well-known anthropologist working in the territory at the time, voiced her concerns about the transition:

> When the trusteeship power, Australia, was confronted in the post–World War II climate of world opinion with demands that Papua-New Guinea be given early independence, the enormity of the problem became evident. Other new nations are less viable in terms of size and economic resources than Papua-New Guinea, but none faces the prodigious problem of governing a territory in which the people to whom authority within the country would fall have all come so recently—some within the last ten years—directly out of stone-age cultures. For this is a country in which cannibalism and headhunting are in some parts only just coming under control, where old feuds over land and fishing rights simmer beneath the surface even in fully missionized villages, and in which no educated elite has been built up.[16]

Despite the economic and societal concerns about the changeover, the first years of PNG independence were filled with political advancement and overall success.

Donald Denoon writing of the decolonization of PNG noted this positive movement afforded by the PNG government during the early years following independence. He explains:

13. Ibid.
14. Ibid., 12–13.
15. Ibid., 12.
16. Mead, "Rights," 422.

> Australians were united in their desire to decolonise, although Papua New Guineans were nervous of independence. Equally startling was the optimism of my new colleagues, who expected Papua New Guineans to learn from, and avoid, the violence, the autocracy, and the corruption that they saw in newly independent Africa. But events seemed to justify that wide-eyed confidence. Within three years, Somare's coalition reorganised the Public Service, negotiated an aid package and renegotiated an important mining agreement. They drafted, debated and enacted a constitution, and created planning capacity, a defence force and all the other limbs of a modern state. Secession was averted in Bougainville and in Papua, an explosive land dispute was defused around Rabaul, anxious Highlanders were mollified and the fragile coalition held together. Pessimists had expected bloodshed, perhaps on the scale of Congo. With peaceful independence, the optimists were vindicated: the coup that overthrew a government took place not in Port Moresby but in Canberra.[17]

Although various economic, political and social challenges would later plague the new nation, the initial transition to self-governance was largely successful and void of major complications.[18] After more than a century of foreign control, the nation of PNG had finally gained back its original state of self-independence.

One of the positive impacts of the independence of PNG was the high emphasis on education after the establishment of self governance. This advancement of higher education in PNG was directly connected to the Australian government's reform efforts in the country. In the years following World War II, the Australian government initiated what became known as the "New Deal," establishing reforms throughout the country.[19] Seeking to show its gratitude to PNG for assistance during the war, Australia set up programs to improve the PNG healthcare system, education system, and political infrastructure. The advancement of education was of particular importance and the goal set to create a "universal primary education in the English language." As such, within the decades that followed "more schools were established" in each province "and English-speaking, mainly expatriate, teachers [were] recruited."[20]

17. Denoon, *Trial Separation*, 16.

18. For a detailed overview of the politics pre- and post-PNG independence, read Griffin et al., *Papua New Guinea: A Political History* (1979).

19. Turner, *Historical Dictionary*, 10.

20. Ibid., 11.

However, while founded out of altruistic intentions, the outcome of these educational reforms also meant a lack of focus on higher education. Ann Turner explains this oversight as she notes that "primary school education was funded at the expense of secondary and higher education." She continues that this "lack of post-primary education [in turn] delayed the emergence of an educated elite."[21] Realizing this quandary, in 1965 the Australian government abandoned its reform of PNG elementary education and switched its focus to secondary and higher education.[22] This refocus allowed the first Papua New Guineans to graduate from the University of PNG in 1970 and from the University of Technology in 1975.[23]

Due to this late amendment, secondary and higher education in PNG were still emerging at the point of independence in 1975. Dame Josephine Abaijah, the only female member of the House of Assembly in 1975, recalls the pioneering efforts of her own educational background in PNG. She writes:

> I was the first girl ever to attend Misima Government School [Milne Bay] and I was the only girl in my class during the whole of my schooling in Papua. I graduated from the first so-called teachers college established in the country, a grass hut at Popondetta. I was with the first people to be sent to Australia for secondary schooling. I passed the first year of the first class of the first tertiary institution established in the country . . . I was the first Papuan . . . to study at the University of London, the University of the Philippines and a score of other places. I was the first woman to be elected as a member of parliament in the country . . . I can assure you that nothing happened before me and my contemporaries. We were the first of everything and the handful who escaped the iron grip of colonialism before me are so exceptional as to be of no general significance.[24]

The struggle inherent in Abaijah's testimony illustrates the variable limitations facing many Papua New Guineans in colonial New Guinea. It was only at the dawn of independence that the opportunities for higher education grew and finally became more accessible to the indigenous population.

Within this historic context of educational limitations, the CRC's high emphasis on indigenous leadership training during the 1970s–1980s

21. Ibid.

22. Ibid., 15.

23. Ibid.

24. Magonet, "Abraham," 183.

began to fall into place. Providing a much-needed educational outlet for its regional students, the CRC focused on establishing Bible training schools throughout the nation to train future missionaries and pastors. Whereas prior to World War II "those trained within the missions were not admitted to ordination,"[25] the CRC, along with numerous other church groups, provided avenues through which nationals could become fully trained for church leadership. The hopeful educational environment of PNG at the time of independence also put the sacrifices of the early CRC national leaders in perspective. Of their own accord, numerous key CRC revival leaders chose to leave their future educational tracks and careers in order to enter full-time ministry. The extent of this personal sacrifice can only be fully understood in light of the historical milieu of the time. Whether considering the establishment of CRC training centers or the educational sacrifice of CRC national pastors and leaders, the educational context of PNG played an important role in the spread of the denomination in the country.

Development of Christianity in PNG

The development of the Christian church in PNG was also influenced by the nation's history in addition to the multiple folk religions of PNG. On the one hand, the early missionaries entered PNG largely as colonizers desiring to evangelize the heathen lands. A product of their times, these early missionaries unknowingly emulated the colonial "master-servant" model with the nationals in addition to introducing a Westernized form of Christianity. In speaking of the southwest pacific mission movement in 1967, Alan R. Tippett comments on this continued trend of foreign colonial dominance upon the national Melanesian churches. He writes:

> yet he [the missionary] to this day tends to retain the master-servant frame of reference in his personal dealings with the Melanesian. A few missionaries have stepped down from this position and a few Melanesians have been elevated from their lowly status; but in general the basic attitudes are still the same. This attitude has hindered the emergence of the indigenous church, especially in the west. The missionaries were fatherly masters who really loved and protected the "lesser breed" (a phrase from a hymn in the hymn-books of both churches involved in this survey) and were in turn loved for this protection. But for long years they remained reluctant to bring islanders

25. Mead, "Rights," 422.

> forward into office, and they in turn accepted their dependent position. My feeling was that the stations, and their plantations, are still very colonial.[26]

This lack of ownership by the indigenous Melanesians was also seen in the continued adoption of traditional beliefs and traditions. Although the population of PNG was primarily Christian by 1960, "many people retained traditional spiritual beliefs and saw no contradiction between these beliefs and Christian doctrine."[27] Syncretism spread in large part from the commonly held belief that Christianity was a Western religion. Yet, beginning in the late 1960s and early 1970s new indigenous revival movements began to emerge around the country. The subsequent indigenization of the church and contextualization of the gospel message took the nation by storm as a plethora of new denominations—including the Assemblies of God, Foursquare, and CRC Churches—grew in popularity within the nation.

The PNG church also arose as "a catalyst" of social change in the nation.[28] Rooted in the early missionaries' emphasis on providing educational and medical services, the church had long maintained a holistic approach to ministry in the nation. Up until the 1950s, the mission stations scattered were "responsible for almost all education and health services" and even in present day PNG, the "churches, subsidized by the government, still run about half the country's health centers and schools."[29] This holistic foundation of physical, educational, and spiritual support gave the church an influential position in many communities. Daniel K. Leke notes the overall contribution of church in training leaders within the growing nation:

> In the process of engaging in different areas of ministry, [mainline churches] have contributed much to the building of Papua New Guinea. The churches got heavily involved in training and equipping Papua New Guineans. They also got involved in building up people's leadership potential and capacity to realize a vision and future challenges for the church and the nation. The church therefore, is seen today as a catalyst for change, a facilitator for national development, and an equipper for the ministry of the Gospel of Jesus Christ.[30]

26. Tippett, *Solomon Islands Christianity*, 25.
27. Turner, *Historical Dictionary*, 11.
28. Leke, "Role of Churches," 283.
29. Turner, *Historical Dictionary*, 55.
30. Leke, "Role of Churches," 283.

The church, according to Leke, worked as a vehicle of social and educational change while aiming for religious transformation in the nation.

Although Leke holds a very positive view of the Christian church in PNG, not all scholars share his enthusiasm. Written prior to PNG's independence Jean Guiart, an anthropologist in the South Pacific since 1947, notes the power issues involved in the Melanesian accepting the white man's religion.[31] He writes:

> I suggest that Melanesians and Polynesians discovered functionalism and structuralism for themselves through being confronted with the white man's culture and society. Among other fine points, they grasped that religion had a definite function inside our world. They realized that if they were ever to come to our level they would have to accept our religion. At first they ascribed to white men a kind of god-like status; but this view passed. The native people were soon trying to think out how they might become the equals of these pale-skinned, rich, powerful, at times naïve or ruthless mortals. The simplest way appeared to be the adoption of their religion.[32]

In considering these two polar perspectives, there is truth evident in both positions. As Leke highlights, the church in PNG was very active in making positive educational and medicinal changes in their communities in addition to spreading the gospel message of Christ. Then again, in line with Guiart's position, these transformations are not independent from the political structures of the community or the traditional religious structures of the people prior to Christianity. However, while both perspectives hold truth due to the complex nature of the church's impact on PNG, the church's influence can neither be identified as entirely beneficial nor inherently harmful. Just as any multifaceted organization with doctrinal and cultural diversity, the PNG church as a whole is a collection of many intricate narratives which sometimes contain victories and at other times tragedies.

Also controversial was the role of the Pentecostal Church within Papua New Guinea. Critiquing the historic lack of contextualization and indigenization within the Pentecostal and Charismatic Churches, Neville Bartle writes:

31. It is important to note that while not discounting the truth within Guiart's position, he is an outsider within the Melanesian context and as such interprets the ecclesiological situation in the South and Southwestern Pacific through his own biases and cultural worldview.

32. Guiart, "Millenarian Aspect," 398.

> Pentecostal and Charismatic Churches often give very little emphasis to traditional culture. They emphasise Western music, songs in English and use electronic instruments, while local songs and bush instruments are seldom used. Videos of Western televangelists are widely distributed, and up and coming preachers try to imitate the styles of their American heroes. They acknowledge the reality of the spirit world, but make little effort to evaluate the traditional beliefs in the light of Scripture. Many of them seem to equate traditional ways with evil and modern ways with Christianity.[33]

While there is some pointed truth in Bartle's critique, it remains impossible to accurately critique in such a generalized fashion the multiple church denominations through several decades. Within the CRC churches in Oro Province, for example, a distinguishing factor of the revival movement was the indigenization of the churches and the local emphasis on language songs.[34] However, Bartle's comments also ring true within the same context, as video projectors were tracked through the Oro jungles in order for films of American evangelists to be shown in the village centers. Thus it is safe to say that the Pentecostal and Charismatic Churches in PNG, like the Melanesian Church in general were neither fully culturally insensitive nor fully culturally contextualized. The strengths of the newer Pentecostal and Charismatic Churches often complemented the weaknesses of the longer established mainstream denominations.[35]

The impact of the Pentecostal and Charismatic Churches in PNG greatly increased in the 1970s and 1980s as spiritual revivals started sweeping the land.[36] Commenting on the tremendous growth of the Assemblies of God (AOG) denomination in PNG, George Forbes notes that from its commencement in 1948 to its fiftieth jubilee celebration in 1998, more than nine hundred AOG churches had been planted.[37] Similar stories were repeated throughout the nation as the late 1960s and 1970s ushered in a new and vibrant era of evangelism in PNG. While noting various prior incidents of Christian revivalism in PNG, Barker highlights the

33. Bartle, *Death*, 57.

34. Indigenous worship songs in the local language.

35. I will elaborate on the Pentecostal and Charismatic Churches' introduction of a power-filled Christianity in the next section.

36. For additional information regarding Melanesian revival history see Barr, "Survey"; Robin, "Revival Movements"; Robbins, "Introduction."

37. Forbes, *Church on Fire*, n.p.

distinctive nature of these later 1970s revivals. He comments that "incidents of Christian revivalism, often intermixed with 'cargoist' elements,[38] have long been reported from various corners of PNG. Yet it is apparent that by the mid-1970s a new and much more extensive regional revivalism was taking place."[39] While not the first historic instances of renewal in the nation, the revivals of the 1970s–1980s emerged out of the newly independent nation as indigenous moves of the Holy Spirit in the region.

Although each revival contained distinct qualities, this PNG revival movement was uniquely unified in its origin, strategies, and reception. First, the spiritual revivals often stemmed from ministries led by the Fundamentalist and Pentecostal groups coming into PNG in the 1960s.[40] While this was the norm, notable exceptions were present throughout the country as spontaneous Holy Spirit revivals sprang up among mainstream denominations such as the Baptist, Lutheran, Catholic, and United Churches.[41] Second, the strategic evangelistic methods of the churches were similar as each movement "set up worship and training centers in the towns, providing bases from which young Papua New Guineans fanned out to spread the 'Good News' back into their language areas."[42] Third, persecution was also a common theme as local evangelists frequently "found themselves under sharp and effective attack from members of their own communities."[43] But

38. Although there is a temptation to identify the PNG revival movements as a new variation of cargo cult mythology, I agree with Barker that the two belief systems do not readily overlap ("Christian Bodies," 273). In considering the CRC revival in particular, there exist distinct and incompatible doctrine and practices between the two belief systems. For example, while the blessing of God is understood as the holistic abundance of life in the CRC movement, there was also an understanding that the blessing of God could not be equated with an absence of pain and suffering as desired in many cargo cults. Revival leaders and evangelists were instead often persecuted and ridiculed for their faith in Christ and suffered many social and physical hardships. Thus, while they received the blessing of God through Christ, there was still suffering; communal blessing in short did not always bring complete harmony in a community nor did it necessarily lead to material prosperity for the clan or a release from hunger. The blessing of God, however, while not entirely eliminating earthly suffering, did lead to the healing of the sick, the releasing of those bound by demonic forces, and the forgiveness of sins; in these ways, the blessing of God did bring *gutpela sindaun* to a community during the actual time of spiritual revival within a village.

39. Barker, "Christian Bodies," 272.

40. Ibid.

41. Bartle, *Death*, 63.

42. Barker, "Christian Bodies," 272–73.

43. Ibid., 273.

in spite of these similarities there also existed a vibrant diversity among the revival movements for, as Bartle notes, "revival is not neat and tidy; revival is like a wildfire. It does not obey rules. It is unpredictable and breaks out in different places at the same time. In all the noise, confusion and excitement about so much power revealed at once, all sorts of things happen."[44]

In the case of the PNG CRC church, the movement was greatly affected by the historic religious development of the church in PNG. A product of its times the CRC exhibited many of the characteristics of its colonial environment; various critiques can be made of the CRC movement's colonial worldview, its dependence upon foreign literature and international teachers and its lack of intentional contextualization in the classroom and the local church. However, launched at the moment of monumental political transition in PNG, the CRC movement also reflected the nation's new emphasis on equal opportunity, national training programs, indigenous leadership, and contextual worship. While not a textbook model of indigenous church mission, the CRC church movement managed to move forward despite its weaknesses and embrace the positive changes that were taking place in the country and in the church's greater understanding of mission theory and praxis.

The CRC also joined many of its Pentecostal counterparts during the 1970s–1980s as spiritual revival swept through its churches. As Barker noted, the CRC's primary strategic methodology paralleled that of other revival movements as Bible training centers were established in major cities around PNG and students were sent from these bases as evangelists and missionaries locally and abroad. Likewise, persecution also followed the CRC movement as revival leaders met resistance from their own communities who belonged to other denominations.

SOCIO-CULTURAL BACKGROUND

In this section I highlight the key socio-cultural values and beliefs that uniquely shaped the PNG CRC revival. While PNG is a land of cultural and linguistic diversity, Papua New Guineans are unified in their holistic worldview, belief in the spirit world and their emphasis on clan centrality. In the following section I present an outline of these central beliefs and explain their impact on the PNG CRC movement.

44. Bartle, *Death*, 64.

Holistic Worldview

At the forefront of the PNG worldview is the understanding that the spirit world and the physical world intersect and affect each other. Within this holistic worldview "there is no clear dividing line between the spiritual world and the unseen world of the spirits; they are in constant interaction." Moreover, "the activity of the spirit world is evidenced by changes in the physical material world."[45] What occurs in one world thus assuredly affects the other. Human beings are also acknowledged to simultaneously exist in both worlds. Bernard Narokobi explains that "the Melanesian is born to the knowledge that he lives and works within a spirit world. His actions and his omissions are always being watched by the spirit world."[46] Just as human beings live in both worlds, the Papua New Guinean also considers him/herself in relationship with the spiritual world. Simeon Namunu notes that "Melanesians see themselves and their social life in relation to nature, to other humans and to spirit-beings. They recognize that their social life is not limited only to the perceived physical world but extends into the invisible part of the universe as well."[47] This harmonic overlapping of the spirit and material world, therefore, is not only a conceptual idea, but a reality that can have physical outcomes for both the individual and the wider community.

45. Ibid., 23.

46. Narokobi, "What Is Religious Experience," 72.

47. Ibid.

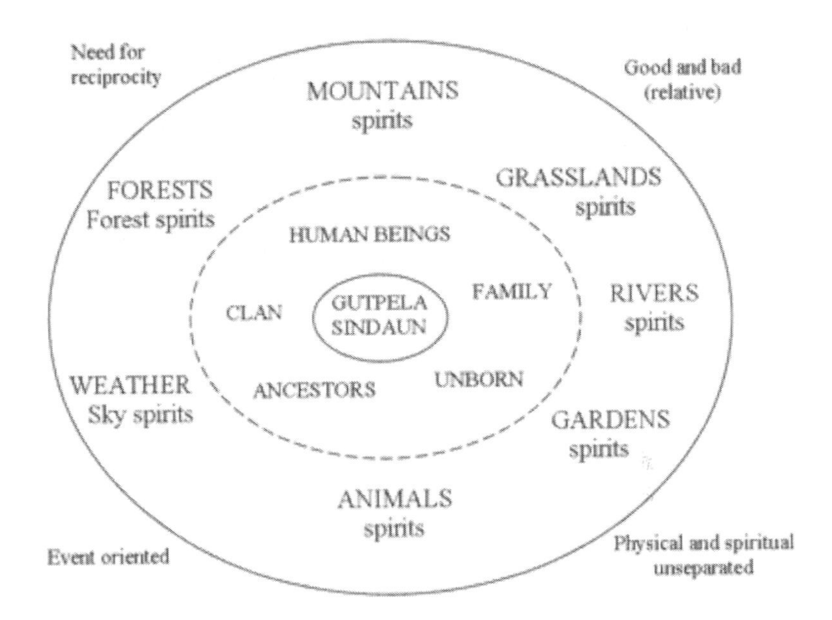

FIGURE 4
MELANESIAN WORLDVIEW
Adapted by Gabrial Kuman[48]

The effect of this worldview is seen clearly as the Papua New Guinean considers the role of religion. While Western dualism allows religion to separate from other segments of life, for Papua New Guineans spiritual identity is irrevocably intertwined with every aspect of daily life (see figure 4 and figure 5). Unlike the Western worldview, "Melanesians . . . do not have a compartmentalized worldview that divides life into categories (of agriculture, education, economics, and so on). Instead, life is an integrated whole, where all is influenced and controlled by spiritual beings and religious rituals."[49] Therefore, an individual converting to a different religious belief system does not only affect the Papua New Guineans' personal faith but it influences their family life, ethical paradigms, educational direction, creative expression, agricultural practices, political beliefs, social interaction, and extended family relationships. Religious faith is directly connected to the Papua New Guineans' holistic identity affecting how they think, act, and relate to both the physical and spirit world.

48. Bartle, *Death*, 24; Shaw, "Melanesian Perspectives."

49. Bartle, *Death*, 23.

FIGURE 5
COMPARTMENTALIZED WORLDVIEW[50]

Belief in the Supernatural

An equally dominant concept in PNG is the belief that the spirit world is filled with spirit beings who can bring both harm and assistance to individuals and communities. Traditionally this understanding has led to the appeasement of ancestral and local spirits in order to maintain spiritual order and social harmony within a limited population.[51] More than a threat to the community, however, spirit beings are also sought after for guidance and assistance. As Bartle notes, within PNG "the spirits, especially the spirits of the dead, are never far away. They live nearby and are concerned about the welfare of the clan."[52] This protection offered by ancestral spirits has led to the creation of local rituals and prayers focusing on seeking this spirit-controlled guidance and prosperity. In *Religions of Oceania*, Tony Swain and Garry Trompf elaborate upon the extensive nature of these prayers of protection. They write:

> This theme of protection is admittedly found in prayers right down the social scale—for planting, fishing and the like—and chants for protection are well known in Micronesia as well . . .

50. Ibid., 24.
51. Namunu, "Spirits," 110.
52. Bartle, *Death*, 23.

> they conform psycho-religiously to a vertico-hierarchical opening of both the social and spiritual orders, reflecting more an attitude of dependence and negotiated rapprochement than "technologic" manipulation. In Melanesia one finds more emphasis on direct transactions with the spirits by groups as virtually unranked wholes, or by small groups helped by the incantations or "manipulative prayers" of specialists or heads of households—to make the garden grow, as a Trobriand spell exemplifies, so that it "rises like the iron-wood palm/[and]. . . swells as with a child."[53]

These direct communal petitions to the spirits for daily protection and well-being permeate every action and event of the collective whole. The Papua New Guinean thus depends upon the continuation of this relationship with the spirit world to bring success to every aspect of life; fertility of the womb and the land, general health within the community, and victory in tribal fights are all reliant upon the healthy affiliation and power of the spirits invoked by the community.

This holistic weaving together of the community's welfare with the spirit world is an important factor to consider in regards to PNG Christianity. Although some observers may be inclined to foresee PNG spirituality as a fertile field for mission work, a community's holistic dependence upon the local spirits cannot be so easily discarded. Instead, "for most Melanesians, the Christian God does not replace this traditional hierarchy of spirits, but rather is added to them . . . Many Christians have divided loyalties and choose whichever source of power they think will be most appropriate at any particular time."[54] This syncretistic behavior is very common in PNG culture partly due to the deep historic roots of the traditional folk religion and partly due to the inadequacy of many Christian traditions in dealing with the spirit world. As Bartle notes:

> Any theology that ignores the traditional cosmology will result in a truncated gospel. Such a truncated gospel gives the impression that although Jesus can help with the ultimate issues (such as eternal salvation), he is powerless to deal with the daily fear of sorcery and witchcraft. The teaching of an imported Western gospel that ignores the spirit world does not prevent syncretism, but actually helps to cause syncretism, thus forming an

53. Swain and Trompf, *Religions*, 150.

54. Bartle, *Death*, 44.

> unhealthy mix of the old and the new which is neither one nor the other.[55]

Syncretism is further promoted by the inherently different foci and questions of the Western church verses those of the PNG church. While the Western church emphasizes correct doctrine and beliefs, the PNG church is more interested in the practical functionality of the gospel message; "the big questions in Melanesia are, 'Does it work? Is it effective? Does it bring abundant life?'"[56] More simply put, does Christ have power to overcome the spirit world and bring harmony and well-being to a community? For in Melanesia "a religion without power is a religion without life."[57]

During the CRC revival this issue of syncretism and holistic dependence upon the spirit world served both as a hindrance and as an impetus in the revival's success. Entering into the highly syncretistic regions of PNG, for example, placed evangelists in situations where spirit powers dominated and competing religions were violently resisted. Within this same environment however, CRC revivalists found that people's belief in the spirit world opened their hearts and minds to the power of God. As with other Pentecostal and Charismatic outreaches, the Papua New Guineans' "expectations for the manifestation of spiritual power" were finally met in the Pentecostal movement's interaction with the spirit world.[58] Once the power of Christ was witnessed in a village or town, those who accepted the gospel adopted more than just an ideology; instead, the new believers made commitments to God and in turn expected holistic transformation. As with the traditional beliefs before them, Christianity was embraced as an all-pervading belief system and lifestyle which influenced both the individual and community in its entirety.

The experiential nature of the Pentecostal experience also connected with the PNG worldview where religion "is felt rather than reasoned and is experienced through one's feelings more than perceived through the mind."[59] In contrast to the doctrinal emphases of previous denominations in the area, the Pentecostal emphasis on the Spirit of God, the gifts of the Holy Spirit, physical healing and victory in the spirit world con-

55. Ibid.

56. Ibid., 38.

57. Ibid.

58. Namunu, "Spirits," 118.

59. Bartle, *Death*, 38.

nected well with the PNG worldview.[60] As a result both Pentecostal and Charismatic Churches met with great success as they presented Papua New Guineans with a gospel of Christ that was both holistic and experiential in nature. Specifically, the Holy Spirit–focused movements provided an avenue through which Papua New Guineans could finally deal with the supernatural through the power of Christ instead of through traditional methods.

Clan Centrality

The final socio-cultural belief which sheds light on my research data is the PNG kinship system. Within PNG in particular, the clan, including individuals both living and dead, stands at the center of society. This often bi-lineal kinship system provides the backbone of PNG society and as such has greatly influenced the spread of Christianity in the nation. In particular, the prevalence of the clans in PNG impacted how the CRC movement spread the gospel throughout the provinces and also the structure of the churches that were planted.

Distinct from the larger Polynesian tribes unified by a common language, PNG is primarily made up of smaller clan units with related kin descended from one common ancestor. Religion, in addition to every aspect of daily life, is centered on and determined by the clan.[61] In fact, "there is no life outside of the clan. Defense, security and wellbeing are all dependent upon the clan members supporting each other. Marriages are contracts between two clans, not just between two individuals." . .. Moreover, "tribal dances and ceremonies are owned by clans, and the daily activities of gardening, hunting and house building are all clan activities. The spirits of the dead are the spirits of the clan."[62] This interdependence within the clan allows each member to be fully supported politically, religiously, and socio-economically by its kin hence maintaining the holistic harmony of the larger group. Loyalty to one's clan is also a principal characteristic of the family system as allegiance to one's family is placed before responsibilities to outside individuals and groups. Thus, in all matters, the clan remains at the center as the source of joint protection, religious tradition, social engagement, and physical well-being of the entire extended family structure.

60. Ibid., 57.

61. Ibid., 26.

62. Ibid.

As a central part of the PNG social structure, the clan also played a large role in the spread of the gospel. Alan Tippett notes that within the South and Southwest Pacific "the Gospel spread through social units—families, lineages, tribes, occupational groups or villages."[63] He concludes that "even though every convert has to be brought personally to Christ as an individual, for the most part people have moved into Christianity in groups and frequently the emerging churches have reflected those social structures."[64] Within PNG, these larger "people movements"[65] took place as entire clans came to Christ during the revival period. The clan structure further influenced the church as the newly converted clans often started their own Christian fellowships within their villages. Ideologically, the concept of the local church also fits comfortably "into [the] already existing social structure" as the inherent autonomy and interdependence of the clan transferred well to understanding the local Christian church.[66] Therefore, as the role of the clan was considered, it became clear that the established kinship system in PNG served not only as the primarily vehicle of the gospel message but also as the foundation for the Christian community which grew out of the CRC revival.

63. Tippett, *Deep Sea Canoe*, 53.

64. Ibid.

65. Tippett, *People Movements*.

66. Gilding, "PNG Impressions," 2.

7

Context of a Revival: CRC Movement

What is now known as the largest branch of the CRC International Movement started in the early 1970s in a small apartment in Port Moresby, PNG. On January 28, 1972, Pastor Barry Silverback and his wife Rosalie arrived in Port Moresby along with their four children to start the first CRC missionary training center in PNG. Having worked since July 1967 alongside the Foursquare Church at the Hageri mission station near Goroka in the Eastern Highlands, Silverback felt "challenged by the needs of Papua."[1] Upon receiving the support of the crusade leaders in Adelaide, Silverback started the CRC led venture. The first few months in Port Moresby proved more difficult than expected, however, and by August 1972 the Port Moresby church boasted only 30 adults. In early 1973, Silverback wrote of the challenges of ministry in Port Moresby:

> Up here in Port Moresby, as in all the Papuan part of New Guinea, religious tradition runs very strong, and change is not readily welcomed. Almost all Papuans claim affiliation with a particular church, but, as in all countries, a large portion of these do not know the salvation of the Lord Jesus Christ . . . Here, we are not welcome in the villages as we would be in the Highlands, and we are not able to go into them and preach at will. In fact, quite strong open opposition is expressed. This makes it harder to have any kind of evangelistic meeting to reach those who are in need.[2]

1. Cooper, *Flames of Revival*, 190.
2. Ibid., 209.

This denominational division felt in Port Moresby and Central Province initially restricted the CRC work to the capital territory. However, despite the evangelistic limitations of mission work in Papua, the CRC church plant took root in the city and started to grow as full-time workers joined the team and new believers started attending the services.[3]

Ministry in the Capital

Working from the Silverbacks' apartment in Port Moresby, the growing team[4] spent the majority of their time witnessing door to door in Tokarara, visiting the sick in hospital and establishing relationships at the Teachers' College and the University of PNG.[5] In a letter to the CRC headquarters in Adelaide, Silverback reports on the early progress of the Melanesian mission team:

> We have about 25–30 adults regularly attending our fellowship meetings on Sunday mornings in a nearby school house and approximately 20 attending the Wednesday mid-week meetings in our flat.[6] These meetings are in English. Most of those attending are students from either the Port Moresby Teachers' College or the University of Papua. These are all contacts which have been made since our arrival.[7]

Despite these small beginnings, the Sunday gathering began to grow steadily and by December 1973 the "Bethel" church building in Tokarara was dedicated by Pastor Leo Harris, the founding father of the CRC denomination.[8]

After the following Christmas and New Year's crusades led by Bethel Center's ministry staff, the new church was filled with more than four hundred congregants, more than a tenfold increase from four months previous.[9] The first Youth Easter Camp held in 1974 continued to bring

3. Wari, interview by author, July 29, 2009. See appendix A for a complete list of interviewees and interview numbers.

4. In 1973 the Bethel Team consisted of Barry and Rosalie Silverback, Barbara Buckland, and Jack and Lorna Kornaats from Australia, and Labu Tuakana, Ovua Rapilla, Ravu Geno, and Thelma Garoa from Central Province ("New Guinea News," *Revivalist*, 1973, 10–11).

5. Ibid., 11–12.

6. A "flat" is an apartment in Australian English.

7. Silverback, "New Guinea News," 1972, 17.

8. "New Guinea News," 1974, 10.

9. Cooper, *Flames of Revival*, 227.

in more young people to the church and proved to be significant as many future CRC pastors and leaders, including Geua (Wia) Wari and Alu (Gima) Purinau, came to Christ during the camp.[10] The church gatherings increased with the developing congregation and Wednesday night meetings (English), Tuesday night meetings (Pidgin), Saturday young peoples' meetings, correspondence courses, and a Joytime Crusade children's ministry were added to the scheduled Sunday morning and evening meetings (English).[11]

Vision for the CRC in PNG

From the commencement of the ministry in Port Moresby there was a clear sense that God, not man, was leading the CRC mission team and had personally established the work.[12] As the Bethel congregation increased and new staff members joined the team, the vision which God provided years before started to come to pass. While completing a six-month Teaching English to Speakers of Other Languages—or TESOL—course in Port Moresby, Teague, a CRC missionary in the highlands, received a vision from God regarding the future work of the CRC in Papua and the entire nation. Received in 1965, seven years prior to the Silverbacks' arrival in Port Moresby, Merrilyn Teague saw the revival that would later hit PNG via the Port Moresby church. She describes her vision:

> One day, whilst I was in prayer, on my knees, seeking the Lord, praying and interceding on behalf of the people of PNG, the Lord gave me a vision . . . The outline of the map of Papua New Guinea came clearly before me in picture-form. Then I saw a small flame alighting on Port Moresby, the capital of PNG, which grew larger. Then the Lord spoke these words clearly: "It must first begin in the capital, Port Moresby! Not by might, nor by power, but by My Spirit, saith the Lord!"[13]

Teague later joined the Bethel team shortly after PNG Independence on October 16, 1975. As the ministry started to flourish in Port Moresby, Teague witnessed firsthand the fulfillment of this vision given to her almost a decade before.

10. Silverback, "New Guinea News," 1974.
11. "New Guinea News," 1973, 12.
12. John Togawata, interview by author, July 13, 2009, 1A.
13. Teague, "Outpouring."

In early 1976, God gave the young missionary another vision of his plan for the people of PNG. In a written account of the event, Teague recalls her vision:

> In this vision, I saw clearly the Bethel church building which I was very familiar with . . . I saw flames of fire bursting forth out of the roof of Bethel Church, it was ablaze with fire! Then, I saw runners, carrying torches of fire, coming out of Bethel church, they were running excitedly in all directions from without the church, into the streets, over the mountains, into the villages, saying, "Take the fire; carry the torch to your own people!"
>
> Then, I saw rivers running down from the mountains to the coast, with small canoes racing down the current, with people inside the canoes, rowing fast, excitedly saying, "Go down to Bethel, get the fire from Bethel, bring the fire back home from Bethel." Both runners and rowers, going from and going to Bethel Church, in Port Moresby.[14]

Upon sharing the vision with Silverback, the Bethel team discovered that many others "had had similar dreams and visions of this outpouring of the Holy Spirit."[15] Little did the team know that the key relationships through which the revival would later spread had already been made through the persons of Thomas and Grace Tamanabae.[16] The vision of Bethel Center becoming the center of a nationwide revival was in fact just months away from coming to pass.

Birth of the Revival

Living adjacent to Bethel Tabernacle in Tokarara, Thomas and Grace Tamanabae began attending church services in 1976 because of its close proximity to their house.[17] However, what started as convenience quickly was realized as a crucial part of God's divine plan. Burdened by their family's involvement in witchcraft in Oro Province, the Tamanabaes began praying regularly with Teague for the salvation of their immediate family.[18] Teague, writing down all the family's names in the front leaf of her Bible, remembers "often call[ing] their names to the Lord in prayer

14. Ibid.
15. Ibid.
16. Ibid.
17. Thomas Tamanabae, interview by author, July 23, 2009.
18. Ibid.

[and] interceding for their salvation and deliverance."[19] God heard the group's faithful prayers and over the course of the months that followed each and every family member came to Bethel Center and was saved. In Teague's own words, "they heard the Gospel, they were convicted of their sins, they accepted Jesus Christ as their Saviour and they were healed; they were delivered, they were baptized with the Holy Spirit, [and] they were touched by the fire of God."[20] As the Tamanabae family came to Christ, several members decide to return home to their village to preach the gospel of Christ to their own people.[21] It was through the Tamanabae family's initial evangelism in the Binandere-speaking villages of the Ioma district that revival ignited and spread like fire across Oro Province.[22]

MISSIONARY OUTREACH PATROLS

Although the CRC's first missionary outreach patrol[23] was to Milne Bay Province in April 1975,[24] it was in August 1976 during a missionary outreach patrol in Oro Province that the PNG CRC revival began. After finding Christ at Bethel Center, members of the Tamanabae family returned home to Kurereda village to share their newfound joy in Christ.[25] Immediately, God began working in the village as people started turning to Christ, finding supernatural healing and delivery from demonic oppression. Remembering the first time he came home after his conversion, Tamanabae states:

> Two weeks after having this experience [with Christ] I went to my village and the people were very surprised to see me walk into the village with a Bible in my hand. They wondered what had happened to me. I began to share what the Lord had done in my life, and I prayed for sick people. The people were also amazed to see my cousin Robert who was an army sergeant and was regarded by the villagers as one of the fathers of sorcery in our village, walk into the village with a Bible in his hand. Robert

19. Teague, "Outpouring."

20. Ibid.

21. Ibid.

22. Richmond Tamanabae, interview by author, July 13, 2009, 2A.

23. A phrase used to describe the evangelistic outreach meetings of the Bethel Center team in which a group of evangelists would travel for several days or weeks sharing the good news about Christ through a specific region.

24. Cooper, *Flames of Revival*, 244.

25. Igarobae, interview by author, August 3, 2009, 2A.

> had been saved only a day before we left for home and did not know much about witnessing, but he knew in his heart what was right.
>
> We began to give orders to the members of our family to repent and throw away all their things to do with sorcery. By the time we left the village ten days later, three quarters of the village had given their lives to the Lord and burned all their implements of sorcery and other evil practices.[26]

The impact of the gospel in the village is great and "after the villagers were baptized in water by immersion, the Lord poured His Spirit upon them all." Tamanabae explains that "this was the first village in the Northern Province of PNG to witness the outpouring of the Spirit and it was just like in the Book of Acts!"[27]

CRC in Oro Province

At the invitation of clan leaders, Silverback and the Bethel team were soon invited to conduct evangelistic meetings in Kurereda village and the outlying area.[28] Three months after the outpouring of the Holy Spirit in Kurereda, the Bethel team came with additional resources to assist the growing church. Outreach patrols soon multiplied in the region as organized Bethel teams and spontaneous local teams traveled throughout the province sharing the good news of Christ. In the midst of these fruitful outreaches, there also existed a steady flow of persecution.[29] During an early outreach patrol, Silverback recalls the presence of such persecution during a local evangelical night meeting:

> It was not until the morning of the fifth day that a truck was available to take us out of Popondetta. We drove for 43 miles then walked for about 2 ½ hours in the hot sun before we reached the first village and prepared for the night meeting. Throughout the whole time of our meeting there was much opposition such as noise, heckling, shouting, and abusive language, which increased until finally we could no longer continue as the people were so disturbed. However we were able to counsel and pray for a few individuals, which resulted in one young man

26. Tamanabae, "Love," 14.
27. Ibid.
28. Richmond Tamanabae, interview by author, July 30, 2009, 2A.
29. Barnabas Tabara, interview by author, June 30, 2009.

> accepting Christ and quite a number receiving healing in their bodies.[30]

Persecution continued to plague the team, particularly during the early patrols, however, as Silverback notes: "In each place the opposition soon turned into interest and then open-hearted acceptance of the message of new life in Christ as the manifestation of the Spirit began to be seen amongst them."[31] He continues that "through the operation of the word of knowledge, word of wisdom, discerning of spirits, and working of miracles, many hearts were turned to receive the Lord Jesus Christ and believe in His power at work today."[32]

Revival Fire

The spiritual renewal that began in Kurereda village soon spread throughout the province as the national and international evangelists trekked from village to village sharing the good news.[33] As the evangelistic groups traveled, they boldly preached the Word, healed the sick, baptized the new believers, delivered the oppressed and witnessed the outpouring of the Spirit. In correspondence to the CRC headquarters in Adelaide, Silverback records some of his experiences during a 1977 missionary patrol in Oro Province. He writes:

> After I had preached in one village I asked for five people with eye conditions to come forward—particularly a woman who had severe pain in her eyes. Among those who came was a very old lady whom some men carried from a house. She had not been able to open her eyes for nine years, and they were extremely painful and "felt as though there were sticks in them." After prayer she opened her eyes instantly and was completely healed. This caused the people's faith to rise and many were healed that night, including three village leaders. The man who had been strongest in opposing us publicly apologized, and the next day acknowledged Christ as his own Lord and Saviour. 104 people from this village were baptized in water, and 55 baptized in the Holy Spirit.[34]

30. Silverback, "Report."
31. Ibid.
32. Ibid.
33. Alkin Orona, interview by author, July 2, 2009, 1A.
34. Silverback, "Report."

Scenes such as this one are repeated throughout Oro Province as the good news moved throughout Ioma to the Kokoda, Afore, Oro Bay, Higaturu, Tufi, and Popondetta districts.[35]

The miraculous often paved the way for the gospel as the numerous signs and wonders served to confirm the message that was preached. During the same 1977 outreach patrol, Silverback notes the powerful effect that witnessing a miracle had on one Oro village:

> Another example of how the manifested power of God was instrumental in opening up a village which would have been otherwise opposed to our presence was the case of an old lady we found as we went down to the river to wash one morning. She was so sick she was to be taken out to the hospital, but when we prayed she was instantly healed, and then was ready and willing to accept the Lord. When we returned from washing, she was nowhere around. In fact she had gone out to her garden, where she worked hard all day! In the meeting that night her husband, too, was led to the Lord and healed, as were many others. Over 55 people accepted Christ there.[36]

With the confirmation of signs and wonders village after village turned to Christ throughout the province. Moreover, once individuals decided to follow Christ, God's power became evident within the community. Peter Igarobae, a national leader during the revival, recalls that during the revival period the power of God was so strong in some villages that there was "a certain radius around the village [of] the presence of the Lord."[37] So much so, that individuals who entered that radius were instantly healed of their aches and pains without even entering the village.[38] Many similar accounts of healings, signs and wonders, and deliverances are recorded in *The Revivalist* magazine and as such bear witness to the powerful work of God throughout the region from the revival's impetus in 1976.

Indigenous Leadership

A distinguishing mark of the Oro revival was the great number and diversity of the individuals involved in the evangelical work. Mothers,

35. Numba Puri, interview by author, August 2, 2009.
36. Silverback, "Report."
37. Peter Igarobae, interview by author, August 3, 2009, 2A.
38. Ibid.

teenagers, the elderly, village leaders, and young children, along with visiting Bethel outreach teams, all participated in formal and informal witnessing efforts.[39] While Bethel Center's outreach patrol teams played a crucial role in building up the newly established churches and witnessing within the villages, they only remained in the region for several weeks at a time. Thus, the local church leaders served as the primary pioneers of the mission movement, constantly preaching the gospel in unreached areas. Although many individuals were involved in indigenous leadership, Robert Tamanabae became one of the foremost evangelists during the early days of the revival.[40] On one occasion Silverback records visiting a village where Tamanabae had already established a church. He writes:

> This village was the first to receive the Word of God, and the people have progressed tremendously under Brother Robert Tamanabae's leadership. He has built a new church in the village, and has taught them how to really praise and worship the Lord. In fact wherever we went Robert would gather the new Christians together the same night that they were saved and teach them how to worship God with uplifted hands and fervent praises. They are also very active in evangelism, and all but 8 people in the village are now born-again and Spirit-filled believers (though many of them were strong in their initial opposition to the revival).[41]

The initial establishment of the revival as an indigenous movement empowered many new believers to share the good news of Christ with their own family and neighbors. This in turn led to a domino effect as the gospel message moved quickly throughout entire kinship systems until whole villages and districts heard of and experienced the work of the Holy Spirit.[42]

The revival's indigenous foundation provided ample opportunity for the church's worship and music to become highly contextualized. Silverback describes scenes of village worship as a common occurrence within the province. Describing a village that had already received the gospel, Silverback writes: "We travelled down-river by outrigger canoe, arriving at the next village two hours later. We found the people in the midst of

39. Barnabas Tabara, interview by author, June 30, 2009; Alkin Orona, interview by author, July 2, 2009, 1A.

40. Uvau Amani, interview by author, June 12, 2009.

41. Silverback, "Report."

42. Numba Puri, interview by author, August 2, 2009.

a time of praising God on the river bank, with their eyes shut and hands uplifted. Some stopped to welcome us, but others continued on praising God."[43] This assimilation of the gospel into the musical culture of the Binandere was also evidenced in the language songs that began emerging from the local congregations as well as the healing that took place in worship during the first few months of the revival.[44]

Missionary outreach teams continued traveling to Oro Province during the next few years assisting the local leadership as well as conducting evangelistic crusades in the area. During this time national leaders began to emerge and take ownership of the large missionary task before them. Bruce Gilding, a CRC pastor leading Bethel Center during the Silverback family's furlough, recalls several such national pioneers reporting on God's continuing work in the province in 1978. Gilding writes in his final report to the CRC Adelaide office of one recent mission outreach led by Suckling Tamanabae:

> Just this month (January) Suckling Tamanabae went on a trip to a village in the North[ern] Province[45]. . . close to his own village. Upon arrival, he found two Christian families. He shared with them then they spend time outside praising the Lord in a circle. The rest of the village (100 or so) stood back and just watched. After some time Suckling asked if any of the folk would like to receive Christ as their Saviour. A large number came into the circle and prayed to receive Christ and they too then joined in the praise and worship. A woman with a small boy, crippled from birth, came and asked for prayer for her son. As Suckling prayed, the power of the Spirit touched the little fellow, his legs began to shake. They put him on the ground, where he stood up and walked for the first time in his life! Subsequently, the rest of the village came into the circle and received Jesus as their personal Saviour followed by much praise and worship. The folk really rejoiced.[46]

This continuation of the revival through the work of indigenous leaders constantly multiplied the pioneering work, as today's new believers became tomorrow's evangelists.

43. Silverback, "Report."
44. Barnabas Tabara, interview by author, June 30, 2009.
45. Northern Province has since changed its name to Oro Province.
46. Gilding, "PNG Impressions," 2–3.

The largely national and local leadership in the CRC church led to a high ownership of the gospel message among new believers as they heard the good news in their own language from their own people.

In the next few years, scores of missionary patrols,[47] city crusades,[48] new churches and new provincial training centers were established by the ever-growing Bethel team of national and international leaders and pastors. Supernatural healings, mass conversions, demonic deliverances, and the presence of the Holy Spirit became regular occurrences during the many outreaches that took place in Oro Province as well as in the Central Highlands, Central, Gulf and Milne Bay Provinces. Bethel Center's missionary outreach patrols continued successfully through to the early 1990s and included ministry trips such as the 1992 patrol to the Gulf Province in which 2,500 dedicated their lives to Christ. Although the 1990s saw the greatest numerical increases in the denomination, it was during the early years of outreach in the mid-1970s and early 1980s that the wide-scale spiritual revival took place. Nevertheless, the spiritual fervor and excitement of the early patrols continued to be a characteristic of all the outreaches both at the beginning and toward the end of the revival period. For as Silverback often notes in his correspondence with the Sturt Street Church in Adelaide, there was a strong feeling throughout the PNG CRC movement that "there remaineth yet very much land to be possessed!" (Josh 13:1).

TRAINING NATIONAL LEADERS

In addition to the success of the missionary outreach patrols, the CRC Bible School first founded in Port Moresby in April 1979 also grew in leaps and bounds. While part-time Bible schools and training programs were conducted in the past, it was the founding of the full-time Bible school (1979), Institute of Evangelism (1981) and World Mission Faith

47. Documented missionary patrols included those conducted in Milne Bay (Apr. 1975; 1981), Oro Province (Aug. 1976; Sept. 1977; Apr. 1978; May 1979; 1981; 1992), Central Province (1981), Central Highlands Province (Feb. 1982), and Gulf Province (Feb. 1982; June 1995). In addition there were numerous boat patrols with the "Mauri Dalana" including those in Dec. 1979, May 1980, and Sept. 1981.

48. CRC Crusade meetings were held throughout PNG and featured international speakers such as Leo and Belle Harris (July/Aug. 1964; June 1966; May 1969; Nov. 1972; May 1973; Dec. 1973; July/Aug. 1976; Dec. 1973), Don and Betty Dawson (May 1969), Bruce Gilding (1978), Brother Worley (Feb. 1979), Norm Armstrong (Mar. 1975; 1979; Aug. 1981; June 1984), Wal Braley (1979), Bill and Joan Beard (Sept. 1983) and Gordon Gibbs (1988).

Training School (1996) which firmly established the PNG CRC as an indigenous training organization. Initially the students consisted of young Port Moresby professionals, university students, and emerging leaders from the revival areas; however, the student population soon included individuals from varying provinces, social classes, denominations, and in later years, nations. As records state in Bethel Center's "Run with the Vision" pamphlet, the training programs also expanded to include in-service training, leadership seminars, a secretarial training program, full-time courses, a tape ministry, and correspondence courses.[49] From as early as 1978, Bethel Center boasted a vibrant and growing list of congregational training courses, women's ministries, youth outreaches, and children's programs which continued to expand exponentially as the Port Moresby congregation grew. In Gilding's remarks regarding his three-month stay at Bethel Center, he concludes, "I have found a wonderful spirit of fellowship and praise coupled with what only can be described as sound teaching in the Word of God. The work is solid and stable spiritually, which is a real tribute and testimony to the ministry of Brother Barry and his wife Rosalie."[50]

As the ministry grew at Bethel Center so did the full-time team members working at the Tokarara campus. In October 1977, Labu Tuakana from Central Province became the first national pastor ordained by the CRC in Port Moresby. The Australian *Revivalist* magazine comments on Tuakana's ordination and his family's recent commission in 1980 to Oro Province:

> First Pastor from Port Moresby . . . Pastor Labu was the first national pastor ordained at Bethel Center, Port Moresby in Papua New Guinea. On 5th of January he was sent out from the Center, bound for Popondetta where he will take charge of the work there. We see Pastor Labu's transfer to Popondetta as an exciting step in God's programme for His church in Papua New Guinea. This is the view of the believers of Bethel Center who have always considered that training of national ministries was one of their essential tasks.[51]

Further ordinations followed as Fuwe Hageyo (Nov. 1978), Richmond Tamanabae (May 1981), Kila Wari (May 1981), Peter Igarobae

49. "Run with the Vision," 12–14.

50. Gilding, "PNG Impressions," 3.

51. Newspoint, *Impact*, 24.

(May 1981), Thomas Tamanabae (Aug. 1982), and Aria Hegame (Oct. 1987) were ordained as CRC pastors. In the following two decades, the PNG CRC ordained approximately eighty national pastors throughout PNG.[52]

The Bible schools also multiplied as CRC pastors, missionaries, and graduates alike started new training schools around the country. CRC Bible schools[53] were established nationally in Central, East New Britain, Oro, Gulf, Western, Milne Bay, Western Highlands, North Solomon, Enga, and Madang provinces. In addition, CRC missionaries and Bethel Bible School graduates founded Bible training schools internationally in Solomon Islands, Fiji, Vanuatu, Indonesia, and the Philippines.[54] Thus, in less than two decades what started as a national revival movement soon became an international mission movement. An added contribution to this shift was the arrival of international Bible students at Bethel Center. In March 1987 the first international students arrived from India with more students from Fiji and India following in March 1989.[55] By December 1996, a total of 105 overseas students from the Solomon Islands, the Philippines, India, Pakistan, Sri Lanka, Fiji, Vanuatu, Australia, New Zealand, the United States, and the Cook Islands attended Bethel Center's Bible school making it a truly international enterprise.[56]

52. See appendix E for more details.

53. See appendix F for a complete record of Bible schools founded by the PNG CRC movement from 1974–1997.

54. "PNG Events in Papua New Guinea."

55. Ibid.

56. "Some Dates and Statistics."

TABLE 8
CRC STATISTICS IN PNG[57]

Information	1981	1984	1985	1987	1990	1991	1993
Number of Provinces with CRC Churches	2	6	10	13	17	17	19
Number of Churches in CRC	40	60	85	158	218	230	350
Number of People in CRC	3,000	7,000	10,000	16,000	24,000	25,000	30,000
Number of Full-Time Training Schools	1	2	*	4	6	9	*
Estimated Number of People Being Trained/year	11	70	*	150	150	200	*
Total Number of Ordained Pastors	5	7	*	24	66	**80	*

* No records provided
** Estimate based upon available data

INTERNATIONAL MISSION OUTREACH[58]

As the CRC movement grew in PNG the mission emphasis progressed from a national to an international focus. While still noting the importance of "the sending of ministries for strengthening and maturing the various local bodies" and "the providing of teachers and teaching aids . . . for the teaching and training of brethren within these local bodies,"[59] Bethel Center also emphasized the multiplying of believers internationally as well as at home. In a stirring call to PNG believers to become "World Christians," the author states the following:

> As we celebrate God's coming to this earth, may we all consider deep in our hearts: Are WE doing what WE can—NOW—to

57. Due to the Bethel Center fire, a complete list of annual statistics is not available for the 1970s–1980s period.

58. Although the overseas expansion of the Papua New Guinean CRC church is significant to illustrate the international growth of the movement, it is not the focus of this study. However, although my case study is restricted to the 1970s–1980s revival in PNG, the missional fruit of the CRC's labor post-1990 demonstrates the mission focus of the denomination after the national revival period and is thus included in this chapter.

59. "Run with the Vision," 6.

> bring the Gospel to the world? The great invitation is open to us, God's people, to be more than just "believers" and "church members" and "Christian workers." We can be WORLD CHRISTIANS![60]

In another letter to the Australian CRC churches on May 11, 1990, Silverback highlights this need to join in international mission work. He explains:

> World Missions is really the heart of God, and the Bible is the revelation of God's heart and His dealings with man in His desire to reconcile to (make one with) Himself every creature in every nation. What a joy and a privilege it is to be invited by the Lord to be a co-worker, joining hands together with Him in pursuit of this great objective! I can think of no greater privilege nor any greater goal . . . When we attempt to do something for our Lord and Saviour whom we love so dearly, then the task before us changes from merely duty and one of drudgery to delight and joy. Such is the joyful experience of being engaged in the task of World Missions![61]

World missions soon came to the forefront of the PNG CRC's training curriculum as national leaders started seeing PNG no longer as a mission field but instead as a sending agency.[62]

This call to participate in God's global mission impacted the local CRC congregations and provincial Bible schools in practical ways. World Missions prayer groups began at many churches and Bible schools and financial assistance for missionaries started pouring in. In 1989 alone, PNG CRC provincial churches gave K12,453.83[63] toward world mission with a total of K12,824.53 going to missionaries and an additional K6,610.89 toward mission work in Irian Jaya, the Philippines, and India.[64] In 1991, the mission offerings from Bethel Tabernacle alone jumped to K28,000 for mission work within PNG and K28,000 for world mission.[65] While historically an impoverished nation, the generosity of the PNG CRC churches clearly displayed their great desire to actively participate in God's global mission.

60. "Nation Aflame."
61. Silverback, "Mission Update," 1.
62. Margaret Sete, interview by author, August 8, 2009, 1B.
63. Offerings are recorded in PNG Kina currency.
64. "CRC (PNG) World Mission Department Annual Report."
65. Silverback, "PNG Annual Report."

In addition to financial assistance and prayer support, Bethel Center soon began commissioning their own missionaries, and in October 1984 the first PNG CRC missionaries left for the Solomon Islands.[66] A natural continuation from the provincial mission outreaches in PNG, the indigenous CRC pastors continued to plant churches, establish Bible schools and train national leaders, but this time among their Pacific neighbors.[67] From 1984–1997 the PNG CRC movement sent full-time missionaries to the Solomon Islands, Vanuatu, Fiji, Indonesia, Australia, and PNG. Additionally, international graduates from Bethel Center's Bible school established CRC-associated ministries in India and Sri Lanka.[68]

The vision for international mission work spread throughout the CRC as the pastors, Bible school teachers, and students started learning about and participating in God's work overseas. Elijah and Beverly Umeume, Bible school students at Bethel Center from 1988–1989 and future CRC missionaries to Fiji, note the great influence of Silverback upon the development of this missionary vision in PNG. In explaining the catalyst of the PNG CRC global mission work, they state that "it was the vision of Pastor Barry that was imparted to the students and to the pastors. And then they [the students and pastors] caught the vision: that reaching the lost was not only in our nation but worldwide. Some have to become local missionaries and some have to become overseas missionaries; and so that's what happened."[69] This multiplication of the vision is further encouraged by the many international speakers that visited Bethel Center during the 1980s and 1990s as well as the students' own practicum experiences abroad in countries such as Australia, the Philippines, Fiji, and the Solomon Islands.[70] Within a few years Bethel Center's focus and vision shifted from ministering solely in PNG to reaching out to the ends of the earth.

As Bethel Center's mission work expanded, the PNG CRC established a mission strategy to express its new vision. In the "Christian Revival Crusade (PNG): Strategy in Relation to Other Nations," the CRC's mission strategy is listed as having a threefold focus: PNG, Australia and New Zealand, and other countries. The goals internationally include:

66. "PNG Events in Papua New Guinea."

67. See appendix G for a list of PNG missionaries sent out for local and foreign mission service from 1980–1997.

68. "Missionaries (Etc) Overseas."

69. Elijah and Beverly Umeume, interview by author, June 24, 2009.

70. Ibid.

"assist[ing] in pioneering evangelistic ministry and the planting of local churches" and "train[ing] and develop[ing] national ministries."[71] Foremost in the listed strategic goals was the desire that the newly established churches share the blessing of Christ with others; that the CRC missionaries would "introduce to the people the concept of themselves being able to be a blessing to the world."[72] Furthermore, the concept of blessing the nations was also shared at the national level as the PNG churches were taught "the responsibility of all churches to be a blessing to the world, and the ability of every Christian himself or herself to participate in fulfilling this great commission."[73] This desire to bless nations through participation in the worldwide work of Christ thus became one of the primary goals of the CRC movement in PNG.

71. "Christian Revival Crusade," 2.

72. Ibid.

73. Ibid., 3.

8

Stories of Revival: Manifestations of God's Blessing

In this chapter I analyze the Abrahamic blessing motif in the PNG interview data through the same missional categories used to trace the Abrahamic blessing motif through Scripture: agents of mission, motivational factors, the message shared, methods of mission, and missional expansion. As mentioned previously, the interview data collected in PNG focused on the CRC revival which took place during the 1970s and 1980s. The following data analysis is based upon the interviews of the key national leaders who were at the forefront of the indigenous missionary movement.[1]

AGENTS OF MISSION[2]

Within the CRC revival period there were numerous national leaders and laypeople that emerged as agents of God's mission. When these individuals are considered as a whole the primary characteristic that they share is their diversity from one another. The evangelists, pastors, teachers, and missionaries who emerged from within the CRC revival movement were both young and old, men and women, educated and uneducated, full-time missionaries and full-time workers, new Christians and revitalized Christians, city dwellers and villagers, foreigners and nationals. This immense variety was also evident in the occupations of the individuals

1. See appendix A for a list of interviewees.

2. As there were innumerable key individuals involved in the PNG CRC revival movement, in this section I analyze the shared characteristics of the revival leaders.

chosen; the pioneer leaders were high school students, mothers, teachers, government employees, university students, bank workers and policemen, among many other professions. Barnabas Tabara, a native of Oro Province, recalls his experience in the local marketplace: "I used to see the gospel preached [among] . . . the mothers in the market place. They would sit around [whispering]. You know, talking to the mothers. They would be sharing the gospel."[3] It was this personal evangelism at every level of society by individuals from every level of society that characterized the CRC revival movement both in Port Moresby and its surrounding provinces.

Call to Ministry[4]

Although there was great variety among the revival leaders, there were also many characteristics that united them. Of primary importance is the large number of leaders who were called by God into full-time ministry and who in turn obeyed that call. Margaret Sete, an early revival leader in the Kokoda area, recalls when God called her to full-time mission work during a trip to the Philippines. Upon seeing a vision of herself blessing Oro Province, Sete explains:

> When I saw that, a voice spoke and it said "Go" . . . and I said, "Is that you Lord?" And I turned around and [heard] "Go" a second time. I said "Lord, is it really you? You know that I can't go to Oro Province because it's [an] Anglican area. I would have to be a nun to be accepted by the Anglican Church to go and preach the gospel. I can't go as a young girl [single woman]. They won't accept me; they won't believe me."
>
> I [then] turn[ed] around to go back to my bed, to sit down and pray. And then, when I turn[ed], [I heard a] third time, "Go." That's it; I just didn't make it to the bed, I just lay prostrate on the floor and I wept and I wept and I wept. I said, "Is that you? [Are] you telling me to go to Oro Province?" . . . I said, "Ok Lord. You have to go with me. I can't go alone . . . Lord even if I go and share your word and nobody believes that's okay at least I obeyed [you]."

3. Barnabas Tabara, interview by author, June 30, 2009. See appendix A for a complete list of interviewees and interview numbers.

4. In order to avoid data manipulation, the subcategories listed in this chapter are unique to this particular data set and were not formulated to mirror other subheadings within this paper.

> So I came. I cried and prayed until I went to sleep on the floor. [When I] got up . . . I just knew in my heart of hearts that I have to go home [to Oro Province]. How it was going to happen, I didn't know. But in mere obedience to God I had to go home.[5]

Sete's testimony of a literal calling from God is reflected in similar experiences from CRC national leaders, as is the understanding that obedience to God's call was obligatory not optional.

In addition to hearing the voice of God, many leaders were also called through visions, dreams, and signs and wonders. One example can be found in the testimony of Fuwe Hageyo the current national leader of the CRC in PNG who explains his own call to Papua as a young man residing in Goroka, Eastern Highlands Province. As a recent Bible school graduate, Hageyo recalls a bright shining light appearing in his bedroom from which a voice called out and instructed him: "Go to Papua. I will look after you. I will take care of you; don't fear."[6] The voice, which Hageyo knew to be the voice of God, repeated its instructions three times, reiterating that he should go to Papua and that God would look after him. At the time, Port Moresby, the capital of Papua, was becoming overrun by local criminals, called rascals, who were violently killing and attacking individuals in the streets of the city. Hageyo remembers that God's promise of protection was of particular importance to him at that moment.

Hageyo responded to the vision by making plans to leave Goroka and join Barry Silverback's ministry in Port Moresby, Central Province. Therefore, on March 4, 1973, he traveled down to join the CRC's ministry in Papua where he has served to this day. Hageyo notes that since his call: "I see God's hand through and through; in everything that happened, I see God's hand."[7] It is thus in visions such as the one witnessed by Hageyo that God called revival leaders to the forefront of his mission in PNG.

Worship and Prayer

Those called by God to ministry were also characterized by their fervent worship of God and prayer life. New Christian leaders often were introduced to ministry by learning how to lead worship in their villages and/or churches.[8] However, the worship of God through music and song was

5. Margaret Sete, interview by author, August 8, 2009, 1A.
6. Fuwe Hageyo, interview by author, July 7, 2009, 1A.
7. Ibid.
8. Alkin Orona, interview by author, July 2, 2009, 1A.

not limited to the CRC leadership. Peter Igarobae, a young man during the revival period, describes an early example of village worship:

> You would see a family here start worshiping and the next door will pick up the same chorus and then in less than ten minutes the whole village in their own houses, buildings, they were worshiping the Lord. And it would go on and on for hours and then Robert [Tamanabae] would go down in the middle of the village and stand there and start preaching. In a rainy day, they don't come together, they sit in their own houses and start whatever songs they sing; [and] it was picked up . . . all around in their own houses there.[9]

This love of worshiping God through song was prevalent both in the cities and the villages. Richmond Tamanabae describes his own family worship time in Port Moresby after becoming a Christian: "Once we came in [the church], the house there became a prayer house. So, what happened was whenever we came together to have a meal, we would get into prayer, and then as we pray, we would sing and worship until the food would get cold."[10] This worship of God and practice of intercession in both public and private spheres of life was a common thread through all the data and continued to increase in prevalence as new churches were established throughout the nation.

Background in Sorcery

Another factor shared by a significant portion of the revival leaders was their former affiliation with sorcery and witchcraft. Sorcery was used particularly in the villages to secure the authority of the clan and the land which was taken through tribal warfare. Thus, even as individuals moved to the cities, they often still actively participated in sorcery gaining knowledge and power for their clan. The Tamanabae clan is an example of such a group who turned to Christ and became pioneer evangelists during the CRC revival period. Identified as the "king of the sorcerers" within their region, the Tamanabae clan was encompassed by a heritage of powerful sorcery passed down from generation to generation.[11] However, upon

9. Peter Igarobae, interview by author, August 3, 2009, 2A.

10. Richmond Tamanabae, interview by author, July 30, 2009, 2A.

11. Swain and Trompf note this familial passing down of a sorcerer's knowledge from generation to generation to be a common practice in both Melanesia and Polynesia (*Religions of Oceania*, 161). In the PNG context, the incredible value placed on

their individual conversions to Christ, each member turned away from the practice of sorcery and pledged allegiance to Christ instead.[12]

While not every member of the clan was a practitioner in sorcery, this rejection of black magic and acceptance of Christ affected the entire community. As Peter Igarobae explained to the yet unconverted Robert Tamanabae: "You know that we are clan, and you know whenever a clan is involved, all of us are involved."[13] As such, each member of the clan was prayed for by the rest of the family members until the whole family had turned and committed to Christ.[14] This commitment later led to the cutting of a covenant between the Tamanabae clan and Yahweh which has been honored to this date.

Boldness in Persecution

An additional characteristic which the revival leaders had in common was their boldness in the face of persecution. Particularly at the outset of the CRC's outreaches into the provinces, there was tremendous physical and verbal persecution against the new Pentecostal believers; houses were burned to the ground; individuals were beaten, whipped with bicycle chains, stoned, arrested, shamed and mocked, and even accused of immoral acts.[15] However, "despite all the persecutions," as John Togawata notes, "the churches just grew and grew. [It] came to the point where the Christians . . . [considered] persecution . . . [to be] part of everyday life. It didn't matter anymore to them."[16] Togawata continues that in the midst of the persecution that he witnessed in East New Britain Province he also saw "the boldness of Christ coming out of young women, young girls, young mothers, mothers, older men . . . [and] young men . . . [as] they [stood] bold[ly] before these people . . . and proclaim[ed] the gospel

this spiritual knowledge can be seen in the fact that Richmond Tamanabae's father, although a practicing Anglican, agreed to pass down his knowledge of sorcery to his sons so that the information would not be lost or forgotten by the clan (Richmond Tamanabae, interview by author, July 30, 2009, 2A).

12. Richmond Tamanabae, interview by author, July 30, 2009, 2A.

13. Peter Igarobae, interview by author, August 3, 2009, 2D.

14. Richmond Tamanabae, interview by author, July 30, 2009, 2A.

15. This list was taken from the following interviews: houses were burned (John Togawata); individuals were beaten (Barnabas Tabara), whipped (Tabara), stoned (Tabara), arrested (Margaret Sete, 1B), shamed (Peter Igarobae, 2B), accused of immorality (John Togawata), and mocked (Togawata).

16. John Togawata, interview by author, July 13, 2009, 1A.

of Jesus."[17] It was this boldness in the middle of the public humiliation and discrimination which marked the new believers and enabled them to continue to spread the good news to their communities.

MOTIVATIONAL FACTORS

The expansion of the PNG CRC revival is often likened to the rapid spread of a forest fire. When the historic path of the revival is traced from village to village and town to town, it appears that nothing stood in its way and that nothing led to its commencement. However, the reality of the PNG CRC revival is that many separate individuals contributed to its success and that numerous barriers stood in their way. As mentioned previously, while historically successful, the revival period contained many hardships for its participants; persecution came from within and without. What then motivated these individuals to persevere in their work? Why did these early pioneers face public shame, family rejection, and personal isolation to spread the gospel?

Communal Concern

When I interviewed the early pioneers of the PNG revival a common concern for the salvation of their families and communities was apparent. Igarobae simply notes: "When I became born again, I just knew I had to go back home."[18] This need to immediately go back to one's family and share the gospel message was evident throughout the interviews. Sete explains:

> Since I came to know the Lord in 1973 I had always prayed for my immediate family to come to know the Lord. I said "Lord I don't want to go to heaven's gate and turn around and see the rest of my family walking away. I want them to come to know and walk with me to heaven's door.[19]

Richmond Tamanabae also notes his own priority of leading his family to Christ as he explains, "When we went in[to] [the church], we had to start from our own house. We had to clean up our own house, our own family. That was our own target."[20] Tamanabae elaborates further on

17. Ibid.
18. Peter Igarobae, interview by author, August 3, 2009, 2C.
19. Margaret Sete, interview by author, August 8, 2009, 1A.
20. Richmond Tamanabae, interview by author, July 30, 2009, 2A.

his first trip to Popondetta town: "The house that we slept at Popondetta, we led them to the Lord. That was our cousin, so we led that family to the Lord. And then that's the place, the people that we led to the Lord, that's the place where the Popondetta church started. Around that family."[21] It was therefore with this desire to lead their loved ones to Christ that many of the new believers chose to share their faith with their family members.[22]

Concern for the salvation of others also extended outside of the family unit as new believers actively shared their faith in their villages, regions, and provinces. Barnabas Tabara notes: "We knew there were changes, but we were not preaching for that purpose, we were just preaching for souls. That's all. All we were interested in was just salvation of souls. Witness and bring them in."[23] Sete agrees and adds, "That's what it means to be God's servant and *wokmeri* [worker]. So, [persecution] didn't matter too much as long as the people would get to know the Lord Jesus in a personal way."[24] This focus on saving souls motivated many of the CRC leaders to enter into full-time ministry and maintained many others through the persecution and struggles that they faced. It also was not limited to the CRC as several denominations during the 1970s experienced a similar phenomenon. Igarobae recalls the evangelical scene during this period: "It was just like the whole nation came alive with men and women coming with ministries, they wanted to reach out. It became just the talk on the streets."[25] Thus, while the CRC was at the forefront of what God was doing in the region the desire to share the good news with the whole community was a motivation that reached past the one denomination.

During the revival period, individuals were also motivated by the idea of missional expansion. Influenced by the Acts 1:8 passage that Christ's disciples would be his witnesses in Jerusalem, Judea and Samaria, and to the ends of the earth, Peter Igarobae explains the parallel with his own experience: "And when we reached our tribe, then my border increased; I had to reach my province. Then, when we reached my

21. Ibid.

22. Bartle also notes this collective desire within Melanesia to bring "good" things to one's family, clan and tribe. He explains that within this kinship system the well-being of the tribe or clan is of the greatest importance (*Death*, 26).

23. Barnabas Tabara, interview by author, June 30, 2009.

24. Margaret Sete, interview by author, August 8, 2009, 1B.

25. Peter Igarobae, interview by author, August 3, 2009, 2D.

province, my border increased . . . You start in Jerusalem, then Samaria, Judea."[26] Igarobae continues:

> I knew my people were lost and I need[ed] to go back . . . but after reaching my people, I thought about my province, [my] border increased. Then, its other provinces; and when I started thinking about other provinces, the Lord took me to the provinces where I hated the people. I think that was the irony of the whole [thing]. But when I broke through in that area, that I loved those I hated, I think it was the Lord's strength that I'm ready for the world . . . And it was while I was doing that that my border increased [to reaching the world for Christ].[27]

This movement from the figurative Jerusalem, Judea and Samaria, to the world is mirrored in many of the CRC leaders' ministry experiences. In Igarobae's case, his motivation was both personal ("I knew my people were lost and I need[ed] to go back") and divine ("the Lord took me . . .").[28] This interweaving of God's plan and his worker's natural desires is a common theme in regards to motivation for mission.

An additional motivational factor was the desire to see individual and communal transformation. Richmond Tamanabae explains: "What I would say is that I really fell in love with the transformation that I saw in the lives of the people. If anything that was the thing; I did it out of love to see the transformation of the people."[29] He continues:

> You go into a place where the people are dry, hopeless and . . . lost and you start ministering the word of God and see what the word of God [does]. You see the glow and the beauty of the people come back again; and the joy that is restored, and people being restored. And people begin to find hope for the first time.[30]

It was this holistic individual and communal transformation that often inspired its witnesses to continue in God's work.

Another factor that influenced individuals was the understanding that evangelism was the work of a mature church. Due to this understanding, local and regional evangelism continued to grow over the

26. Ibid., 2C.

27. Ibid.

28. Ibid.

29. Richmond Tamanabae, interview by author, July 30, 2009, 2A.

30. Ibid.

decades and did not diminish following the initial village revivals. Margaret Sete describes her own motivation for village work: "My aim there was to work so that I can bring young people from the different villages to train as pastors and evangelists to go back and continue to mature the Christians."[31] This goal of maturing the church also fed into the understanding of what a mature church should look like. Sete explains, "As a mature church we have a responsibility. *Mipela no olsem ol pikinini.*[32] We are not babes. We are not sucking *su su olgeta taim.*[33] As a mature church we also have an obligation."[34] This obligation according to Sete was to share the gospel as in Acts 1:8 to one's home region and then to the world: the purpose of "the church of Jesus Christ matured in PNG . . . is to send missionaries out."[35] Thus, the movement toward becoming a matured church movement inspired leaders to continue in their local and global evangelistic work.

Personal Factors

Revival leaders were also inspired by their all encompassing love of Christ. Upon turning to Jesus, new believers often attended every church meeting, poured over Scripture continually, and shared the good news with everyone they knew. The world around them dimmed in comparison with their love of Christ; Richmond Tamanabae explains: "[These were] really powerful days. As far as motivation is concerned, in those days it seemed like everything in the world meant nothing to you . . . and [you] didn't really care what was happening around. Money, those things meant nothing."[36] What did mean something was the person of Jesus Christ. Peter Igarobae comments on many of his colleagues' conversion experience: "[When we were] filled with [the] Holy Spirit, Jesus was your idol, your model, your superstar; you [would] write "Jesus" all over you, all over your books."[37] Arriving in Rabaul, East New Britain Province, John Togawata noticed a similar mindset:

31. Margaret Sete, interview by author, August 8, 2009, 1B.
32. English translation: "We are not like little children."
33. English translation: "We are not drinking milk all the time [as children do]."
34. Margaret Sete, interview by author, August 8, 2009, 1B.
35. Ibid.
36. Richmond Tamanabae, interview by author, July 30, 2009, 2A.
37. Peter Igarobae, interview by author, August 1, 2009, 1A.

> I admire the boldness of the Christians [in Rabaul]. They didn't identify with any particular Pentecostal Church they were just people who had found the Lord Jesus Christ and there was something about them. Nothing could quench their hunger, their love, their passion for Jesus.[38]

It was this tremendous love and passion for Jesus that led many believers to share their faith with others despite the challenges that came in their path.

Likewise, it was often simply the joy of the Lord that led many new believers to join God's mission. In recalling the village outreaches he participated in, Barnabas Tabara explains, "I used to love leading people to the Lord; especially evangelism. I really loved it."[39] Margaret Sete also remembers her excitement about sharing the gospel as she looking forward to graduating from high school: "we were just finishing grade 6 looking forward to go to university and we were all very excited about taking the gospel."[40] Perhaps, however, Richmond Tamanabae best describes the enthusiasm of the time as he recalls entering a village after a long track through the jungle:

> I remember the first time we went [to the village]; we were very exhausted as soon as we went there, tired, blistered, everything, hungry. But by the time we got . . . there, people started singing and all the strength and everything, revived again; you forgot the pain and agony of your trip and you said, "oh, I can do it again."[41]

It was thus this communal and individual joyfulness that maintained and inspired many of the CRC leaders as they continued in their ministry. Although the cause of this joy was not overtly indicated in the interviews, it was implied throughout that the believers were given this joy by God through his Holy Spirit.

The final personal motivation that was mentioned was the sense of past and future responsibility. Some of the leaders felt a duty to the missionaries who had come before them and also to the individuals who had not yet heard the gospel. Sete explained this conviction in her interview: "I'm linked in a chain; My coming to know the Lord, it was through

38. John Togawata, interview by author, July 13, 2009, 1A.

39. Barnabas Tabara, interview by author, June 30, 2009.

40. Margaret Sete, interview by author, August 8, 2009, 1A.

41. Richmond Tamanabae, interview by author, July 30, 2009, 2A.

Scripture Union but it is because some person in another country heard the call of God and left their home and comfort to come."[42] Therefore, due to this communal responsibility, Sete notes that "I owed it to all these people who heard the call of God and obeyed him to come to our shores to bring the gospel to PNG."[43] Moreover, "if I didn't go, then I would be denying other people from other cultures and countries [from] coming to know the Lord Jesus Christ in a personal way."[44] This sense of collective duty was articulated distinctly in Sete's interview but was also confirmed indirectly in many other interviews as CRC leaders indicated a strong sense of duty to share the gospel in their own regions.

God as Motivator

Although there were many motivations that led the PNG Christians into ministry, the principal motivator during the revival period was God. Whether it was God indirectly leading his mission through visions or dreams, or directly orchestrating the events through the Holy Spirit, it was evident that my respondents gave God the credit for establishing the revival.[45] One way that God led the leaders was through prophetic visions; Margaret Sete had one such vision as God laid before her the future ministry in Oro Province.[46] Similarly, God confirmed his leading to people through his Holy Spirit as Barnabas Tabara found when Thomas Tamanabae spoke to him about entering the Bethel Bible School. Tabara describes the experience: "When Papa Thomas said 'I enrolled your name in the Bible College,' it was that time that I receive[d] a sudden urge in my heart. That was really exciting to me . . . it dawned on me, 'This is what I will do for the rest of my life.'"[47] This inner confirmation from the Holy Spirit was repeated in many of the interviews as leaders recalled God's supernatural confirmation as they planted churches, participated in outreaches, and entered into full-time ministry.

42. Margaret Sete, interview by author, August 8, 2009, 1B.

43. Ibid.

44. Ibid.

45. Tippett likewise notes that "the growth of the church, like the growth of a crop unto harvest is the work of God Himself, although He uses human agents in the process of cultivation" (*Solomon Islands Christianity*, 30).

46. Margaret Sete, interview by author, August 8, 2009, 1A.

47. Barnabas Tabara, interview by author, June 30, 2009.

More than interaction with individuals however, God is noted repeatedly as the overarching motivator in the revival movement.[48] In reflecting on the revival years, John Togawata states: "Our lives [and] our movement w[ere] all directed by God. We never really saw it then but, boy, it was so clear to us. Looking back now we . . . recognize so clearly God was in every turn. He commanded and . . . directed everything."[49] Richmond Tamanabae also notes the providence of God during this period; he recollects that "the Lord sort of moved naturally and supernaturally . . . there were natural things that people were doing. And God was . . . doing supernatural things [through those natural things]."[50] God was thus acknowledged as the key player in the revival movement as he directed his people through his Spirit leading them each step of the way.

MESSAGE SHARED

During the early revival years of the CRC in PNG, there were countless local and regional outreaches throughout the country. As such, scores of topics were shared by the traveling evangelists ranging from the gospel message to talks on God's judgment, heaven, prayer, martyrdom and how to establish a local church. In the interview process, however, several topics were repeatedly mentioned as key messages shared during the revival period. I will elaborate upon these fundamental themes in the following section.

Salvation Message

Of primary importance in the CRC revival movement was the simple sharing of the gospel message. In reflecting upon the success of the CRC outreaches, Barnabas Tabara comments: "I think it was the gospel, really, that God used; the salvation message, healings and deliverance. Simple preaching of the gospel I saw in those times was the key to revival."[51] He

48. Although the tendency when recording history is to begin with humankind, the history of the church has to begin with God. Tippett writes that "[church growth] is not our work. It is God's work. He is in control, and we are trying to do what He wants us to do . . . basically everything depends on God. He protects us, He guides us, He gives us blessing in the work . . . the history of the planting and growth of the church is the story of God at work" (*Deep Sea Canoe*, 6).

49. John Togawata, interview by author, July 13, 2009, 1A.

50. Richmond Tamanabae, interview by author, July 30, 2009, 2A.

51. Barnabas Tabara, interview by author, June 30, 2009.

continues that "in those days [personal] witness and salvation messages were really . . . the key to breaking out [in revival]."[52] More than simply being the key to revival however, the good news was also at the heart of every outreach sermon. Passages such as Mark 16:16[53] and John 14:6,[54] which encapsulated the gospel message, were pivotal in people's conversion experiences.[55] The power of the good news transformed individuals and communities as they often heard the news about salvation through Christ alone for the first time.[56]

It was this good news that the new believers also shared with individuals locally and globally. On a three-month cultural exposure trip to Japan, Sete recalls sitting in a train traveling to Oita and reading *Knowing God* by J. I. Packer. Seeing the text, a Nepalese man sitting behind her asked if she was a Christian and then inquired if she knew of a church where he could go and be baptized.[57] Sete replied that going to a church wasn't necessary but instead he could come to know the Lord right here and now. Even many years later, Sete recalls the general message which she shared that day:

> God had a plan of salvation. God had a plan [for] this whole universe. You have been born in Nepal and we been born in PNG and it's all in God's plan. God had this plan for mankind and man fell into sin and God had to bring his son to redeem us back to himself and the only way to go to the Father, the only way to be a true Christian, is . . . to accept Jesus [as] your savior. And you have to repent of your sins in your heart and receive Jesus into your heart. That is what makes you a Christian; that can happen right here.[58]

52. Ibid.

53. "Whoever believes and is baptized will be saved and he who does not believe will be condemned" (Mark 16:16).

54. "Jesus answered, 'I am the way, and the truth and the life'" (John 14:6).

55. Barnabas Tabara, interview by author, June 30, 2009; Margaret Sete, interview by author, August 8, 2009, 1B.

56. Margaret Sete, interview by author, August 8, 2009, 1A. This transformative power of Christ therefore replaced people's dependence upon the power of the spirits. All the aspects of life, "health, wealth, hunting, gardening, fertility, death, sickness, childbirth and weather" (Bartle, *Death*, 37), were now blessed abundantly through Christ alone.

57. Margaret Sete, interview by author, August 8, 2009, 1A.

58. Ibid.

The Nepalese man, touched by the gospel message, answered that he wanted to make that commitment to Christ. After Sete led him through the sinner's prayer, the Nepalese man started crying and right there on the train gave his life to Christ.[59] Testimonies such as that of Sete were repeated throughout PNG as new believers shared with others the good news they had found.

Identity of God

Another message which was frequently shared was the nature and character of God. Formally and informally, God was identified as all-powerful, the ultimate healer, sovereign over all creation, a source of unconditional love, and inclusive of all people. In a particularly touching story, Sete's younger brother discovered the truth that God cares for all people. Eddie Ogameni, just thirteen years old at the time, was given the task of delivering some food to his sisters at the Popondetta Youth Camp during Christmas 1977. Instead of quickly returning home to the village, Eddie hid behind the croton bushes outside the meeting hall where he overheard that morning's devotional message. A young man from Kavieng was preaching at the time, declaring that "it doesn't matter if you're a small boy, big boy, old man, or whatever, God loves you and he can still come into your heart."[60] After the meeting, Margaret's sister Greta found Eddie crying behind the bushes. Asking who had hit him, the boy, through his tears, responded that "no, no, nobody hit me. I want Jesus in my heart. Can you tell Jesus to come to my heart?"[61] To his sisters' delight, their brother gave his heart to Jesus right there and then proceeded to hurry back to the village to share his newfound faith with his parents.[62] This reality that God loves both young and old, male and female, educated and uneducated, poor and rich continued to be a powerful message throughout the PNG revival.

The message of God as healer also often accompanied the gospel message. In particular, the understanding that God has healed all sicknesses and diseases on the cross was proclaimed verbally and many times reiterated through demonstrations of God's power. Sete recalls an

59. In the narrative, Sete also explains how she went through a tract entitled "How to become a Christian" in addition to explaining the *Four Spiritual Laws*.

60. Margaret Sete, interview by author, August 8, 2009, 1A.

61. Ibid.

62. Ibid.

instance in 1978 when her younger sister's mother-in-law "was dying and they brought the witchdoctors . . . [but] nothing happened. So [the mother] asked the son: "Go and get Margaret. That God that she knows is going to heal me."[63] Upon entering the village, Sete felt God speak to her:

> The Lord just reassured me and said, "Just go and pray for her." So, I went up and told her, "Your daughter is here . . ." [But as] my brother-in-law was not back from the creek, they went to the river to wash . . . I waited for him to come. When he had come, I climbed up the stairs [to the bush material tall shelter] . . . it was like a platform, set with steps . . . So, I went up; I said, "In the Name of Jesus, be healed." That's all I said. And I walked down and I moved the line across the platform and I said, "Nobody is to cross over this line. This is where Jesus is going to reveal himself."[64]

The elderly mother instantly clearing her throat "said, 'I'm hungry.' So, they brought food . . . and she ate it."[65] During that evening, the woman was completely healed; Sete's words to the village had indeed come to pass: "The Lord Jesus is going to heal this woman and no one is going to come and share the glory of what the Lord Jesus is going to do because he is worthy, he is the one who took all our sickness and diseases on the cross."[66]

The power of God was likewise a recurrent theme as CRC teams entered regions with strong allegiances to traditional sorcery and black magic. Peter Igarobae, for example, recollects his initial interest in Christianity stemming from his curiosity in the power of the God. One evening after driving back to the university campus with Barry Silverback, Igarobae remarked:

> He was sitting there listening to me while I told him stories about trying to destroy witchcraft and sorcery by contacting connection to the . . . highest powers in the cosmos. He was listening and then he said, "You know Peter; I know what you are talking about." So I was interested. He said, "In fact I know someone that I can connect . . . you [to] and that power will go through you." And I said, "Okay, I'm interested."[67]

63. Ibid.

64. Ibid.

65. Ibid.

66. Ibid.

67. Peter Igarobae, interview by author, August 1, 2009, 1A.

In this case, Silverback was referring to the power of the Holy Spirit that is given to all believers through Jesus Christ. This emphasis on the power of God was expressed verbally and also in conjunction with miraculous events. During one of Sete's visits home to Oro Province, she encountered an elderly woman who was very ill. At the request of the woman, Sete prayed for her and she was completely healed.[68] The local witch doctor, upon hearing about this great healing, tried to claim the victory for himself. Sete explains: "He heard about it and he was trying to compete against the power of God. And I said, 'Don't . . . you're playing with fire . . . you are using the created things of my Father God but the power that's healing her is the one that raised Jesus Christ from the dead. It's the Creator, his power. Not the created being.'"[69] The power of God was thus declared supreme and above that of the evil spirits and powers that traditionally had held the people captive. Furthermore, believers in Christ were also empowered by God's Spirit as they made disciples and healed people and cast out demons in the name of Christ.

Call to Mission

The call to evangelize PNG and the world was also a common theme throughout the CRC revival movement. Barry Silverback, the senior pastor at Bethel Center, preached regularly on the missional call upon the nation of PNG. He noted that PNG was a servant nation and as such was to be a servant to the nations.[70] In addition, Silverback expressed that Papua New Guineans were called to become actively involved in mission work both locally and overseas.[71] Geua Wari, a full-time Bethel team member at the time, remembers the first time she heard Pastor Barry speak about world missions:

> We used to be just a team which worked within the country. [I] remember the first time Pastor Barry came and in a team meeting said he had been asked to go to . . . Indonesia . . . We released him and then he went and then he came back and started talking to us about missions. It's been a part of him from the start. But because Papua New Guineans were so involved in receiving, receiving, receiving, we just thought, "Oh, this is just a message." But when

68. Margaret Sete, interview by author, August 8, 2009, 1A.

69. Ibid.

70. Ibid., 1B.

71. Peter Igarobae, interview by author, August 3, 2009, 2A.

> Pastor Barry did those trips . . . he started talking to us about the needs of the people out there. And . . . that started to change our thinking [about only being] based in PNG just ourselves and [made us] to move outward to others out there in the world.[72]

The fervency of Silverback's missional message was documented several times as revival leaders still recalled with clarity the great emphasis placed upon world missions during these revival years onward. As the Port Moresby church was the hub of the CRC ministry, this call to be involved in national and international mission spread throughout the provinces of PNG. The establishment of the Institute of Evangelism in September 1981 on the Bethel Center campus further facilitated the training of future PNG evangelists and missionaries. Eventually the first PNG missionaries were sent overseas to the Solomon Islands in October 1984.

This message of participation in the *missio Dei* was expressed both one-on-one and to large Christian communities. While working at Everyman Ministry in Port Moresby, Sete remembers "challenging the young people going home for holidays" to share the good news about Christ with their families and friends.[73] "I said, 'You know, if you are going home, the best gift that you can bring home—I know that many people are bringing clothes and radios and all kinds of things home—but the one thing that you can take home that is of eternal value is the Lord Jesus Christ.'"[74] She thus implored them to, "Go and tell your family about the Lord that you know; that newfound faith that you have. That will be the best present for your families. And it will be of eternal value."[75] As is evident in Sete's entreaty to the high school and university students, the gospel of Christ was regarded as extremely valuable and transformative. While the families back home in the village could use material possessions, it was the gift of eternal life through Christ which had the greatest worth.

METHODS OF MISSION

The CRC revival in PNG combined multiple outreach methods and means of communication. Due to the large number of methods employed, only a selection of the primary methods directly relevant to realizing Abrahamic blessing will be discussed in the following section.

72. Geua Wari, interview by author, July 29, 2009.

73. Margaret Sete, interview by author, August 8, 2009, 1A.

74. Ibid.

75. Ibid.

Outreach Forms

The local and regional mission outreach of the CRC incorporated a variety of evangelistic forms during the revival period including outreach teams, crusade meetings, church meetings, a boat ministry, and camp gatherings. The outreach teams specifically were a fundamental part of the CRC's ministry in the 1970s and 1980s as Bethel Center initially sent out small teams of evangelists to unreached areas of PNG.

Initially these teams focused on the Binandere and Kokoda villages in Oro Province; once these villages had turned to Christ and churches were established, the teams continued to visit the region to strengthen the existing congregations. Richmond Tamanabae, a former member of the CRC Oro outreach teams, commented that "it became very important for Bethel Center to start continually sending teams to visit those villages so that they are continually updated and encouraged and built in what they were doing."[76] From the initial outreach trip in 1975 the CRC outreach teams expanded their ministry across the nation focusing specifically on Oro Province, Milne Bay Province, Central Province, Gulf Province, and the Central Highlands. Nevertheless whether through an official CRC outreach team or individual CRC congregation members, within twenty years of the establishment of the CRC church in Port Moresby in 1972 each of the nineteen PNG provinces boasted a thriving CRC ministry.

Large crusade meetings were also held regularly both in the cities and village areas. International speakers such as Pastor Leo Harris, Brother Worley, and Pastor Norm Armstrong from Australia were often invited to share the gospel over the series of local evangelistic meetings. Occasionally, as in the case of village crusades, Billy Graham, Theo Osborne, or Oral Roberts films were also shown as evangelistic tools.[77] Peter Igarobae remembers the large crusade held in Rabaul upon John Togawata's appointment as police commander of East New Britain Province in 1986:

> When John arrived there I said, "John, we need to hit Rabaul quickly." With some sort of crusade to bring awareness of what God is doing. So, John being there and [with] his influence convinced the Lord Mayor of the town; the United Church to hold a crusade; and it's the first of its kind . . . they don't know what [a] crusade is. And they gave us "Queen's Park." And we invited

76. Richmond Tamanabae, interview by author, July 30, 2009, 2A.

77. Ibid.

> Papa Norm Armstrong from Sydney, an Assembly of God guy, and an evangelist and [a] 500-member choir . . . from the United Church Rapitok. It shook Rabaul town.[78]

The purpose of these larger evangelistic meetings was often to jump-start or extend the CRC ministry already begun in the area. The international speakers, special music and films attracted individuals who would normally never attend the regular CRC church service. Smaller versions of crusades, open-air meetings, were also held in local market places or street corners both in urban and rural areas. While the larger crusades were run by the CRC churches, these smaller open-air meetings were often led by local congregation members or laymen evangelists.

Ministry Methods

The gospel message was proclaimed through a variety of methods including the preaching of the word, published literature, radio advertisements, ministry-based films, and Christian music. However, it was the preaching of the gospel message which was the most adopted means of sharing the good news about Christ. Barnabas Tabara recalls the first time he heard the gospel preached in his home village in Oro Province:

> Christmas 1980. Christmas Eve . . . I gave my life to the Lord. And the next day, which was Christmas . . . I was in the water there; [there was a] big baptismal service. And again I saw Pastor Thomas stand on the rocks on the creek with one leg in the water and one leg on the stones and he started to point to the crowd. There were hundreds of people both believers and bystanders and persecutors all alike. You know, stones were flying too, all at the same time; persecution. And Thomas would point his fingers straight to the people and he would be preaching, and for the first time, looking at the gospel being preached that way, I actually thought that Thomas was John the Baptist.[79]

This proclamation of the good news of Christ was a consistent theme throughout the CRC revival. Even when nobody was listening to the message—as was in the case of Barnabas Tabara's newly converted father—individuals would just preach to nobody if necessary.[80] There was also great diversity among the preaching styles of the evangelists but as

78. Peter Igarobae, interview by author, August 3, 2009, 2C.

79. Barnabas Tabara, interview by author, June 30, 2009.

80. Ibid.

one of the young revival leaders noted, "Every pioneer pastor that came . . . [was] very unique in their presentation, they [all] had their different personalities and they were all powerful."[81]

Local evangelism was a very hands-on experience as CRC believers visited people's homes, evangelized their neighbors, and witnessed in their own schools. While church services were held regularly, the majority of the ministry to the neighborhood occurred outside of church hours in the community itself. Alkin Orona recollects how his own parents came to Christ through the gift of a puppy and the witness of their neighbors in the village.

> So mom wanted to give a puppy to them. So they were having [a worship] service and Mom and Dad got that puppy and they went down. It was the puppy that made the way for them to go down. And Pastor Barnabas stood up and said "Thank you, you see us we are doing this. You know I'm a drunk and I just gave my heart to the Lord and I'm wonderfully saved. This is the new church that I'm in." When he was sharing with them, they [were] convict[ed] by the Holy Spirit . . . it was God's timing that they would just get a puppy . . . and exchange [it] for Jesus. So they went and gave [the] puppy to Pastor's dad and then in return Pastor's dad prayed for them and then led them through the sinners' prayer. They wonderfully got saved; filled with the Holy Spirit instantly. And from then on they started serving [in the church].[82]

After coming to Christ, Orona's parents started evangelizing themselves, going from house to house praying for the sick and witnessing the power of God at work in their village.[83] This pattern of door-to-door evangelism was also common in Port Moresby, as Bethel teams regularly walked around the city's neighborhoods knocking on doors and sharing their own testimonies.[84] Individuals who had accepted Christ were also followed-up regularly by Bethel's ministry teams, and schools were visited by CRC teams and also witnessed to by fellow Christian students.[85] This style of evangelism which focused outside the church walls encouraged new believers to feel ownership of their faith and the gospel mes-

81. Ibid.

82. Alkin Orona, interview by author, July 2, 2009, 1A.

83. Ibid.

84. Thelma Garao, interview by author, June 12, 2009, 1A.

85. Margaret Sete, interview by author, August 8, 2009, 1A.

sage. Ministry was thus not left to the full-time "experts" but instead was taken on by everyone touched by the gospel of Christ regardless of their profession, age, social status, or nationality.

Development of Leaders

An important focus of the CRC ministry in PNG was the training of indigenous leaders. In Port Moresby, the Crusade Bible School was founded in March 1974 and was later followed by the establishment of CRC Bible schools throughout the country and the nations where the PNG CRC had established churches.[86] In PNG, promising young leaders from the village were invited, often by Barry Silverback, to Bethel Center to attend the Bible school[87] and then were sent back after graduation to start ministries in their villages and towns.[88] Richmond Tamanabae explains: "There were a lot of people that God recognized, that Pastor Barry recognized [as leaders]. We tried to equip them properly and . . . [with] whatever opportunities that were available to encourage them."[89] It was therefore through this process of inviting potential Christian leaders from both urban and rural areas to Bethel Center that the CRC work multiplied throughout the country.[90]

86. At Bethel Center, the first full-time Bible school was established in April 1979 and the Institute of Evangelism in April 1981. Additional Bible schools were established across PNG and the world: Vision Bible School in Rabaul (July 1984), Oro Province Bible Training School (Feb. 1986), Gulf Province Bible Training School (Dec. 1988), Indonesian Bible School (July 1990), Western Province Bible Training School (July 1990), Philippines School of Ministry (Sept. 1991), Hailens Skul Bilong Evangelism in Western Highlands (Sept. 1991), Milne Bay School of Discipleship (Sept. 1991), Bethel Women's School of Ministry (Aug. 1993), Peniel Bible School in North Solomons (Mar. 1994), Enga Provins Disaipelship Trening Skul (Mar. 1994), Fiji School of Discipleship (Mar. 1994), KarKar Ministry Training Center (Jan. 1995), Bethel World Mission Faith Training School (Mar. 1996), Lahai Roi Bible School in Trobriand Islands (1997), Livingston Discipleship Training School in Vanuatu (1997), Christian Ministry Training Center in Solomon Islands (1997), and School of the Teacher at Bethel Center (1997).

87. Barnabas Tabara, interview by author, June 30, 2009.

88. Richmond Tamanabae, interview by author, July 30, 2009, 2A.

89. Ibid.

90. Tippett also notes the importance of developing indigenous leadership. He states that "only when converts are effectively incorporated into the church fellowship and are provided with opportunity for participation and development" can the strength of the church be seen (*Deep Sea Canoe*, 87).

The teaching style at Bethel Bible School in Port Moresby was unique in its equally theoretical and practical training. Students were taught in the Bible classes and then sent out almost immediately to do local and regional ministry. Peter Igarobae, a lecturer at the Bethel Bible School at the time explained: "While I'm busy teaching, it's the students who are doing it and coming [with] the report. By listening to the [field] report . . . I correct them. I said, 'Next time you go don't do this and when you do this you get the HS on your side . . . And [through this] . . . we took this nation by force.'"[91] It was this circular pattern of training indigenous leaders and then sending them back out that the ministry within the provinces continued to expand, and new churches, ministries and training schools were established.

The training of leaders also took place on the field as new believers were taught practical ministry skills by the visiting outreach teams and through firsthand experience. When the revival first swept through the villages of Oro Province for example, believers in the region were simply asked by the visiting Bethel teams to lead or assist in leading various activities. Richmond Tamanabae recalls one such revival meeting where "after the meeting we just prayed for some young men and just said, 'Okay, you look after this fellowship now' . . . And those fellows now became pastors; they actually grew with the church, grew with what God was doing."[92] Barnabas Tabara recalls his own rapid introduction to ministry in Oro Province:

> I would go for patrol with Pastor Brian [Homba] or Pastor Robert [Tamanabae]; or into the villages. They would ask me to lead worship; this is just someone who just gave his life to the Lord and he's already into leading worship. Then they would ask me to help baptize people. I would get them baptized with Pastor Robert on the side and help baptize people, and I would say "Wow, this is exciting." So that's how we got trained.[93]

This hands-on ministry training model created a sense of excitement and ownership among the new believers. Additionally, it enabled the gospel to spread rapidly throughout the region as new believers felt empowered to pray for healing, cast out demons, lead worship, baptize

91. Peter Igarobae, interview by author, August 3, 2009, 2C.

92. Richmond Tamanabae, interview by author, July 30, 2009, 2A.

93. Barnabas Tabara, interview by author, June 30, 2009.

believers, and preach the word apart from any official CRC outreach team.

Manifestations of the Spirit

The supernatural manifestations of the Spirit of God were also a powerful means of evangelism through which many people were saved. In a letter back to the CRC mission board in Adelaide, Australia, Silverback writes about an Oro Province outreach trip in September 1977:

> We visited completely new places, where we met with much initial opposition or indifference and were called many derogatory names. But in each place the opposition soon turned into interest and then open-hearted acceptance of the message of new life in Christ as the manifestation of the Spirit began to be seen amongst them. Through the operation of the word of knowledge, word of wisdom, discerning of spirits and working of miracles, many hearts were turned to receive the Lord Jesus Christ and believe in His power at work today.[94]

Thus, as the gospel was preached, the word of God was often confirmed through the miraculous. Physical healings,[95] communal and individual transformation, salvation of entire villages, visions, angelic visitations, gifts of the Spirit, the casting out demons, and signs and wonders were all regular occurrences throughout the revival years.[96] Uvau Amani, a high school student at the time, remembers returning to his village of Lalaura in Central Province right in the middle of the CRC revival period. His house was situated next to the church and he was surprised to hear someone speaking in English during the service; looking out of the window he saw that it was his father who he knew didn't speak a word of English. His sister Thelma had spoken to him about Christ, and filled with the Holy Spirit he was proclaiming in perfect King's English without an accent:

94. Silverback, "Report," 3, italics added.

95. The healing of the sick within a community also illustrated the power of Christ over the power of the village spirits. As sickness and death were often considered a result of sorcery or displeasing the spirits (Bartle, *Death*, 29), the healing of an individual represented not only a physical miracle but also demonstrated the dominion of Christ over the spirit world.

96. During the interviews, countless testimonies were shared regarding the miracles and signs and wonders which filled the CRC revival years. Due to the sheer number of miraculous events mentioned, only select examples will be noted within this book.

"I love the Lord. The Lord is not in my head, he is in my heart."[97] It was through signs and wonders such as this one experienced by Amani and Thelma Garao that the gospel of Christ was confirmed throughout the provinces.

The work of the Holy Spirit also led to the transformation of individuals and communities. With the coming of the gospel message and the empowerment of the Spirit, the Lord touched people inside and out.[98] For example in the Binandere villages in Oro Province, objects of witchcraft and sorcery were burned and "from the mountain down to the coast, the Hebrew God became [the] God of Binandere."[99] Even the way gardens were made in the agricultural community was transformed. Influenced by their new dependence on God, "the families would go and hold hands and pray and then plant banana trees, kau kau, and tapioca. Before they would call on the ancestral spirits but now they were calling upon the Lord their God.[100] The revival came and the whole lifestyle changed.[101] Some of the changes were immediate and others developed over time as the Holy Spirit continued to teach the new believers. Barnabas Tabara remembers witnessing this gradual change in Spirit-filled Christians:

> They would say "Praise the Lord" and at the same time [still be] smoking [and] chewing betelnut.[102] Along the way those things suddenly dropped off . . . [it] suddenly sort of dawned on them. Those desires for nicotine, the desire for chewing betelnut sort of died off. And then they were testifying and they would say, "The Lord has done it. The Lord has impressed in my heart that

97. Uvau Amani, interview by author, June 12, 2009, 1A. The miracle of speaking and reading English was also mentioned in the interviews with Alkin Orona and Peter Igarobae; in both cases individuals who didn't know how to speak or read English instantly were given the ability through the power of the Holy Spirit (Alkin Orona, interview by author, July 2, 2009, 1A; Peter Igarobae, interview by author, August 3, 2009, 2A).

98. John Togawata, interview by author, July 13, 2009, 1A.

99. Peter Igarobae, interview by author, August 3, 2009, 2A.

100. The ability to observe the visible power of God within these communal and individual transformations illustrated God's higher position over that of the ancestral spirits. As power within Melanesia "must have the ability to change things" and individuals expect "to see the power of God in observable ways" (Bartle, *Death*, 37), these visible demonstrations of the power of God were significant on both a societal and spiritual level.

101. Peter Igarobae, interview by author, August 3, 2009, 2A.

102. Betelnut is a mild stimulant made from combining the areca nut with lime and sometimes tobacco; it is the stimulant of choice throughout PNG and Melanesia.

> this is over now, so I am finished." [It was] so pure and innocent; I like those times.[103]

This Spirit-inspired transformation and "surrendering to God of old habits and traditional customs"[104] indicated that God was indeed at work in individuals' lives. Additionally, it was clearly God himself who was guiding and teaching the new believers how to follow and obey Christ.

MISSIONAL EXPANSION

In his first interview, Richmond Tamanabae described PNG as "firewood that is always ready to catch revival fire."[105] This image of ready anticipation proved true during the 1970s–1980s CRC revival in PNG as revival indeed spread like fire throughout the nation. Whole villages turned to Christ, local believers rose up as missionaries and evangelists, and the gospel was spread from individual to individual, family to family, and clan to clan. This missional expansion however did not stop at the nation's borders but instead instigated the beginning of the international mission work of the CRC in PNG. In the following section, the spread of the gospel of Christ in PNG is discussed as it relates to the fulfillment of the Abrahamic blessing to the nations.

Role of the Village

While the CRC was based in the capital city of Port Moresby, the rural areas of the nation were most impacted by the 1970s–1980s revival.[106] Therefore, in addition to the fruitful ministry in Moresby, the villages in Central Province and later Oro Province experienced the first of the CRC revival. Oro Province in particular became the center of revival in November 1976 when the village of Kurereda came to Christ and started sending out evangelists to the surrounding areas.[107] Peter Igarobae describes one of the massive baptisms after an outreach in the Binandere area:

> We were there for two weeks . . . mainly baptizing; hundreds [of people]. And we came down to my native village Ginemai

103. Barnabas Tabara, interview by author, June 30, 2009.

104. Silverback, "Report," 3.

105. Richmond Tamanabae, interview by author, July 13, 2009, 1A.

106. Ibid.

107. Peter Igarobae, interview by author, August 3, 2009, 2A.

> and 160 or 170 [people] got baptized. But the river Mumba was flooding . . . and the current was so fast, they tied Pastor Barry with a cane. And [they] held him and he would baptize people . . . and sometimes they come up in his hands but other times, we put two or three [people] down the river and you see them disappearing and popping up down there and those further down will catch them. It was so funny.[108]

This initial revival in the Binandere villages was a crucial event that impacted the surrounding region greatly; as entire Binandere villages came to Christ, hundreds were baptized and filled with the Holy Spirit and traditional witchcraft and sorcery was rejected.[109] From this first outpouring of the Holy Spirit, the CRC revival spread across the whole province and nation of PNG.

Although Bethel Center was involved in the continued growth of the revival in Oro Province, the greatest expansion came through the work of the new Binandere believers. Robert Tamanabae, a retired Binandere army commander, was at the forefront of these village outreach groups during the year following the 1976 Kurereda outreach. Peter Igarobae notes the important role and natural strategy of these indigenous evangelists in the extension of the gospel message throughout the region:

> After about two weeks we came back to Bethel and Robert [Tamanabae] and . . . about 30 guys . . . went from village to village . . . when we left . . . There's three rivers in our tribe—Mamba, Gira, Eia river—and there are about more than three thousand people in the tribe; so Robert just went from village to village where intermarriages and relatives all cross[over]. Looking back the Holy Spirit used that pattern and . . . would take Robert to chiefs or landowners who had some sort of influence over the villages. And village after village was coming to the Lord.[110]

This strategy of sharing the gospel with family members, neighboring villages, and important local leaders was an organic occurrence during the revival as new believers would often accept Christ and then instinctively "go to [their] village and then start preaching."[111] It was through this ever-growing pattern of new believers sharing the blessing

108. Ibid.

109. Ibid.

110. Ibid.

111. Barnabas Tabara, interview by author, June 30, 2009.

of Christ that they had found with others that the revival in Oro Province grew in leaps and bounds.

Before long the revival fire spread through the Binandere speaking villages to the Kokoda and Orokaiva regions and then later to the coastal areas of Oro province.[112] Richmond Tamanabae recalls sharing the gospel in Ajeka village in Kokoda:

> When I gave an altar call, the whole congregation stood up to come forward and there was no place and everyone wanted me to pray for them individually. And while I began to pray, the miracles would happen . . . And after that the revival in the Kokoda area just went. All the churches in Ajeka, Fija, Papaki . . . [in] all those villages it happened.[113]

Over the next decade the "CRC actually became the main Christian movement in the nation" as churches were planted and Bible schools established throughout the country.[114] Moreover, although the CRC focused its outreach in Oro Province, East New Britain Province, and Morobe Province, the CRC planted churches in Central Province, Milne Bay, Sepik, the highlands and in Gulf and Western Provinces.[115] John Togawata comments on this rapid spread of Pentecostalism through the country: "The Pentecostal movement . . . was just like a fire. It would burn one corner of society . . . [and then] go to the next village and then if they stopp[ed] there it would come out to another village somewhere else. And it would stop there; and then it [would] start somewhere else. It happened that way."[116] Thus, while the CRC revival movement started in one small Oro Province village, the revival rapidly affected the villages, regions and provinces around it as the gospel was shared through kinship and larger societal relationships.

Evangelistic Patterns of the Revival

When asking how the CRC revival spread so quickly across PNG, there are a variety of answers that emerge. The primary reason, however, for the widespread expansion of the gospel message was the pattern of clan

112. Richmond Tamanabae, interview by author, July 30, 2009, 2A.

113. Ibid.

114. Ibid., July 13, 2009, 1A.

115. Ibid.

116. Ibid.

and kinship evangelism which developed.[117] John Togawata explains the evangelistic pattern that developed during the revival period:

> If you receive the Holy Spirit, you go to . . . your village [and] you start [a] fellowship with your family. Your family accepts the Lord Jesus and they receive the Holy baptism. They build . . . [the] fellowship then . . . others join you [and] they all join. Then the village now has a church. But then other people want [a church] in the next village. So they go . . . into the next village and when they start their fellowship they don't want to come here to us. It's too long for them to walk here or they have to drive so they say no we'll start ours here. You guys come and sing to us and visit us. This is the way it happened in the Book of Acts.[118]

This sharing of the gospel message with one person who then shares it with another person enabled the good news to travel rapidly throughout kinship systems, spreading the gospel to wider and wider social circles. An example of this societal expansion is seen in the testimony of Montague who was originally touched by the Holy Spirit before a traditional dance.[119] Richmond Tamanabae narrates the story:

> Montague was one of the men that got touched . . . So the next day, he invited me to go to his house where I shared with him and led the whole family to the Lord . . . [He] took the message and he was the one that . . . started the work, started fellowshipping. And then the fellowship grew, grew, grew and become one of the main churches at [the] Mamba estate.
>
> Now again Montague's other brother-in-law from Bogera [Estate] came all the way from Bogera [and] visited them in the village at Kurereda. [When he] was there he got touched and then went back and invited the team [from Bethel] to come and it . . . eventually became Pastor Stephen Gill['s church] at Bogera.[120]

117. Donald A. McGavran describes this method of relational evangelism as one of the primary means of missional expansion in Scripture and church history (*Understanding Church Growth*; *Bridges of God*). Alan R. Tippett also notes the importance of people movements in Melanesian as a method through which communal cultures accept Christ (*People Movements*).

118. John Togawata, interview by author, July 13, 2009, 1A.

119. Richmond Tamanabae, interview by author, July 30, 2009, 2A.

120. Ibid.

This evangelistic domino effect of sharing the gospel within and across kinship systems allowed the CRC revival to evolve from a clan revival to a regional revival and then later to a national revival.

Another pattern that developed during the revival period was a "come and go" evangelistic model. On a micro level this was seen as individuals in Oro Province would visit a nearby village in revival, be touched by the Holy Spirit, and then return to their own village with the gospel message.[121] Richmond Tamanabae explains that "the pattern sort of emerged. That people from another village would come and take from this village and go and start fellowship in their own thing. And so when the next [outreach team] arrived in Oro Province . . . instead of two villages [with churches] there were three or four villages . . . So that's how it grew and it grew."[122] On a national scale this pattern of coming and hearing the gospel and then going out and evangelizing was also evident at Bethel Center which served as the main operational base of the CRC in PNG. Peter Igarobae reflects:

> After the Lord's outpouring of the Holy Spirit in the Oro Province, [the] same thing was happening in Manus among evangelical Lutherans. And . . . this was the pattern: the Lord will bring some people group to Bethel Center and as they become born again, filled with the Holy Spirit and . . . excited for the Lord and the Lord pours his Holy Spirit among their place. So they're the ones [that start the ministry].[123]

Thus, on both the micro and macro-level this pattern of coming into an already reached base and then taking the gospel message back into one's home region was a common motif that was threaded throughout the revival's history.

Nevertheless, the outpouring of the Holy Spirit also took place independently from CRC outreaches, and only after the fact did the CRC become involved. The 1970s–1980s revival in PNG was in fact quite complex as the CRC was not the only denomination which experienced spiritual revival within their churches. Over the two decade period there were many autonomous revivals that took place including that of the Foursquare in the Highlands, the Lutherans in Manus, the United Church in East New Britain and Central Province, and the Anglican Church in Oro

121. Ibid.

122. Ibid.

123. Peter Igarobae, interview by author, August 3, 2009, 2C.

Province. In Manus, for example, a young man named Paul Kehi who was connected to Bethel Center invited the Bethel team to come and assist in the revival already taking place in Manus. Peter Igarobae explains that "there was an outpouring of the Holy Spirit [in Manus]. . .[and Paul] sat with Papa Barry and . . . said [that] he wants to take us in there."[124] This invitation to minister within the Manus revival led to the CRC pioneering churches throughout the area.[125] Similar events took place in Rabaul as there was an "outpouring of the Holy Spirit . . . in Rabaul in the Rapitok area among the United Church."[126] Due to the "tremendous persecution [that] took place" from the United Church leadership, "the elders in that area . . . heard about Barry [Silverback] and they contacted him."[127] Barry Silverback visiting the churches later sent Richmond Tamanabae to assist and run training programs for the growing churches. Therefore while God did bring revival to the CRC churches and church plants, the CRC also assisted in the training and nurturing of other revivals taking place among sister denominations.

Denominational Adoption

The main motivation for inviting Bethel Center to be involved in non-CRC revivals was the sister churches' desire to have a spiritual covering. A repeated theme throughout the interviews was the persecution that many newly Spirit-filled churches experienced from their own denomination.[128] As such the non-CRC churches, rather than disbanding, sought a Pentecostal movement to come under. At the time in PNG, the country required religious groups to be properly registered in order to function.[129] This required the persecuted and/or excommunicated churches to become their own denomination, register as a local church and be independent or to come under an already established Pentecostal church.[130] In the CRC's history in PNG, during the revival period several

124. Peter Igarobae, interview by author, August 3, 2009, 2C.

125. Ibid.

126. Ibid.

127. Peter Igarobae, interview by author, August 3, 2009, 2C.

128. Thelma Garao, interview by author, June 12, 2009; Margaret Sete, interview by author, August 8, 2009; John Togawata, interview by author, July 13, 2009; Richmond Tamanabae, interviews by author, July 13, 2009 and July 30, 2009.

129. Richmond Tamanabae, interview by author, July 30, 2009, 2B.

130. Ibid., July 13, 2009, 1A.

churches in Enga Province,[131] East New Britain Province,[132] and Manus Province[133] officially joined the CRC denomination. More than solely a governmental requirement, the churches seeking covering were "looking for a leader. For someone to give them . . . fatherly care and oversight."[134] This was expressed by the CRC in the sending of permanent missionaries to the area to plant churches, establish Bible schools, and run local training programs. Thus, as the revival spread through the CRC additional churches experiencing revival were also added to the fold increasing the overall impact of the CRC in the nation.

131. Ibid.

132. John Togawata, interview by author, July 13, 2009, 1A.

133. Peter Igarobae, interview by author, August 3, 2009, 2C.

134. John Togawata, interview by author, July 13, 2009, 1A.

PART III

Abrahamic Blessing in Application

9

Genesis Revisited: CRC Revival and God's Blessing

In this chapter I compare the Abrahamic blessing motif in Scripture with its representation in the PNG case study. Using the five missional categories of agents of mission, motivational factors, message shared, methods of mission, and missional expansion, I present the similarities and differences that exist between the two contexts. In addition, I interpret the data and make observations regarding the transcultural missional patterns of the Abrahamic blessing motif.

AGENTS OF MISSION

Although several centuries and oceans separate the Hebrew recipients of the Abrahamic blessing and the young revival leaders of PNG, several parallels join the two narratives. Of these similarities, I will present the following key elements: the presence of covenant, PNG's collective nature, the leading of God, revivalists as agents of blessing, and dependence upon God. However, due to the equally vast differences between the time-periods there are also characteristics unique to the PNG church leaders which I will also discuss.

Covenant Treaty

Of foremost interest is the covenantal bond which linked both groups to Yahweh. Abraham's own covenant with God is clearly recorded in Hebrew Scripture and traced through his descendants to the new covenant established through Christ. While the ritual of cutting covenant was a common practice in the ancient Near East, it was also a ritual present within several PNG communities. Tamanabae, a member of the Binandere people group in Oro Province, explains that covenants were established between his people and evil forces during their most recent period of sorcery.[1] It was through these covenantal treaties that the leaders in the community were able to harness the spirits' powers in the physical realm.[2] However, Tamanabae notes that "when we turned to the Lord we had to cut our bridges with that, renounce that. And cut a new covenant with the Lord. Not only with the Lord, but also with each other."[3] Igarobae continues the story:

> So when the [Bethel Center] team came with Pastor Barry [Silverback] to Kurereda village and after Daniel [the village chief] accepted that Jesus Christ would be the Lord of the clan, both Graceford [a village elder] and Daniel had to submit three things that w[ere] like gods to the clan, that protected the clan, made the clan prosperous in their gardens and things and [which brought] the fear of the clan to the [surrounding] people so they won't touch us.
>
> Daniel knew firsthand the power of God; so both Daniel and Graceford traded these three things for Father, Son, and the Holy Spirit. They said alright these three persons are now [our] clan God and our children's, and our children's children.
>
> Our descendants will serve this single God and will forsake other things . . . serving the Lord will be family, clan business . . . So they made their declaration and . . . we all came in and held fast onto this Hebrew God and we declared him to be the God of the clan.[4]

Thus, "from the mountain down to the coast, the Hebrew God became God of [the] Binandere [tribe]."[5] This covenantal agreement established in November 1976, while different in its ritual form from its Hebrew equivalent, held the same meaning: through this covenant, the Binandere turned from their pagan gods to Yahweh and entered into a

1. Richmond Tamanabae, interview by author, July 30, 2009, 2A.

2. Ibid. The spiritual world in PNG is made up of many different sources of spiritual power: "the power of tribal spirits; the ancestral spirits, including the remembered dead; and the bush spirits . . . magic and also the evil power of sorcery" (Bartle, *Death*, 37). The object of life is thus to keep "these powers working for the benefit of one's clan or family, rather than working against them" (37).

3. Richmond Tamanabae, interview by author, July 30, 2009, 2A.

4. Peter Igarobae, interview by author, August 3, 2009, 2A.

5. Ibid.

solemn oath covenanting that their clan and descendants would serve and worship God alone.

Collective Orientation

Another parallel between the Old Testament patriarchs and the PNG revivalists was their collective orientation. As a nomadic traveler, Abraham and his descendents were a communal people group dependent upon each other for survival, moving as a whole unit, and focused more upon their collective group than neighboring non-group members. The effects of this collective orientation in the Abrahamic blessing motif can be seen in the fact that when God blesses a patriarch his entire family and entourage is also blessed; the clan leader is in essence the conduit of blessing to his group. Likewise, within the PNG context, the orientation throughout all the nation's provinces is collective. As illustrated in the Binandere covenant with God, once the tribe's elders had decided to follow Christ, the entire community followed suit.[6]

Similarly, in a village outreach, Igarobae records a whole village waiting for the chief's response before deciding whether or not to accept Christ. In this case, once the chief raised his hand everybody in the village came forward to become Christians.[7] As in the case of the patriarchs of Hebrew Scripture, the head of the clan or tribe brought the blessing of Christ into the community and chose the religious allegiance of the group. In the cities, due to the displacement of individuals from their tribal communities, this pattern is seen on a smaller scale with the head of the family often leading the rest of the family members to Christ. Exceptions to this collective model also existed as individuals sometimes turned to Christ apart from or despite the opposition of their family units. But overall the prevalent mode of receiving the blessing of Christ within the PNG revival movement was through the witness of the collective family unit.

6. This collective mode of decision-making illustrates the mindset within PNG that "religion is a social activity and involves the whole clan. [Moreover], decisions that concern the religion of the people should not be made on the individual level, but on the clan level" (Bartle, *Death*, 38).

7. Peter Igarobae, interview by author, August 3, 2009, 2A.

Led by God

An additional connection between the agents of mission from both the Old and New Testaments and the PNG revival leaders was the fact that they were all led by God. Of particular importance is the literal calling of the individuals within the revival movement. Just as God spoke to Abraham, Isaac, and Jacob through visions, angels and dreams, so God also spoke to the new believers he called into full-time ministry.

Numba Puri, for example, a part-time Bible student at the time, heard the call of God in 1981 while working on a YMCA agricultural farm just outside of Port Moresby. Originally from Mt. Hagen, Western Province, Puri remembers walking to the Laloki river one afternoon around 3 p.m. in order to have his regular fellowship time with the Lord. Carrying his guitar in one hand and his Bible in his pocket, he heard somebody call his name: "Numba." Thinking it was just the wind, Puri continued until he heard the voice again, this time louder: "NUMBA." Not seeing anyone around, he checked everywhere to see who was calling him but he couldn't see anybody.

Finally wondering to himself who could be calling him, he heard Jesus speak: "It's me, Jesus Christ." He then saw in his mind's eye a package with "90 kina" written on it, his own fortnightly salary, and he heard the words: "It's me calling you to leave this job where you are earning 90 kina per fortnight. I have another plan for you. You are going to preach my gospel."[8] After Puri heard these words, he simply replied "I'm coming."

God revealed several things to Puri that afternoon ending with a confirmation of his call. Puri remembers clearly the word of the Lord that day:

> The Lord says, "[Do] you remember me calling Samuel to replace Eli? Do you remember me calling Moses in the burning bushes to deliver my people? Do you remember me calling Matthew, James, and Peter and the disciples? Do you remember me calling Paul? Okay. I'm calling you like these fellows."[9]

Puri quit his job the very next morning and answered God's call to ministry, eventually enrolling in the Institute of Evangelism at Bethel Center where he was later ordained as a full-time minister.[10] Experiences such as that of Puri correlate directly with the testimonies recorded in

8. Numba Puri, interview by author, August 2, 2009, 1A.

9. Ibid.

10. Ibid.

Scripture of those called by God. In both cases, God supernaturally and clearly chose and instructed certain individuals to follow him. Whether it was through dreams, visions, or a literal voice, it is evident that it is God who is in charge of his mission and it is his chosen people who join him in it.

Agents of Blessing

Called by God, the PNG leaders acted as vehicles of God's blessing to PNG. Just as God used Abraham as a vessel to bless the nations, the theme of receiving blessing in order to bless nations is repeated in the PNG ethnographic interviews. In describing his ministry in Rabaul, East New Britain Province, Igarobae describes the rich blessings of God upon his family through the abundant donations of fruit and vegetables and the harvests donated toward paying his children's school fees. Igarobae notes, "We broke through; we connected to . . . heavens' vaults . . . not to be blessed but to be a distributor . . . [to] become a blessing to others."[11] It was this understanding of acting as a vehicle of God's blessing to one's neighbors that was understood by the leaders and was also spoken upon people by God. Sete was one such leader who saw a vision of herself blessing her home province. Sete explains:

> I was caught in the Spirit . . . I found myself standing at . . . [the] Owen Stanley ranges. I found myself standing in those ranges and I was putting my hand, blessing everybody in Oro Province . . . And you know the leaves of the forest turned to heads of people. Lots and lots of people; kneeling down . . . I was [blessing them as] . . . they were kneeling down.[12]

In the rest of the vision God called Sete to full-time ministry in her own Oro Province. Responding to God's call, Sete started a ministry in the Kokoda area of Oro Province in the early 1980s and a few months later revival broke out in the entire region.[13] This combination of the physical blessing of God and the spiritual blessing through Christ is present throughout the testimonies of the PNG revival leaders. Although they, like their New Testament counterparts, suffered persecution, it was this concept of having something of value to give to others—God's blessing—that kept them focused on their missional task.

11. Peter Igarobae, interview by author, August 3, 2009, 2B.
12. Margaret Sete, interview by author, August 8, 2009, 1A.
13. Ibid.

Dependence on God

A final comparison which stands out in the testimonies of the PNG leaders is their dependence on God. As Jesus and his disciples displayed a constant devotion to communing with God through prayer, so prayer was evident within every aspect of the revival leaders' lives in PNG. The national leaders prayed about all aspects of their lives and ministry; they prayed for physical healing, church planting opportunities, revival, direction, spiritual and physical protection, baptism of the Holy Spirit, family members to be converted, breakthroughs to come in difficult regions, and against persecution and demonic forces. Tamanabae reflects on a particularly challenging village outreach: "Sometimes you go into a place [and] it's very hard. You go into a place and you cannot [breakthrough]. So all they [the evangelists] could do was pray and . . . that's what happened. In a situation like that, God had to do something miraculous to break the place up."[14] This constant communication with God at every stage of ministry suggests that, as with the early church in Jerusalem and Antioch, the PNG church knew that it was through total dependence on God that God's mission would be accomplished.

Distinctions

Although there are many parallels between the agents of mission in Scripture and those within the PNG revival context, there are also some distinctions. The PNG revival for example started in many ways as a youth movement; in fact, many of the pioneers in the revival movement were university students or employed young people residing in Port Moresby.[15] Young teenagers also played an important role in local evangelism as both boys and girls shared the gospel in their villages. Orona recalls his own involvement in the music ministry as a young teenager:

> I didn't know how to play [guitar], I just started playing . . . And when I started playing, people would come . . . And then people would start crying and then someone would come and say, "Hey . . . I just heard the sound then I don't know, something just happened [within me] . . . What's . . . causing this?" And then my pastor, Pastor Barnabas, he would get up and say . . . "It's Jesus who is making himself known through these little boys."[16]

14. Richmond Tamanabae, interview by author, July 30, 2009, 2A.
15. Thelma Garao, interview by author, June 12, 2009.
16. Alkin Orona, interview by author, July 2, 2009, 1A.

Jesus did make himself known through the young people in both the villages and city areas during the revival period. Silverback notes the involvement of the youth in a congregation under Athanasius Igarobae's leadership in Oro Province:

> Amongst them is a 14-year-old boy who takes his young friends on a weekly circuit of five surrounding villages and gathers the people for worship and praise, to the accompaniment of a guitar and a bass tea-chest. It is really stimulating to see such a young lad taking the initiative and leading this group of young people on his own (some of them are much younger than he is and some are older).[17]

In addition to involvement in the CRC evangelistic ministry, many of the youth involved in local and regional evangelism came to make up the next generation of leaders within the CRC movement and are still strong in the faith today.[18]

The fact that PNG was a former colony also influenced the mindset of national leaders. For example, until the 1980s PNG was seen by the national pastors and evangelists as a mission field, not as a sender of missionaries.[19] The indigenous leaders were greatly influenced by the revelation that God could call Papua New Guineans to pioneer local and global evangelization efforts. The years of colonization and subsequent British influence on the education system also had positive repercussions; for example, foreign missionaries and PNG nationals were able to work together. The Papua New Guineans' familiarity with the cultural values, traditions, practices, and education system of the mostly Australian missionaries enabled healthy partnerships between the two groups to be established. The additional advantage of the previous spread of the English language throughout PNG was also a benefit for the cross-cultural outreach teams negotiating the rural regions of New Guinea.

MOTIVATIONAL FACTORS

There are multiple overlaps between the people of God in Scripture and the PNG revival leaders during the 1970s–1980s. One of the central parallels is the role of God as the primary motivator of his mission in each time period. In addition to the overarching providence of God, the

17. Silverback, "Report," 3.
18. Thelma Garao, interview by author, June 12, 2009.
19. Richmond Tamanabae, interview by author, July 13, 2009, 1A.

individuals involved reflected similar desires and goals as they participated in the *missio Dei*.

God as Motivator

Of principal importance is the role of God as the primary motivator for his mission regardless of the country, culture, tradition, language, or politics of the people involved. As God led the patriarchs, the Israelites, and the early church, so the PNG Christians also felt the hand of God directing their work. Tamanabae summarizes the situation when he stated: "We played our part in the growth and establishment of CRC in PNG. But when I look back . . . I see . . . God's hand was on it."[20] It was this joint collaboration between God and his people that was evident throughout the PNG revival; God inspired, led, and informed his church as the converts reached out to their local communities. Thus, just as God was clearly deemed the originator and inspiration for the expansion of the Abrahamic blessing in the Old and New Testaments, so God continued to guide his people in Melanesia as they participated in his mission.

While God did work in conjunction with his people as he distributed his blessing, he also worked independently. The Hebrew Scriptures and New Testament mention several instances where God connected directly with individuals not already in his covenant. This is evident in God's encounter with Melchizedek king of Salem (Gen 14:18–20), Hagar the Egyptian (16:7–14), Abimelech king of Gerar (20:3–7), the Egyptian Pharaoh (41:1–7), Paul (Acts 9:3–6), and Cornelius (10:3–6).[21] Similarly, God worked in conjunction with, but also independently from, his church in PNG during the revival period. Togawata remembers his own experience in East New Britain with churches that had received the Holy Spirit independent of any missionary team. He recalls encountering villages where nobody had evangelized previously but they had already received the Holy Spirit and were spreading the gospel through word of mouth.[22]

Tamanabae also witnessed God going ahead of the mission team in Oro Province. He notes, "When we went [to the village] . . . we walked in with a Bible in our hand. And apparently the prayers that we had been

20. Ibid.

21. This list is just a select sample of God's independent interaction with individuals as recorded in Scripture.

22. John Togawata, interview by author, July 13, 2009, 1A.

praying here [had come to pass]. The Lord had already moved before and so somehow everybody was already feeling something. Expectation was there."[23] These examples of God going ahead of his people to prepare the way as well as working independently from his people highlight that this was in fact God's mission. God is not confined by convention or by human plans; he instead is the source, the motivator and sustainer of his mission.

Obedience

Another parallel between the two periods is the emphasis on obedience to God. As Abraham was known for trusting God, so the repeated theme of following Christ through obedience was evident in the CRC revival. While working at the University of Lae, Sete travelled to Ukarumpa where she heard a Youth With A Mission team speak from Genesis 12:1–3 about world missions. Listening to the message about Abraham's call, Sete felt convicted not only to support missions financially but to become a missionary herself. Resigning from her full-time position and turning down an opportunity to earn her Master's degree at the Hague University, the Netherlands, Sete decided to obey God's call. Referencing "the step of faith that Abraham took . . . and [his] sheer obedience to step out and go," Sete remarks on obedience explaining that "the call of Abraham that morning was very clear. It was a command to leave; not when you feel like it, not when all the conditions are right. It's a [command] . . . It's loving Jesus. It's a mark *bilong yu*[24] about how you obey him."[25] This emphasis on obeying God immediately as evidenced in Abraham's own narrative, is manifest in multiple PNG testimonies as individuals respond to God's call without delay.

Power of the Gospel

The personal impact and value of the gospel message was also a motivational factor for both the disciples and the PNG church. In the New Testament, individuals such as Paul (Acts 9:20–22), Lydia (16:14–15), the Philippian jailer (16:30–34), and Apollos (18:24–28), upon hearing the gospel, immediately began to share the good news with their

23. Richmond Tamanabae, interview by author, July 30, 2009, 2A.

24. English translation: "It says something about you; about how you obey him [Christ]."

25. Margaret Sete, interview by author, August 8, 2009, 1B.

communities, and in the case of Paul, the entire known world. Likewise, during the CRC revival there was a deep understanding of the great worth and power of the gospel of Christ. Tabara describes coming home from university in 1980 and hearing the gospel message for the first time:

> [During] the Christmas of 1980 Pastor Thomas, came with a team and that evening he preached [in] my place, [the] Saiho Health Center . . . And that night he preached on Mark 16:16: "He who believes and is baptized will be saved, and he who does not believe will be condemned." And I got a shock of my life. That was the first time I ever had [heard the] full gospel. [The] first time . . . And I [had] never heard that type of message before in my life. To me that was the most powerful gospel I ever heard. I was the first person to respond that night.[26]

The impact that the gospel message made upon Tabara was multiplied throughout Oro Province as village after village turned to Christ. Moreover, the hearers of the message soon became the messengers themselves as individuals started to share the good news of Christ with their family and friends. Sete explains how this took place in her life during high school: "I realized that I had found the most beautiful, the most important thing in my life. Like the Bible says about finding a pearl. I couldn't keep this to myself I had to tell it to share it with others."[27] She elaborates further, stating that "the word of God says that it is more blessed to give than receive."[28] It was this understanding that the gospel of Christ was invaluable and must be shared with one's community which motivated many believers to partake in local and global evangelism.

Distinctions

Although there are many similarities between the two periods, there are also motivations that were uniquely evident in the PNG revival. For example, the fact that PNG during the 1970s was already a highly evangelized nation created a distinct setting for CRC evangelism and outreach. The CRC missionaries were not always sharing the gospel message in an unreached area but instead were evangelizing areas that were already nominally Christian or syncretistic. In regards to motivations for outreach in PNG, there was a decided understanding that the gospel already

26. Barnabas Tabara, interview by author, June 30, 2009.

27. Margaret Sete, interview by author, August 8, 2009, 1A.

28. Ibid., 1B.

preached was not complete and was lacking in an intimate knowledge and relationship with Christ. When Sete encountered resistance from the Anglican Church in her village in Oro Province, it was her father who defended her sharing the gospel of Christ:

> And my father got up and he said to . . . the archbishop of Oro Province . . . "My friend, I've served you well. There is no one in this building who would deny that. I served you well. I was the first friend you had. I was there with you. Why didn't you tell me the truth? If I died tomorrow, I would have gone to hell because I didn't know Jesus in a personal way, as my Lord and Savior. And now I know I'm a Christian; I'm a born again Christian. And I now know that I will go to heaven. Ask yourself, [although] you've spent years preaching the word, if you yourself know the son of God personally, lest you don't make it to heaven."[29]

The fully preached gospel of Christ radically impacted both the audience and messengers of the gospel. Furthermore, this belief that PNG, regardless of the denominational background, still needed to hear the good news led many to participate in the outreaches that took place all over the country.

One of the positive aspects of the former evangelization of PNG was that a foundation of the gospel had already been laid in many regions. Tamanabae likens this occurrence to one sharing their light source with others:

> If you see it in terms of Anglican, Lutheran and Pentecostals, you would see it in terms of these ones did well but these ones didn't do well. But you [have] got to see that they are from their . . . period, the time that they were in. And when the Anglicans first encountered our area they were still powerful [impactful] with the light that they had. You see, whatever . . . light . . . they had of the gospel, the Lord [worked] . . . powerful[ly] in that place they went to.[30]

While the previous missionaries may not have conveyed the full revelation of the gospel message, Tamanabae suggests that what they did share was still used powerfully by God. Due to this previous evangelical work in PNG, a distinct readiness for the gospel was sometimes observed in a region. In Oro Province, for example, Igarobae credits the

29. Ibid.

30. Richmond Tamanabae, interview by author, July 30, 2009, 2A.

ease in which the gospel spread in the region to the previous witness of the Anglican Church. He notes that in Oro Province "everybody became preachers overnight because the word [was] already in them."[31] Likewise in his own village of Kurereda, he points out that "these [villagers] were all Anglicans. And we [didn't] have to really preach to them; it's just like . . . the word is there but it just needed to be ignited."[32] Thus, while a serious lack was expressed in regards to former evangelistic attempts, the work of previous generations was also noted as laying the foundation for the spiritual revival to come.

A further motivation which the CRC leaders felt was a desire to display the power of the gospel of Christ. Similar in many ways to Elijah's demonstration in 1 Kings 18:21–40 that Yahweh was more powerful than Baal, the PNG revivalists desired to demonstrate the power of Jesus Christ. The main reason for this aspiration was the widespread prevalence of syncretism prior to the spiritual revivals of the 1970s. For as individuals converted to Christianity, many still held onto their traditional sorcery and black magic to deal with the spiritual powers. Elijah's rebuke to Israel still echoed in many PNG villages and towns: "How long will you waver between two opinions? If the Lord is God, follow him; but if Baal is God, follow him" (1 Kgs 18:21). This dual allegiance[33] was evident throughout PNG at the time as membership was held in denominational churches while the practice of sorcery continued.

There are many examples of syncretism both individually and communally within the research data. Igarobae, for example, prior to following Christ was the president of the Anglican Student Society at the University of PNG at the same time as being an avid student of sorcery, magic, and the paranormal.[34] Likewise, Tamanabae's father, while personally having renounced sorcery, agreed to pass on his knowledge of black magic so that it wouldn't be lost for future generations.[35] Additionally, Togawata, while a member of the Catholic Church, kept traditional sorcery artifacts in his house in Port Moresby.[36] This prevalence of traditional spirituality directly correlated to the void that the missionaries originally left in

31. Peter Igarobae, interview by author, August 3, 2009, 2A.

32. Ibid.

33. For a detailed explanation of dual allegiance, see Kraft, *Anthropology* (201–2).

34. Peter Igarobae, interview by author, August 1, 2009, 1A.

35. Richmond Tamanabae, interview by author, July 30, 2009, 2A.

36. John Togawata, interview by author, July 13, 2009, 1A.

regards to the spirit world.[37] As one Oro leader highlights, "We Papua New Guineans were involved in sorcery which was very real; with powers that were very real. When we abstained from it, there was a vacuum there."[38] The need to fill this vacuum led individuals to hold onto their former traditional powers while simultaneously adding Christianity to the mix. It was thus the desire of many CRC evangelists to claim the power of Jesus' name and display his supreme power within the spirit world.[39]

MESSAGE SHARED

During the PNG CRC revival, laypeople and Christian leaders alike took to the streets, towns, and villages sharing the gospel of Christ. The topics and theological positions which the revivalists embraced mirrored in many ways those of the early church leaders. The PNG believers were in fact living out the prophetic message declared in the Hebrew Scripture that the nations would be blessed through Abraham and his descendents.

Continuation of Acts 1:8

One of the foundational truths which the CRC leaders shared was the Papua New Guinean's role in continuing the work of Christ on earth. This was evident in the general call to mission preached from Bethel Tabernacle's pulpit and also the teachings given to new believers in Christ. Igarobae recalls Teague, an Australian missionary, sharing with him for the first time about the significance of Acts 1:8. Having just returned from Oro Province where Igarobae witnessed the incredible healing power of God, the young student inquired as to how these miracles had taken place through him. Teague replied:

> "You have received that power now to carry on what Jesus did." I said, "Hang-on, hang-on; please explain [this] to me. Jesus was [the] son of God. You mean I believe [in] the son of God and I will carry on what he started?" She said, "Yeh! But not only that; he is with you to confirm everything you are saying.[40]

37. Paul G. Hiebert speaks extensively regarding the flaw of the excluded middle in *Anthropological Reflections* (189–202).

38. Richmond Tamanabae, interview by author, July 30, 2009, 2A.

39. Peter Igarobae, interview by author, August 1, 2009, 1A; Margaret Sete, interview by author, August 8, 2009, 1A.

40. Merrilyn Teague, interview by author, June 4, 2009, 1A.

Teague's explanation that the Holy Spirit works through believers to do the work of Christ reflects Jesus' words in John 14:12–14[41] that those who have faith in Christ will do what he has been doing and "even greater things than these" (John 14:12). The PNG church realized that as the disciples before them they too would be empowered by the Holy Spirit to share the good news about Christ to the nations, to heal the sick, do signs and wonders and to cast out demons.[42]

Reminiscent of the Messianic prophecy of Isaiah 61:1–2 and Christ's own fulfillment during his life time, the PNG believers witnessed their role in the fulfillment of Christ's work on earth. The prophet Isaiah declared about the coming Messiah:

> The Spirit of the Sovereign Lord is on me, because the Lord has anointed me to preach good news to the poor. He has sent me to bind up the brokenhearted, to proclaim freedom for the captives and release from darkness for the prisoners, to proclaim the year of the Lord's favor and the day of vengeance of our God, to comfort all who mourn (Isa 61:1–2).[43]

As Jesus Christ expressed to the synagogue in Nazareth (Luke 4:16–21) and to John the Baptist's disciples (7:20–22), Christ himself was the fulfillment of Isaiah's prophetic words. With the commissioning of his disciples,[44] believers in Christ continued Jesus' work on earth; the *missio Christi* did not end with the ascension. In PNG, the believers witnessed this continuation of Christ's work in the nations. A young teenager at the time, Orona remembers the miracles and signs and wonders which took place through the prayers of the believers during the outreaches in Oro Province: "So we had people come with crutches. We had people come [with] walking stick[s]. The blind started seeing. The lame started walking. The deaf and dumb were talking."[45] When villagers questioned how such young children were performing such great miracles, Tabara, the young leader of the music team at the time, explained "the difference

41. "I tell you the truth, anyone who has faith in me will do what I have been doing. He will do even greater things than these, because I am going to the Father. And I will do whatever you ask in my name, so that the Son may bring glory to the Father. You may ask me for anything in my name, and I will do it" (John 14:12–14).

42. See Luke 10:1–17.

43. This prophecy regarding the Christ is also found in Isa 29:18–19 and 35:5–6.

44. See Matt 28:18–20, Mark 16:15–20, Luke 24:46–49, and Acts 1:8.

45. Alkin Orona, interview by author, July 2, 2009, 1A.

is this. It's Jesus who is making himself known through these little boys."[46] Indeed Jesus was making himself known through the PNG evangelists as they, like the generations of believers before them, participated in the blessing of the nations through Christ.

Blessed to Be a Blessing

The transition from a local church-centered movement to a missions-centered movement led the CRC toward sharing the blessing of Christ with the world. As the early church before them, the PNG church felt the call to proclaim Christ—God's blessing—to all the world. In reflecting upon this transition in PNG, Geua Wari explains how this change of focus to world mission took place:

> We had grown up with the mentality that it was always give me, give me, give me. And [Barry Silverback] came with that [message] to teach us that we could be a blessing as well. We are blessed to be a blessing. Not just give me, not just blessing and keep blessing. He taught us to just let it out. If you've got the goodness of God, you've got so much of that; don't just keep it to yourself.[47]

As a nation divided and portioned out to different mission organizations, this message that Papua New Guineans could be missionaries and bless the nations was revolutionary and in turn changed the direction of the CRC movement.[48] Although blessing in its fullest form was also reflected in the interview process,[49] Wari describes God's blessing as simply being Jesus Christ.

Wari also notes that God's blessing of Christ[50] should be shared with one's surrounding community. Wari explains that "you've been given that

46. Barnabas Tabara, interview by author, June 30, 2009, 1A.

47. Geua Wari, interview by author, July 29, 2009.

48. Richmond Tamanabae, interview by author, July 13, 2009, 1A.

49. Blessing was also referenced as including the physical blessing of food and finance (Peter Igarobae, interview by author, August 3, 2009, 2A; Richmond Tamanabae, interview by author, July 30, 2009, 2A).

50. In the PNG context, God's holistic blessing through Christ has been equated with the Pidgin English concept of *gutpela sindaun*. This idea of sitting down together in peace and social harmony (Bartle, *Death*, 39) refers to overall "fulfillment in every aspect of life, be it health, success, fertility, respect, honour and influence over others" (Fugmann, "Salvation," 282). While this phrase was not referred to directly within the CRC interviews, the foundational understanding that God's blessing affects life

[blessing] . . . you have received Jesus and I have received Jesus . . . you need to tell someone [about] the same blessing that I received from the Lord; so I can be a blessing to everyone."[51] She continues, "I can give to them what I have received from the Lord. And then they can give it as well. Teach them. You see, teach one and then they will teach the other."[52] Therefore the blessing of Christ, according to Wari, is not to be withheld but instead it is to be shared and those who receive it likewise need to be taught to share it again.[53]

One Way to God

Another central message of the CRC revival was the One Way emphasis. Known for their "One Way" and "Jesus is the Answer" T-shirts, the CRC young people declared that there was no other way to God except through his son Jesus Christ.[54] Echoing the proclamations of the New Testament writers that "salvation is found in no one else, for there is no other name under heaven given to men by which we must be saved" (Acts 4:12),[55] the CRC leaders declared Christ to be the only way to the Father.[56] This message of Christ alone was specifically emphasized in PNG due to the syncretistic nature of many of the regional churches. An extension of this message of Christ alone was the message of demonic deliverance which was timely due to the prevalence of sorcery and witchcraft in the nation.[57]

In addition to this one way message, there was an urgency which accompanied sharing the good news. An interesting passage that frequently arose in the interviews was 2 Corinthians 6:2: "I tell you, now is the time of God's favor, now is the day of salvation." Tamanabae recalls this idea

holistically was present in the narratives.

51. Geua Wari, interview by author, July 29, 2009.

52. Ibid.

53. In addition to reflecting the biblical understanding of blessing, this idea of passing on God's blessing also reflects the Melanesian concept of reciprocity. Reciprocity, as described by Bartle, provides "equality and harmony in life . . . [as] goods are given and received" between two parties (*Death*). However, the distinction in the case of biblical blessing is that rather than something being received in return for the given blessing, the blessing is expected to be forwarded to another individual or group.

54. Geua Wari, interview by author, July 29, 2009, 1A.

55. Also see Matt 1:21, John 14:6, Acts 10:43, 1 Tim 2:5.

56. Geua Wari, interview by author, July 29, 2009.

57. Richmond Tamanabae, interview by author, July 13, 2009, 1A.

expressed in the church meeting in which Robert Tamanabae, a retired army officer, came to Christ:

> As soon as Pastor Barry finished [the sermon] he went to the side door and . . . said [to Robert], "The Lord was speaking to you." . . . And then [Robert] said, "Oh, my Lord's got his time." . . . This was Robert's reply. So, [Pastor Barry] got the Bible, opened up, and said that "God's got his time but . . . now is the day of salvation, now is the acceptable year. How do you know that when you fly from here to Popondetta, the plane won't crash? [Robert] said, "Okay, okay, okay." So, he put his head down . . . and then the next day, [Robert] and I went over to Popondetta.[58]

Sete also remembers preaching to the Oro villagers that Christ was the only way to God and there was no time to lose in turning to him. She preached: "Today is the day of salvation. Today, you hear God speaking to you. Today, you can open your hearts and you can receive Jesus Christ into your hearts. So, you can be sure without any shadow of doubt . . . you are destined to heaven."[59] Both of these narratives express the need for individuals to turn to Christ, the urgency of this call and the consequences of not accepting Christ as one's savior.

Additionally, among the new believers during the CRC revival there was a focus on heaven and Jesus' return. Reminiscent of the early church's teaching on the second coming of Christ,[60] there was an excitement regarding one's heavenly home and the imminent arrival of Christ. Igarobae recalls the topic of heaven and Christ's return as one of the hot topics of conversation in the revival villages:

> Some of us sort of miss those days and . . . [that] feeling of home. Not [an] earthly home but [a] heavenly home . . . Literally people [would] sit [for] hours talking about [their] heavenly home. They want to go home . . . In those days many talked about . . . want[ing] to go home quickly. It sounds funny but that was the common thoughts in those days. We knew that Jesus was going to come tomorrow.[61]

Echoing Paul's words to the Corinthian church in 2 Corinthians 5:1–5, the PNG church longed for their heavenly home and for the

58. Ibid., July 30, 2009, 2A.

59. Margaret Sete, interview by author, August 8, 2009, 1B.

60. See Acts 1:11, Matt 16:27, Luke 21:34–36, and 2 Pet 3:10–14.

61. Peter Igarobae, interview by author, August 3, 2009, 2A.

fruition of Christ's return. Although not elaborated upon specifically, the expectation that Christ would soon return and the urgency felt by believers to share the gospel appears to be interconnected; for if believers expect Christ's immediate return, there is an urgency to share the gospel while people can still repent and turn to Christ.

Distinctions

Although not exactly in contrast to the messages shared in the New Testament, the centrality of the New Creation message during the PNG revival movement was unique. In 2 Corinthians 5:17, the Apostle Paul proclaims to the original audience that "if anyone is in Christ, he is a new creation; the old has gone, the new has come!"[62] This concept of becoming a new creation through Christ was at the forefront of the revival movement. Geua Wari explains the importance of the concept in the PNG context:

> Our old life, our old culture, the tradition, whatever thing; it's all been dealt with. The power of our culture . . . it's been done away with . . . even our sin . . . Newness comes, new life in Christ. And when we talk about new creation, the new life that Christ has for us, he gives us in place of all those other things the fruit of the Spirit . . . love, joy, peace.[63]

First expressed in sermons by Barry Silverback and Leo Harris[64] and the "New Creation" pamphlets written by Barbara Buckland,[65] the new creation teaching was spread throughout the CRC outreaches. Tamanabae describes the phenomenon as a divine anointing which the CRC received to share the new creation message with the wider PNG church.[66]

The effect of this message during the mission outreaches was dynamic as individuals started to understand their identity in Christ and become involved in evangelism.[67] Wari notes:

> Our country at that time . . . we would sort of talk religion . . . but there was no life . . . I believe that the message [Barry] came to teach us was to know our position in Christ. Then when we knew who we were, we wanted to tell others about that. Because

62. Also see John 1:12–13, Rom 6:1–4, and Gal 6:12–15.
63. Geua Wari, interview by author, July 29, 2009, 1A.
64. Richmond Tamanabae, interview by author, July 13, 2009, 1A.
65. Barnabas Tabara, interview by author, June 30, 2009.
66. Richmond Tamanabae, interview by author, July 13, 2009, 1A.
67. Geua Wari, interview by author, July 29, 2009.

> it was bubbling in our lives to know that we had been set free and that you can have Jesus in our heart. You can be filled with the Holy Spirit. You can be baptized in water . . . so the emphasis was on the word of God and to teach us about the truth of the Word.[68]

The result of understanding one's identity in Christ, as Wari notes, led to many people sharing this joyous news with others. In contrast to the nominalism and syncretism within the PNG church at the time, having a meaningful relationship with God and being filled with the power of the Spirit was empowering.

METHODS OF MISSION

The methods used for evangelism in Scripture and the revival movement in PNG share many similarities. As did the disciples in the early church, the CRC revivalists proclaimed the good news of Christ to all people, healed the sick, cast out demons, witnessed signs and wonders, and were dedicated to prayer. As there are so many strategic overlaps with sharing the blessing of Christ with the nations, the following section will focus on the three primary characteristics of PNG evangelism: prayer, signs and wonders, and personal testimony.

Prayer

Prayer was the most prevalent evangelistic method used during the revival period. The PNG believers saturated themselves in prayer as they prayed individually, in the power of the Holy Spirit, and in community. This practice of constantly turning to God at every stage of their ministry and personal life was evident throughout the interview process as the revival leaders casually and specifically commented on how prayer penetrated every aspect of their lives during that period. Revivalists prayed for a great variety of issues including guidance, revival, healing, the Holy Spirit, spiritual and physical protection, church planting opportunities, evangelistic opportunities, and the salvation of family members.[69] This dependence upon God was evident in small and large matters alike. Tabara remembers prayer becoming a pivotal event during a typical afternoon village soccer match:

68. Ibid.

69. This list is compiled from the interviews with Barnabas Tabara, Margaret Sete, Peter Igarobae, Richmond Tamanabae, and John Togawata.

> I remember the late Brian Homba when he was coming down to visit us. On his way in one of the villages there was a soccer match in the afternoon and they were playing and one of the young fell[ows] fell down and broke his collar bone. Pastor Brian prayed for him and he got miraculously healed. The bones knitted again.[70]

It was this incorporation of prayer in everyday life that most mirrored the life of the early church believers who were likewise devoted to constant prayer (Acts 2:42). Just as the early church leaders depended upon God for guidance, assistance, inspiration, encouragement, and strength, so the revival leaders also needed that communion with God to follow him in completing his mission.

An interesting factor in the PNG revival was the novelty of prayer. Whereas the early church believers were deeply rooted in the Jewish prayer rituals, many PNG believers were learning how to pray to God for the first time. Igarobae describes how he learned how to pray for the sick while visiting a hospital in Popondetta, Oro Province:

> I was an altar boy in the Anglican [Church] from 6 years old until 18 years, so when I knelt down beside the bed, the woman got up and knelt beside me . . . we both [said] "In the name of the Father, Son and Holy Spirit, the Lord is with you" and she said "and with you also." . . . That's it. I never felt so embarrassed because I don't know how to pray, to pray for the sick. I was thinking [about how to pray] . . . until a picture came to my mind of seeing Pastor Barry laying hands on me . . . and I said, "Yeh, I'll do the same." So I asked the lady, "Excuse me Ma'am; let's do it again." So, . . . I said "Father, Son and Holy Spirit," I said the same things "and the Lord is with you and with you also." I bent down to put my hand on this fellow's head. I put my hand on this head and a few seconds later he grabbed my hand and he went ahhhh [deep breath].[71]

To the shock of both Igarobae and the sick man's wife, the man was instantly healed. Learning how to pray through practical experience was a common occurrence for many PNG believers as the majority of CRC converts moved from nominal faith and priest-led congregations to passionate faith and believer-led ministries. The additional fact that God

70. Barnabas Tabara, interview by author, June 30, 2009.

71. Peter Igarobae, interview by author, August 1, 2009, 1A.

answered the believers' prayers further indicates that God himself was the chief motivator and the means behind the revival movement.

Signs and Wonders

The power of God was also very evident through the signs and wonders that took place among the CRC believers. While God-led, the healing of the sick and the demonized was one of the principal means through which the gospel message was shared. Recalling the days of the Acts of the Apostles, the PNG revival movement was filled with the miraculous. The narrator of the book of Acts records a similar situation among the early church believers in the New Testament:

> The apostles performed many miraculous signs and wonders among the people . . . As a result, people brought the sick into the streets and laid them on beds and mats so that at least Peter's shadow might fall on some of them as he passed by. Crowds gathered also from the towns around Jerusalem, bringing their sick and those tormented by evil spirits, and all of them were healed (Acts 5:12–16).

This witness of God through signs and wonders was particularly evident in the miraculous physical healings that took place throughout the provinces. In Oro Province Orona describes some of the many miracles that took place during the village ministry: "We had people come with crutches. We had people come [with] walking stick[s]. The blind started seeing. The lame started walking. The deaf and dumb were talking."[72] Reminiscent of Jesus' own description of his ministry to John the Baptist's disciples (Luke 7:22), the PNG believers saw the miracles of Scripture before their very eyes.

The abundance of physical healings during the revival often led to the conversion of the miracle's recipients and on-lookers. Both Richmond and Leila Tamanabae experienced God's healing power in Port Moresby which eventually led to their acceptance of Christ. Richmond was prayed over by Barry Silverback and instantly healed from an injured leg and his wife Leila's poor eyesight was healed after Merrilyn Teague prayed for her.[73] It was the healing of Leila's eyesight that directly led the family to God; Richmond explains that "she got healed and that's how we came into

72. Alkin Orona, interview by author, July 2, 2009, 1A.

73. Richmond Tamanabae, interview by author, July 30, 2009, 2A.

God."[74] Such stories of physical healing leading to salvation were repeated again and again throughout the interviews with the revival leaders.[75]

Additionally there were testimonies of mass healings which impacted entire regions with the blessing of Christ. In Oro Province, Tabara's father was radically converted and as he worked at the Saiho Medical Center he started praying for the patients. Tabara tells the story:

> One day my dad went up to the hospital to work. He was sitting down and . . . writing prescriptions for the others to treat them; he would see the patients and interview them and get their prescriptions. He was sitting down and he saw a man walking into the hospital . . . with a walking stick. He had swollen feet; they were swollen right from the waist down to the feet. He was in pain and agony. He walked slowly and painfully to the hospital. As soon as my Dad saw this man he felt the anointing of the Holy Spirit come upon him like a mantel. And he thought hope was coming upon him and he literally looked around.
>
> Then he said, "Maybe this is what anointing is." . . . He took the man into the injection room privately and asked him, "Do you want me to give you a treatment and an injection, or do you want the Lord to heal you?" And he closed his hands, and the man looked at my dad and he said, "I don't want an injection; I want the Lord to heal me." My dad prayed on him and instantly the power of God came on him and the swelling and the water just ran out, just drained out and he got instantly healed, and he ran out of the hospital and he started running. My dad came out of the hospital, called him and said, "Come back, come back." And he came back.
>
> My dad held the stick that this man brought. And the man was standing there . . . and he preached that hour . . . he preached and 120 patients got completely healed. They left the hospital the next day. And the local radio station from Popondetta came up the next day; they interviewed my Dad and the whole province heard the interview. And from then on the people came from all over the province to my dad's house. He prayed for them and

74. Ibid.

75. A selection of parallel testimonies include the healing of John Togawata's wife Nellie (John Togawata, interview by author, July 13, 2009, 1A), the healing of Robert Tamanabae's wife (Peter Igarobae, interview by author, August 2–5, 2009), and the healing of Peter Igarobae's mother (Richmond Tamanabae, interview by author, July 30, 2009, 2A).

> they got healed and they left their walking sticks and crutches and left.[76]

Testimonies of God's healing power touching an entire region were told by the revivalists on a small scale when one person was healed and on a large scale, when hundreds of people were healed. The common factor in all the healings was that the glory of God was revealed and many people came to Christ through witnessing these miracles.[77]

Distinctions

One of the unique characteristics of the PNG revival period was the use of indigenous worship songs as a means of spreading the gospel message. Previous to the 1970s revival in Oro Province, the worship songs sung in the Anglican Church were written in English; however, with the spread of the national-led CRC revival through Oro, indigenous worship songs or "language songs" were also developed. Tamanabae explains this transition from English worship to language songs:

> When the revival first started, we were singing mainly "This is the Day," that was the only song that they would know. And we began to sing some of the English ones. None of the language songs were coming out because the language songs were all there [with the other group] in the string band.[78] . . . And so you can see a real pattern about how it grew. That when we first begun . . . but later on language songs became very, very popular and powerful. So, now when you go to the villages, English songs are sung as the Spirit leads them . . . but most of the worship is in their language.[79]

This transition from English worship songs to language songs was a very "significant feature of the revival . . . and had an impact particularly amongst the young people . . . They said, 'don't use [our] language to sing string band songs because people get blessed hearing that song [in the Binandere language].'"[80] An already highly musical region, the people groups in Oro province were especially receptive to worshiping God in

76. Barnabas Tabara, interview by author, June 30, 2009.

77. Margaret Sete, interview by author, August 8, 2009, 1B; Barnabas Tabara, interview by author, June 30, 2009.

78. String bands are secular village bands.

79. Richmond Tamanabae, interview by author, July 30, 2009, 2A.

80. Ibid.

their own languages and as musicians were converted the new believers quickly formed evangelical worship teams in addition to writing Christian worship music.[81]

Worshiping God was a common means through which individuals communicated with God and came to God. Barry Silverback records that after individuals came to Christ, worshiping God was the next task at hand. He writes the following regarding a village outreach in Oro Province in 1977: "Wherever we went Robert [Tamanabae] would gather the new Christians together the same night that they were saved and teach them how to worship God with uplifted hands and fervent praises."[82] This emphasis on worshiping God through music and song became a strong characteristic of the CRC revival. In addition, Christian worship often attracted people to the church and opened them up to hearing the gospel of Christ.[83] Sete recalls three brothers who were gardening in the village and hearing the Christians' singing came over to see what was happening.[84] Upon listening to the gospel for the first time, the brothers later returned to the village with their families and the entirety of their family was saved.[85] During the revival movement, worship became not only a natural response of praise to God but also a light which led people to Christ.

The style and fervency of revival worship was also unique. In the Kokoda region of Oro, Sete recalls the joyful focus on worship after her village came to Christ: "From that day on, we'd go to gardens maybe from 8 a.m. to 3 p.m. . . . all the people singing all the way to the garden, all the way back."[86] Igarobae also tells of the strong presence of worship in village life; he remembers the presence of worship in his own village of Kurereda:

> So, you would see a family here start worshipping and the next door will pick up the same chorus and then in less than ten minutes the whole village in their own houses . . . [would be]

81. Alkin Orona, interview by author, July 2, 2009, 1A; Richmond Tamanabae, interview by author, July 30, 2009, 2A.

82. Silverback, "Report," 2.

83. Barnabas Tabara, interview by author, June 30, 2009; Margaret Sete, interview by author, August 8, 2009, 1A; Richmond Tamanabae, interview by author, July 30, 2009, 2A.

84. Margaret Sete, interview by author, August 8, 2009, 1B.

85. Ibid.

86. Ibid.

> worshiping the Lord. And it would go on and on for hours and then Robert [Tamanabae] would go down in the middle of the village and stand there and start preaching. In a rainy day, they don't come together, they sit in their own houses and start whatever songs they sing [and] it was picked up . . . all around in their own houses there . . . language songs.[87]

This chain reaction of worship was a regular characteristic of Oro village life during the early revival years. Igarobae recalls that "in the daytime, you [would] go down to swim in the river and you get blessed and you shout 'Hallelujah' and somebody in the middle of the jungle . . . [would] say 'Praise the Lord.'" This would then start "a chain reaction; all down the river banks and the gardens, people will just stop what they are doing raise their hands in the middle and just worship the Lord."[88] Worship thus permeated everyday life as the new believers were filled with the joy of the Spirit and sung songs of praise to their God at all moments of the day.

MISSIONAL EXPANSION

Throughout the interview process the parallels between the revivalists' testimonies and the early church narratives were clearly apparent. Indeed, the enthusiastic proclamation of the gospel and the scores of miracles and signs and wonders in the CRC outreaches instantly bring to mind the work of the Holy Spirit within the early church. However, it is the ensuing results of the CRC revival, or the "fruit" of the ministry, which provides the strongest parallel. Just as the gospel of Christ spread from Jerusalem throughout the known world, so the blessing of God through Christ spread from village to village, region to region, and province to province in PNG. While there are numerous parallels that can be brought to light, in the following section I will be focusing on the strongest overlaps between the two periods while still highlighting the unique distinctions of the PNG context.

Missio Dei

As God poured out his blessing upon Abraham and the surrounding nations in the Hebrew Scriptures and orchestrated the proclamation of the good news in the New Testament, so God was the architect and

87. Peter Igarobae, interview by author, August 3, 2009, 2A.

88. Ibid.

inspiration behind the CRC revival in PNG. While in both the Middle Eastern and Melanesian contexts key individuals were involved in the expansion of God's blessing, the principal director was God himself. Tamanabae acknowledging the centrality of God noted that "we played our part in the growth and establishment of [the] CRC in PNG. But when I look back . . . I see there was . . . God's hand . . . on it."[89] Togawata added: "Our lives [and] our movement w[ere] all directed by God. We never really saw it then but boy it was so clear to us. Looking back now . . . we now recognize so clearly [that] God was in every turn. He commanded and he directed everything."[90]

Sete also acknowledges the providence of God as she explains that she "just followed the leading of the Holy Spirit" to new villages and communities in the Kokoda region.[91] Perhaps Tamanabae summarizes God's involvement in the revival best when he states that "the Lord sort of moved naturally and supernaturally" both in the "natural things that people were doing" and the supernatural things.[92] It was this interaction between God and his followers that so strongly resembles the Spirit-led missional expansion in the book of Acts. While the believers play a large role in the events, in both cases God directs the work and fulfills his mission.

An additional factor in the fulfillment of the *missio Dei* was the acknowledgment of the Lord's strategic plan. Just as God proclaimed that all nations would be blessed through Abraham and Christ foretold the international expansion of the gospel message, so the revivalists saw that a purpose greater than their own was at work in the revival areas. In reflecting on this divine orchestration of events, Igarobae notes the perfect plan of God within the CRC revival:

> In 1972 [Barry Silverback] came back with Pastor Leo Harris's covering and started a fellowship going on in Tokarara . . . 1975; that's when Thomas came in. 1976 is when we all came in. It's how everything just took off; without plan, without strategizing. It looks like we were just moving everywhere. But now looking back, you can see the Lord's strategies . . . It looks like it was written already . . . It's just like we knew what we were doing and yet, we don't know what we were doing. We were divinely guided.

89. Richmond Tamanabae, interview by author, July 13, 2009, 1A.
90. John Togawata, interview by author, July 13, 2009, 1A.
91. Margaret Sete, interview by author, August 8, 2009, 1B.
92. Richmond Tamanabae, interview by author, July 30, 2009, 2A.

> So, when I look back, I have this eerie feeling like it was like all these things were written before. And we were just following what was instructed.[93]

Several revivalists spoke about this eerie feeling when they reflected on the missional expansion during the revival days and of their involvement in God's greater plan. In Rabaul, Togawata witnessed God's hand in the seemingly negative imprisonment of six believers. He explained that the imprisonment was "God's doing" as their incarceration led to the establishment of the prison ministry and the salvation of the prison commander and some of his officers.[94] In examples such as these the overarching purpose of God was highlighted as the driving force behind the PNG churches' actions and the strategic plan via which the revival grew.

Continuation of the Early Church's Blessing

As the CRC pastors and leaders described the events of the revival period there was a repeated parallel made between the events recorded in the Book of Acts and those that took place during the PNG revival. Togawata exemplifies this observation when he states that miracles took place as they were "written in the book of Acts. Signs and Wonders follow[ed] the proclamation of the gospel . . . [It] literally happened the way that . . . it [did] in the Bible."[95] In addition, the actual events of the revival appear to mirror those of the early days of revival in the book of Acts when "everyone was filled with awe, and many wonders and miraculous signs were done by the apostles . . . and the Lord added to their number daily those who were being saved" (Acts 2:43–47). Silverback describes the church growth of the early revival in Oro Province in a similar manner; he states:

> We ministered in nine villages, and throughout the trip we saw approximately 300 people saved, 270 baptized in water and over 130 filled with the Holy Spirit. There were also healings too numerous to count, including some dramatic healings of crippled bodies and the opening of blind eyes and deaf ears of long standing (up to 30 or 40 years). Among those saved and healed were six sorcerers, who genuinely turned from their old ways and destroyed all the evil implements of their former practices. Three new churches were established, and we found

93. Peter Igarobae, interview by author, August 3, 2009, 2D.

94. John Togawata, interview by author, July 13, 2009, 1A.

95. Ibid.

> that the others which were founded on our previous trips are now flourishing under local leadership. This makes seven local churches established in the past 13 months in this province, and there are several other meeting places where there is potential for a local church to eventuate.[96]

This incredible fruitfulness visible in the PNG revival as well as the Jerusalem church and the missionary journeys of Paul suggests that God is still involved in his mission on earth. Moreover, it indicates that while the early church began the distribution of God's blessing to the nations, the church still carries out the fulfillment of the Abrahamic blessing today.

Blessing through Kinship

The PNG revival parallels the Old Testament narrative as the blessing of God is passed through family lines. One of the core components of the original Abrahamic blessing was God's use of one man and his family as vehicles through which all peoples would be blessed. Furthermore, the blessing of God was passed through the family line as God blessed Abraham, his son Isaac, his grandson Jacob and his great-grandson Joseph and all their households. While the PNG revival is unique due to its post-Messianic context, there is also a strong emphasis on passing the blessing of Christ through the kinship system. Igarobae notes the parallel missional pattern in both the Old Testament and the PNG revival:

> [God] started with Abraham; with a family, then Abraham made a clan, then he had twelve clans that formed a tribe, the twelve tribes of Israel. And I believe that that's the same pattern [in the CRC revival] but it's more accommodated by the body of Christ. But the mechanics of reaching out is the same. And one of the [reasons] why I'm so successful here is that we just reach and influence and guide the family. Maybe it's the chief, or spokesman, we reach in and put word in here and you've got the clan in your hands already.[97]

This prominent role given to the clan and family correlates with God's similar use of Abraham's family as a missional vessel. Similarly in the PNG context, as Igarobae states, the "Lord used the family, clans, and

96. Silverback, "PNG Annual Report," 5.

97. Peter Igarobae, interview by author, August 3, 2009, 2D.

tribes to break through in the urban areas"[98] of PNG in order to bring his blessing to the nation.

Families in the PNG context played a similar role to the family of Abraham as God poured out his blessing upon extended families and then blessed individuals and communities through them. Tamanabae highlights God's employment of family connections in PNG noting specifically their role as conduits of God's blessing.

> Family connections . . . they would all go and invite people to come and take on [Christ]. It just grew like that. So, the key was that there were families that broke through completely and took possession of it and it became theirs and then the Lord blessed them. The Lord gracefully moved through the miraculous signs and wonders open[ing] up . . . opportunities so that others would come and get blessed by it.[99]

As Tamanabae notes God used these families as vehicles through which others would come to Christ and receive the blessing of God. Even outside of the CRC movement Igarobae noticed the same pattern being visible as the Lord used family units missionally; he concludes: "I believe with all my heart that the Lord used families and clans. You go to the Assembly of God and you see the same trends. You get the same picture with Christian Life Center . . . in those days it was clans and families that moved."[100] The divine blessing poured upon believing families spread the gospel message throughout the region both within the CRC movement and outside the denomination.

While the gospel message was spread primarily through kinship networks, the CRC's proclamation of the good news was not limited to one extended family or clan. Instead, outside individuals often invited the CRC to conduct outreaches or crusades in their area which eventually led to the establishment of a church in their village or community. For example, the initial revival located in Oro Province came about through Chief Daniel's invitation to Barry Silverback to have an outreach team visit Kurereda village.[101] This concept of receiving an outside invitation was repeated frequently; for example, Paul Kehi invited the CRC to

98. Ibid.

99. Richmond Tamanabae, interview by author, July 30, 2009, 2A.

100. Ibid., 2D.

101. Peter Igarobae, interview by author, August 1, 2009, 1A.

Manus, the Rapitok churches invited the CRC to Rabaul,[102] and George Iki invited the CRC to Enga.[103]

These provincial invitations along with the local invitations bring to mind similar invitations recorded in the New Testament; for example, Peter's invitation to share the gospel with Cornelius' household (Acts 10), Paul's invitation to the households of Lydia (16:15) and the Philippian jailer (16:31–32), and the Jewish community's invitation to Paul to share with them in Rome (28:21–28). Like their biblical counterparts, these outside invitations in PNG led to the expansion of the church geographically, culturally, and numerically. Moreover, as God provided these divine connections, the CRC movement was able to continually expand the borders of the kingdom of God in PNG.

Distinctions

One of the key factors which led to the success of the CRC movement in PNG was the sense of ownership which the new believers felt toward both the gospel message and the national revival. In explaining the CRC's success in Oro Province, Tamanabae points to the adoption of Christ by the entire Tamanabae clan as a central cause of the missional expansion. He explains:

> When it becomes a family thing, . . . everybody makes a commitment and [takes] ownership of it. So, when we took ownership of that CRC became ours. And the Anglican [Church] was not like that; we were just part of the thing. But it's not so much the CRC but it was the message and the revelation that was flowing and the life that was flowing through that. That became ours. And it became a family thing. And when that happens everybody else who are not really willing to be part of it, they have no choice but to be in it. So, that's how it had a powerful impact.[104]

This identification with the movement, and more importantly the gospel message, encouraged new believers to take responsibility for their local outreaches.[105] Even young high school students such as Amani and Sete felt ownership for sharing their faith and "were all very excited about

102. Ibid., August 3, 2009, 2C.

103. Richmond Tamanabae, interview by author, July 30, 2009, 2B.

104. Ibid., 2A.

105. Ibid., 2A.

taking the gospel" to the university campus.[106] Thus, young and old, urban dwellers and villagers alike felt personal responsibility to share the good news that they had received. Although God did raise key families and leaders up in the revival areas,[107] there was an overwhelming sense that each individual had the power to change the fate of their family and friends by sharing with them the blessing of God.

106. Margaret Sete, interview by author, August 8, 2009, 1A.

107. Richmond Tamanabae, interview by author, July 30, 2009, 2A.

10

Conclusion

By identifying the missional patterns of the Abrahamic blessing in Scripture and in the Papua New Guinean case study of the CRC missionary movement I have been able to distinguish significant parallels in regards to the agents of mission, motivation for mission, message shared, evangelistic methods, and missional expansion. The conclusions I present in this section focus on my three primary research areas: the nature of the blessing motif in Scripture, the expression of the Abrahamic blessing in the PNG case study, and the shared missional patterns of the Abrahamic blessing motif in both Scripture and the PNG case study of the CRC movement. In addition I identify the missional implications of my research.

Blessing Motif in Scripture

At the center of my research is the subject of God's blessing to the nations as proclaimed to Abraham in Genesis 12:3. As illustrated in the narratives of the book of Genesis, God's blessing upon creation and humankind is intrinsically holistic, God-given, and continuous. The very nature of this divine blessing points to God's desire to bless all peoples of the earth.

First, God's blessing in Scripture is holistic. Within the text, God blesses every living creature (Gen 1:21–22), humankind (1:27–29; 5:1b–2), Noah and his family (9:1–7), and Abraham and his family (12:1–3).[1] This blessing encompasses the physical, political, relational, and spiritual aspects of life. It is entirely complete in its reach, not missing any

1. See table 7 for a full list of references of the Abrahamic blessing being proclaimed and given to each of the patriarchs.

area of the recipients' communal or private life. God blessed every living creature—and all of humankind—from the point of its creation. From the beginning, God's blessing was and continues to be universal in its scope, touching all of creation and all of humankind. Even as God chose Abraham, the underlying purpose of this selection was that all peoples, not just one, would be blessed (12:3).

Second, blessing is God-given. Throughout Scripture, both in the Old and New Testaments, it is clear that God is the source of all blessing. As illustrated in the book of Genesis, creation and humanity were blessed only when God proclaimed his blessing aloud. Linked with this divine origin comes the mystery that surrounds the blessing of God. Westermann notes that with the imparting of blessing God gives a "vital power" to humankind.[2] Kidner explains it as "God turning full-face to the recipient . . . in self-giving."[3] No matter how God's blessing is described, it is clear from the biblical text that God's blessing of creation is supernatural. Whether it is Laban prospering (Gen 30:27), Potiphar's household thriving (39:1–23), or the Sidonian widow's son coming back to life (1 Kgs 17:17–24), the blessing of God is more than the spoken word—it is action incarnate, as God meets humankind with his generosity and abundant provision. The Abrahamic blessing to the nations is likewise filled with mystery as God chooses in his sovereignty one man and one nation to embody his rich blessing for all peoples.

Finally, God's blessing is at its core continuous. As God first proclaimed his life-giving blessing upon creation (Gen 1:21–22) and humankind (1:27–29), the blessing given to them was also theirs to give. In Genesis 1–11, this passing on of God's blessing is seen in creation's God-given ability to be fruitful and multiply (1:22b, 28b; 9:1b, 7). This inherent fruitfulness in turn is passed on to every following generation of plant, animal, and human life. In the Abrahamic narrative, God's blessing is likewise transmitted from generation to generation as each new patriarch is blessed anew by God.[4] Similarly, God's blessing is also poured out upon the surrounding nations as the blessing of God overflows upon the peoples closest to Abraham and his kin.[5] This continual extension of

2. Westermann, *Blessing in the Bible*, 18.

3. Kidner, *Genesis*, 52.

4. See appendix C for a complete list of references in which God blesses each patriarch.

5. See appendix D for a diagram explaining the missional overflow of the blessing of God upon the nations in the patriarchal narratives.

God's blessing across generations and national boundaries comes into its greatest fulfillment in the New Testament with the coming of Christ. It is through Jesus Christ that all peoples can become heirs of the original promise given to Abraham (Gal 3:29). As recorded in the New Testament, the early church continued this extension of the Abrahamic blessing as they too shared the blessing of God proclaiming the gospel of Jesus Christ in its community and abroad.

It is thus through these characteristics of holistic extension, divine origin, and continuity that the very nature of blessing points to God's desire to bless all peoples of the earth. The holistic dimension of blessing itself indicates that it is God's desire to bless every level of his creation and every aspect of life. Furthermore, as the source of blessing is God himself, the distribution of blessing is not reliant on the whims of humanity but instead it finds its guaranteed fulfillment in God. And the nature of divine blessing is continuous on a variety of levels within Scripture. In the Old Testament this continuity is evident in the life-giving power bestowed by God upon creation, the blessing passed from generation to generation in the patriarchal narratives, and the overflow of blessing on the surrounding nations throughout the Old Testament. In the New Testament this continuity of God's blessing changes with the coming of Christ and the inclusion of the Gentiles as heirs of Abraham's promise. Finally, the blessing of God continues as the early church proclaims the message of Christ to all peoples. It is therefore in the core characteristics of God's blessing that God's desire to bless all peoples completely and eternally is apparent.

Abrahamic Blessing Motif in the PNG CRC Case Study

As I explored the Abrahamic blessing motif in the PNG case study of the CRC revival movement, I observed several insights regarding the PNG church's participation in the fulfillment of the Abrahamic blessing. In this section I will continue to use the categories of mission theology discussed previously to provide the framework for my conclusions. These categories include: agents of mission, message shared, motivations of mission, methods of mission, and missional expansion.

In the PNG case study there were several unifying factors that characterized the agents of God's mission. First, those called by God during the revival as preachers, teachers, and evangelists were all unique in age, gender, profession, educational level, and origin. The PNG CRC leaders included both young and old, men and women, educated and uneducated, full-time missionaries and full-time workers, new Christians and revitalized Christians, city dwellers and villagers, foreigners and nationals. Second, many of these leaders were supernaturally and sometimes literally called by God into ministry through visions, dreams, and signs and wonders. These individuals, once called by God, were also characterized by their fervent worship of God and devoted prayer life. Additionally, many of the revival leaders were formerly affiliated with sorcery and witchcraft before they turned to Christ. Finally, primarily due to the denominational divisions in the nation during the 1970s and 1980s, the CRC revival leaders faced wide persecution for their faith. In the face of this persecution, the leaders exhibited boldness in their proclamation of Christ. In fact, it was this boldness in the midst of public humiliation that set the new believers apart and which enabled them to continue to spread the good news in their communities.

As I studied the factors which motivated the CRC leaders to participate in the fulfillment of the Abrahamic blessing, I observed several consistent characteristics. To begin with, a common concern motivating the revival leaders was the eternal salvation of their families, villages, regions, and provinces. The PNG evangelists were also motivated by the all encompassing love of Christ which they had experienced and in turn desired to share with others. The pure joy of sharing the gospel also motivated others to continue sharing their testimony. Another personal motivation was the sense of past and future responsibility: past responsibility to continue the work of the missionaries who had come before them, and future responsibility to the individuals who had not yet heard the gospel. The greatest motivator of mission, however, was the Holy Spirit. It was through the leading of God himself that individuals were called, equipped, and sent to share the good news about Christ throughout PNG.

Although there were a variety of messages preached during the PNG CRC revival movement, there were also several select messages that were repeatedly mentioned. The most prominent of these was the salvation message; that it is only through Christ that one is saved and reconciled with God. Another repeated topic was the divine nature and character of God, particularly that God was all-powerful, the ultimate healer, sovereign over all creation, a source of unconditional love, and inclusive of all people. Last, a key message was that Papua New Guineans had been called by God to engage in local and global mission. Taught from the pulpits and in the Bible school classrooms, this revolutionary message strongly impacted the new believers in the CRC movement and influenced many of them to become full-time missionaries.

During the PNG CRC revival movement there were also many methods of mission which were widespread during the period. In the local and regional outreaches, for example, a variety of evangelistic forms were adopted including outreach teams, crusade meetings, church meetings, a boat ministry, and camp gatherings. Several ministry methods were also incorporated such as the preaching of the word, published literature, radio advertisements, ministry-based films, and Christian music. The holistic training of indigenous leaders was also significant in the CRC movement, and ministry training schools were established throughout the nation and eventually abroad. The supernatural manifestations of God were also a powerful means of evangelism during the local church services and mission outreaches. As the gospel was preached in the villages and cities, the word of God was often confirmed by miraculous signs and wonders. Physical healings, communal and individual transformation, salvation of entire villages, visions, angelic visitations, gifts of the Spirit, the casting out demons, and signs and wonders were all regular occurrences during the revival period and in turn led many to Christ.

The missional expansion of the gospel during the PNG CRC revival also reflects the fulfillment of the Abrahamic blessing motif. In my interviews, several key missional patterns came to light specific to the PNG context. First, the 1970s–1980s CRC revival in PNG primarily took place in the village. While Bethel Center was located in an urban context, the revival spread like wildfire through the rural villages of Oro Province. Likewise, the principal evangelists were predominantly local villagers, not individuals from outlying provinces or abroad. The gospel message was thus spread via familial lines and in turn moved from clan to clan throughout the province. Another way that the gospel was spread was through individuals coming to the urban centers and taking the gospel message back home to their villages. At the foundation of all this missional expansion however was the work of the Holy Spirit. The interviewees noted that on every level it was God himself who organized, led, and enabled the missional expansion of the revival movement.

In conclusion, my research revealed that the PNG CRC movement was indeed an extension of the fulfillment of the Abrahamic blessing. While studying the representation of the Abrahamic blessing in the revival movement, I noted that the PNG CRC movement was at its core dedicated to local and global evangelism. In particular, the revival movement emphasized obedience to Christ in word and deed, sharing the good news with all peoples, dependence upon the Holy Spirit, and participation in the mission of God. In many ways, the CRC revival movement in PNG mirrored the early life of the church in the book of Acts as the blessing of Christ spread throughout the known world through signs and wonders, preaching of the word, and the transformative work of the Holy Spirit. It is with this similarity in mind that I originally decided to compare and contrast the Abrahamic blessing motif in Scripture with its representation in the PNG case study.

Shared Missional Patterns of the Abrahamic Blessing Motif

As I conducted this integrative research comparing the Abrahamic blessing motif in Scripture with the missional motif in the PNG case study, I observed several missional patterns that overlapped both contexts. In this section, using the missiological lenses of agents of mission, motivation for mission, message shared, methods of mission, and missional expansion, I present my conclusions based upon my research findings.

In regards to the agents of mission there were several key areas in which the messengers of God in both contexts were similar. Perhaps the most surprising was the covenantal bond which linked both Abraham and the Oro revivalists to Yahweh. While the ritual of cutting covenant was well known in the ancient Near East, it was also a familiar ritual among the Binandere people of Oro Province. With the Tamanabae clan's conversion to Christ, a covenant was thus cut with Yahweh declaring the Hebrew God as God of the Binandere.[6] In addition to this covenantal treaty, another parallel between the Old Testament patriarchs and the PNG revival leaders was their collective orientation. The leaders in both contexts were also most often called into ministry, reaffirmed in their ministry, and directed in their mission by God. In this calling, the leaders both in Scripture and PNG acted as vehicles of God's blessing both locally and to the nations. Finally, in both contexts the agents of mission all noted their dependence on God and highlighted the fact that they prayed about every aspect of their lives and ministry.

The primary motivator of God's mission within Scripture and the PNG revival movement was God. As God led the patriarchs, the Israelites, and the early church, so the PNG revival leaders were also directed

6. Richmond Tamanabae, interview by author, July 30, 2009, 2A.

by God to complete his work. Another shared motivational factor was obedience to God as leaders heard God's call and followed God's direction. In connection with the early church of the New Testament, the PNG church was also highly motivated by the power of the gospel message. As Sete aptly summarizes: "I couldn't keep [the gospel] to myself; I had to tell it to share it with others."[7] This joyful excitement and urgency to share the blessing of God through Christ characterizes both the early church and the PNG revival movement and in turn motivated many believers to participate in local and global ministry.

As I compared the messages shared in the New Testament with those of the revival movement, I observed several significant connections. At the forefront was the belief that Papua New Guineans can and should play a role in the continuing work of Christ on earth. Just as the early church worked as the body of Christ on earth, so the PNG church was called during the revival to participate in the extension of the good news to the nations as expressed in Acts 1:8. Another key message which overlaps with the missional message of the Abrahamic blessing motif in Scripture was the concept of being blessed to be a blessing. In reflecting on the original blessing of Genesis 12:3, interviewees noted that they had been blessed by God with the knowledge of Christ and thus needed to extend that blessing to the nations. The final message which strongly coincided with the New Testament's teaching on Christ was the One Way emphasis. In a nation filled with folk religions and deities, the cry of the CRC revivalists was that there is no other way to God except through Jesus Christ.

The methods of mission evident in the New Testament fulfillment of the Abrahamic blessing and the PNG movement also correspond in many areas. The revival leaders' emphasis on prayer, for example, echoed the prayer life of both Jesus and the early church. As the followers of Christ before them, every aspect of the PNG Christians' lives were permeated with prayer. PNG believers prayed to God for all their needs and repeatedly witnessed God's answers to their prayers. Also evident in the early church and the Papua New Guinean revival was the permanent presence of the Holy Spirit. In both narratives God confirms the validity of the gospel message of Christ with signs and wonders and the healing of the sick and demonized.

7. Margaret Sete, interview by author, August 8, 2009, 1A.

In comparing the missional expansion of God's blessing in Scripture and in the PNG case study, the strongest parallels between the two periods become apparent. In both contexts, God was the architect and force behind the spread of his blessing to the nations. The *missio Dei*, or the mission of God, was in fact simply that, the all-encompassing mission of the Creator God to bless his creation. Participation in this mission was extended by God to his people both in Scripture and the PNG case study as God empowered and equipped individuals to join him in his task. Finally, continuing the Abrahamic blessing to the nations, the CRC revival movement also paralleled the Old Testament narratives as the blessing of God was passed primarily through kinship lines.

As the missional patterns from this integrative research are considered, several facts come to light. First, the research points to the fact that the God of Abraham, Isaac, and Jacob is the same God that we serve today. In contemporary culture there is always a desire to find new messages, new methods, and new motivations for mission. While God is a God of diversity and creativity, his desire to bless all peoples has not changed. The historic context may vary and the methods used may be contextualized but God's missional heart remains the same. Second, God's proclaimed promise to Abraham in Genesis 12:3 has, is, and will continue to be fulfilled through the Holy Spirit empowered body of Christ. And God invites his people to join him in his mission to the nations. Just as God chose Abraham and his descendents as his vehicle of blessing, so God has chosen the Church through the centuries to bless the nations through simply sharing about the joy they themselves have been given by God.

Missional Implications

The greatest contribution of my integrative research is to the field of biblical theology of mission. In this section I highlight the implications of my research in regards to the Abrahamic blessing motif in Scripture, narrative theology, the identity of the church and God's mission.

Abrahamic Blessing Motif

Although references to the Abrahamic blessing are scattered throughout the works of various missiologists and theologians, my research is one of the few to provide an in-depth analysis of the biblical motif within the whole context of Scripture. By identifying the missional patterns of the Abrahamic blessing motif in Scripture and in the PNG case study, I illustrate the continued fulfillment of the Abrahamic blessing through the Old and New Testaments and the contemporary PNG church. Far from being limited to the pages of Scripture alone, the promised Abrahamic blessing to the nations is extended by the people of God, both past and present, who as heirs of Abraham inherit and pass on God's blessing.[8] The implications of my research directly affect our understanding of the body of Christ's role and function in the world today. As recipients of the Abrahamic blessing, the people of God are both beneficiaries and one of the means through which God's blessing reaches humanity. The description of the church as "missional" is therefore not an optional acquisition, but is instead an essential core characteristic of God's people established at the outset of creation.

The very nature of blessing also sheds light upon the role of the church today. God's blessing was created from its inception to multiply and extend beyond itself. Blessing in Scripture works the same way as a seed; just as a seed planted brings forth one life it also has the infinite capacity to multiply itself. Likewise, the blessing of God given to one person has the ability to expand and reproduce. This phenomenon is evident in Genesis 1:21–22, 27–29 as creation is blessed by God with the ability to multiply and be fruitful; inherently transferring that life-giving ability to the next generation. With the blessing of Noah and his sons (Gen 9:1–7) and Abraham and his descendents (12:1–3), the blessing of God maintains its capacity to multiply and spread. While still extending life through childbirth, Abraham is promised a greater life-giving gift; God declares that "in [Abraham] all the families of the earth shall be blessed" (12:3 NRSV). As heirs of Abraham's blessing through Christ (Gal 3:26–29), the church continues this extension of God's blessing to the nations. However, just as God's blessing encapsulated life in Genesis and the Old and New Testament narratives, so God's blessing to the nations still inherently incorporates fruitfulness and the multiplication of new life through Christ. God's blessing simply put was created to spread; it was designed to be planted, take root, grow, bear fruit, and multiply itself again. The church's role in this process is therefore not peripheral; the spreading of God's blessing through Christ is instead a natural outcome of a community blessed by God. As God has blessed his people so they will consciously and unconsciously be a blessing to the nations around them.

8. See Gal 3:26–29; Acts 13:47.

Narrative Theology

In addition to the contributions of my research to mission theology, the integration of biblical literature and a historical case study was also a significant contribution to the field of narrative theology. Discovering the same missional patterns in both Scripture and the PNG CRC case study enabled me to create a hermeneutical bridge between the biblical narratives and the contemporary Melanesian context. Using standard mission theology categories as a comparative framework, I was able to identify significant parallels between the two otherwise varying contexts. While much remains to be developed in the field of narrative theology, my research provides a successful example of biblical theology in context.[9] Differing from the concept of contextualization, biblical theology in context explores biblical themes and patterns as they are represented in contemporary church contexts. As narrative theology currently offers few practical guidelines to enable this exploration, the methodological advances that I made in my research will greatly add to the field.

Identity of the Church

A biblical understanding of the Abrahamic blessing reshapes how we understand the identity and role of God's people, the church. A common question raised by the Christian community today is "how can we be a blessing to the nations?" According to the scriptural account of blessing, this is the wrong question to ask. In both Hebrew Scripture and the New Testament, the source and impetus of all blessing is God himself. It is through the work of the Holy Spirit that the people of God, in connection with God, will bless the peoples of the earth. Blessing the nations is not simply a task but is instead a part of the core identity of Abraham's heirs. As the church lives in relationship with God through Christ, it joins in God's mission to pour his love and blessing upon his creation. Although action on the part of God's people is involved via proclamation and witness, it is only through the power of the Holy Spirit that God's blessing flows to the nations.

9. For a detailed examination of biblical theology in context, see Shaw and Van Engen, *Communicating God's Word in a Complex World*.

God's Mission

The prominence of God's mission is also highlighted in my research. By following the Abrahamic blessing motif in Scripture and the PNG CRC case study, the overarching purpose and significance of the *missio Dei* became evident. While numerous themes run through the pages of Scripture, God's blessing upon his creation stands as one of the foremost in its universal importance. From God's blessing of every living creature and humankind in Genesis 1:21–22, 27–29 to the eternal blessing given through Christ and carried on by the early church in the New Testament, God's loving-kindness toward humanity is a prevalent reality. The fact that God's blessing was divinely created to multiply, be adhesive, and holistically affect every area of its recipient's life further indicates God's deep desire to pour his love upon all peoples and to reconcile them to himself.

A powerful example of the continuation of God's blessing to the nations is seen in the events of the PNG CRC revival. As two thousand years separate Scripture from contemporary society, it is easy to downplay the magnitude of the promise of the Abrahamic blessing. However, through documenting a present-day version of the book of Acts filled with supernatural miracles, proclamation of the gospel, mass conversions, and signs and wonders, the continued fulfillment of the Abrahamic blessing to the nations is easily recognizable. The fact that the Abrahamic promise is still being fulfilled points again to the missional significance of the biblical motif.

My research also highlighted the principal role of the Holy Spirit in the fulfillment of God's promise to Abraham. As I studied the Abrahamic blessing motif in Scripture and in the PNG case study, it became evident that the work of the Spirit of God was the common factor in each narrative. In the PNG CRC revival for example, it was through the leading and guidance of the Holy Spirit that many of the believers became Christians, entered into ministry, and proclaimed the gospel message to others. It was through the work of the Holy Spirit that demons were cast out, people were convicted of their sins, and whole villages accepted the good news. The mission of God was in fact driven, guided, and maintained by the Spirit of God. As evident from the point of creation, the blessing of the nations was God's plan which he has and continues to carry out to fulfillment.

Along with the prominence of the Holy Spirit in both Scripture and the PNG CRC revival, the mystery of God was also evident. As I researched the missional methods and expressions of the Abrahamic blessing in Scripture and the PNG case study, it became evident that no one missional method completely represented the work of God. While the majority of biblical narratives recorded examples where God blessed the nations through Abraham and his descendents, there were also multiple instances where God directly blessed non-Yahwists such as Hagar, Melchizedek, and Nebuchadnezzar. An explanatory image that comes to mind is that of a rain shower; although the people of Israel served as the primary vessel to collect and distribute the shower of God's blessing, God's blessing also fell on those outside of that relationship. It is this mysterious unpredictability surrounding God's blessing that again underlines the fact that although many details are known about God and his mission there is a lot more yet to know and understand.

RECOMMENDATIONS FOR FURTHER STUDY

Based on my research, I have several recommendations for further study. These suggestions consider the current work in the areas of the Abrahamic blessing motif, biblical theology of mission, and the hermeneutics of narrative theology. I also address the need for a comprehensive indigenous history of the Papua New Guinean revival period of the 1970s–1980s.

Abrahamic Blessing Motif

Although the Abrahamic blessing motif has received some attention by scholars, there is still a significant need for further research on this biblical theme. While often identified by missiologists and theologians as a major missional motif, the Abrahamic blessing is not extensively elaborated upon in missiological literature. The largest gap in the literature is the fulfillment of the Abrahamic blessing in Hebrew Scripture. While various authors such as Clines,[10] Brueggemann,[11] and Newbigin[12] acknowledge that God's blessing is partially fulfilled in the Old Testament, a thorough evaluation of the motif has not yet been published. Additional missional sub-themes pertaining to the Abrahamic blessing motif also require attention, such as the act of blessing in contrast to cursing, the presence of suffering in the midst of blessing and the political, economic,

10. *Theme of the Pentateuch.*
11. "Ministry Among."
12. *Open Secret.*

and social impact of biblical blessing. While my research in the Old Testament briefly addresses some of this disparity, further research is still needed to document all of the examples and references of the fulfillment of the Abrahamic blessing motif in the Hebrew Scriptures.

Likewise, the realization of the Abrahamic blessing motif in the New Testament is a significant missional theme that requires further research. Although discussed briefly within my work, the extension of the Abrahamic blessing through Christ and the early church is a rich missional theme that deserves more attention. New Testament passages such as Jesus' proclamation of Isaiah 61:1–3,[13] the parable of the rich fool,[14] the narrative of Ananias and Sapphira,[15] and Paul and Barnabas' sermon to the Lycaonians[16] all contribute to our understanding of the Abrahamic blessing. The potential goal of such research would be to strengthen the understanding of God's mission to the nations and the church's continued role in this work. As illustrated in my research, although the greatest fulfillment of the Abrahamic blessing is in Christ, God's blessing was created to constantly flow through the people of God. As such the church is still called to participate in the *missio Dei* and to be vehicles of God's blessing through Christ.

Abrahamic Blessing Motif in Context

Another natural extension of my study is the exploration of the Abrahamic blessing motif outside of the PNG CRC revival movement. While there are missional patterns joining the Abrahamic blessing with the PNG context, the question must be asked: do these missional parallels also exist outside of Melanesia and outside of a revival situation? For example, in my research I was able to affirm the continuation of the Abrahamic blessing among the ministry of the PNG CRC churches, but is this extension also present in non-Pentecostal contexts and other regions such as Asia, Africa, North America, Europe, the Middle East, and greater Australasia? By developing these connections further, the present-day fulfillment of the Abrahamic

13. See Luke 4:14–30.
14. See Luke 12:13–21.
15. See Acts 5:1–11.
16. See Acts 14:14–18.

blessing motif would be identified as a global and trans-historical reality rather than an isolated event limited to one denomination in PNG.

The misconception surrounding the prosperity gospel message also needs to be addressed. As illustrated in the Hebrew narratives, there is a great disparity between God's proclamation of blessing in Scripture and the modified concept of blessing preached from many pulpits. For example, in contrast with the modern version's emphasis on monetary wealth, physical health, and earthly success, the biblical understanding of blessing presents a God-initiated holistic blessing which is proclaimed upon humanity in the midst of their suffering and hardships. A biblical work outlining the characteristics and purpose of God's blessing to the nations would bring biblical insight and clarification to this global conversation.

Mission Theology

My first observation in the area of mission theology is the need for additional contemporary biblical theology of mission texts. While authors such as Wright[17] have recently done much to mend this gap, more research needs to be done in this area. Besides a handful of mission theology texts written in the last decade, the field continues to rely almost exclusively on missiological works written during the 1960s, 1970s, and 1980s. While these texts contribute greatly to the field, innumerable missional motifs and narratives remain unexplored. These missional motifs need to be considered afresh by the next generation of the global church. In particular, there is an urgent need for more mission theology texts to be written by non-Western scholars. As the center of Christianity is now located in the global South, a new missiological paradigm needs to be outlined which reflects the changing world church and provides new culturally appropriate approaches to studying God's Word and understanding God's mission in Scripture.

In addition, there needs to be further research that explores biblical theology of mission in contemporary and historical contexts. Moving beyond the contextualization of the gospel message, the identity, purposes, and goals of the church need to be understood as they relate to the missional purposes of God as expressed in Scripture. Although connections between the Bible and the contemporary church should not be forced, there are numerous biblical motifs that extend beyond Scripture to the present-day twenty-first-century church. The outplay of these missional

17. *Mission of God.*

themes, which includes motifs such as the kingdom of God, the *missio Dei*, and the new covenant through Christ, need to be considered within their biblical context and also within the contexts of the historical and present-day church.

Narrative Theology

Further research is also needed in the area of the hermeneutics of narrative theology. Specifically, the establishment of a hermeneutical bridge connecting biblical narratives with contemporary contexts is essential. While literature on narrative theology currently provides a helpful theoretical framework, hermeneutical guidelines remain abstract and vague. There are currently few practical strategies in narrative theology literature to guide scholars from the biblical narrative to a contemporary theological interpretation. Therefore, the biblical narratives of Scripture, particularly those of the Old Testament, remain largely untapped resources which could provide theological insight and clarity for today's church. It is vital to continue this exploration of how biblical narratives serve as conduits of theological truth.

In addition to solidifying the practical guidelines of narrative theology theory, there is also a need to implement the methodological approach. Narrative theology has traditionally been divided into three categories: (1) canonical story; (2) life story; and (3) community story.[18] While various insightful theological interpretations of biblical, life, and communal narratives have been documented in mission theology literature, there is a continual need to study the theological implications of biblical, historical, and contemporary story. For example within Hebrew Scripture alone there are numerous missiologically rich narratives including those of Noah, Hagar, Joseph, Rahab, Ruth, David, Daniel, and Jonah that speak of the mission of God and the role of God's people within that mission. The theological insights expressed in such narratives have much to contribute to mission theology and praxis.

Indigenous Revival History

The last area of research requiring further study is the indigenous revival history of PNG. Although several key works have been published on Melanesian church history, there still remains a strong need for the

18. Fackre, "Narrative Theology," 343; *Christian Story*, 6–7.

inclusion of an indigenous perspective. While my research takes a step in this direction by presenting the history of the PNG CRC revival through the voices of the national leaders, it remains the work of a non-Melanesian. The obvious challenge of this approach is the limited contextualized understanding of God's work in PNG. Although this does not mar the validity of my data, the Papua New Guinean church as well as the global church would benefit significantly from the unique theological insights of Papua New Guinean scholars.

In regards to the PNG CRC movement there is also a pressing need to record and publish the events of the 1970s–1990s revival period. Prior to my field research, the revival narratives of the PNG CRC leaders and members had never been gathered together as one body of literature. The few written narratives that did exist had long been forgotten amidst the dusty piles of archival pamphlets and denominational magazines. The events of the PNG CRC revival movement should not remain a forgotten chapter of Christian history. The stories of miraculous healings, signs and wonders, and mass conversions point directly to God's continued fulfillment of his mission in PNG.

CLOSING REMARKS

At the start of my research I was unaware of the significant role that the Abrahamic blessing motif played in Scripture and the PNG CRC case study. What was previously described in missiological writings as a varying stream proved to be a vibrant and consistent river that impacted the whole metanarrative of the Old and New Testament. This realization has greatly influenced my understanding of the purpose of the global church in mission and the blessing of God.

The research I conducted on the Abrahamic blessing motif has in many ways created a paradigm shift in my understanding of global mission. Growing up in the Christian church in Australia and North America, missional evangelization and outreach was often sidelined as an optional elective aside from church activities. Even in North American seminaries, the departments of theology and missiology often function independently from one another. In studying the Abrahamic blessing motif I was presented anew with the reality that the church and its role in God's mission could not and should not be separated. My research has in turn moved my understanding of the church's participation in the *missio Dei* from the periphery of its purpose to the center of its identity.

Listening to the testimonies of the PNG CRC leaders I was also moved by the power and presence of God among his people. During the CRC revival, God miraculously healed people, gave them visions, brought freedom from demonic oppression, ended bondage to sorcery, and spoke to people through the power of his Spirit. The individuals that met God were never the same again; even during my interviews 35 years later tears came to people's eyes as they remembered what God had done in their lives. God's blessing was felt tangibly and permanently within this community.

Hearing these firsthand testimonies of God's blessing has breathed new life into Scripture for me. What originally were words on paper are now material realities visible in the lives of those around me. In recording the revival testimonies I saw the God of Abraham, Isaac, and Jacob continuing to bless his people. It is my desire that this research exploring the Abrahamic blessing motif in Scripture and in the PNG CRC case study will allow readers to fully comprehend the magnitude of God's blessing in their lives and in the life of the church.

Glossary

Abrahamic Blessing	The term "Abrahamic blessing" (Gen 28:4) refers to the divine blessing first given to Abraham in Genesis 12:1–3. It also encapsulates the later promised blessings of God to Abraham of land (Gen 12:7), greatness (Gen 12:2), fruitfulness (Gen 13:16), dominion (Gen 22:17), and covenantal relationship (Gen 17:7).
Abrahamic Blessing Motif	The divine proclamation originally recorded in Genesis 12:1–3 and then extended throughout Scripture in which Yahweh proclaimed that "all peoples on earth will be blessed through [Abram]" (Gen 12:3b). Both the repetition of this declaration in addition to its fulfillment within Scripture will be included in the study of this motif.
Australasia	A geographic region of Oceania which includes the nations of Australia and New Zealand, and the islands of Papua New Guinea.
Christian Revival Crusade	A Pentecostal Australasian denomination originally founded by Pastor Leo Harris in 1945 in Adelaide, South Australia. Originally named the Christian Revival Crusade, the movement has recently been renamed CRC Churches International.

Melanesia	A geographic subregion in Oceania which includes the nations of Papua New Guinea, Solomon Islands, Vanuatu, New Caledonia, Fiji, and the Territory of Norfolk Island.
Missio Dei	Latin for "the mission of God" the term denotes the purpose of God as evidenced in Scripture and human history to draw all nations to himself in a covenantal relationship.[1]
Mission	The participation of an individual or nation, consciously or unconsciously, in the *missio Dei*.
Missional Motif	A recurrent theme of missional importance that is repeated throughout both the Old and New Testaments.
Papua New Guinea	The independent state of Papua New Guinea located in southwestern Melanesia and consisting of 19 national provinces and more than 830 known language groups.
Tok Pisin	Also referred to as Pidgin English, Tok Pisin is an official language of PNG and is spoken and/or understood by the majority of the population.

1. For further discussion regarding the *missio Dei,* see Georg Vicedom (1965), Van Engen (1981, 1996), David Bosch (1980, 1991), H. Rosin (1972), Johannes Verkuyl (1978), Lesslie Newbigin (1978), C. Wright (2006), James Scherer (1993) and Andreas Köstenberger and Peter O'Brien (2001).

APPENDIX A

PNG CRC Revival Leaders Interviews

Interview Date	Name	Gender	Interviews	Time	Interview Location
June 12 and 14, 2009	Thelma Garao*	Female	1 2A 2B	2h 1h45m 17m	Cairns, Australia
	Uvau Amani*	Male			
	Katie Amani*	Female			
June 23, 2009	David Jaruga	Male	1	1h37m	Port Moresby, PNG
	Manoka Jaruga	Female			
June 23, 2009	Geno Kanage	Male	1A 1B	1h14m 58m	Port Moresby, PNG
	Elena Kanage	Female			
June 24, 2009	Elijah Umeume*	Male	1	1h26m	Port Moresby, PNG
	Bev Umeume*	Female			
June 29, 2009	Jennifer Zairere	Female	1A 1B	33m 48m	Mt. Hagen, PNG
June 30, 2009	Pikal Gela	Female	1	1h19m	Mt. Hagen, PNG
June 30, 2009	Barnabas Tabara*	Male	1	53m	Mt. Hagen, PNG
July 2, 2009	Alkin Orona*	Male	1A 1B	1h6m 1h13m	Mt. Hagen, PNG
July 3, 2009	John Marmar	Male	1A 1B	48m 1h47m	Mt. Hagen, PNG
July 3, 2009	Kelly Lotu	Male	1	34m	Mt. Hagen, PNG
July 7–8, 2009	Fuwe Hageyo*	Male	1 2A 2B	1h4m 49m 45m	Port Moresby, PNG

Interview Date	Name	Gender	Interviews	Time	Interview Location
July 10, 2009	Aria Hegame	Male	1A 1B	1h27m 43m	Port Moresby, PNG
July 11, 2009	Kila Laena	Male	1A 1B	1h42m 55m	Port Moresby, PNG
July 13, 2009	John Togawata* Nellie Togawata*	Male Female	1A 1B 1C	1h18m 1h12m 11m	Port Moresby, PNG
July 13, 2009	Richmond Tamanabae*	Male	1 2A 2B	1h43m 3h3m 19m	Port Moresby, PNG
July 13, 2009	Priscilla (Igaro-bae) Ban	Female	1	2h8m	Port Moresby, PNG
July 19, 2009	Micky Purinau Alu Purinau	Male Female	1	1h14m	Port Moresby, PNG
July 22, 2009	Hilarion Mairaro	Male	1	1h22m	Popondetta, PNG
July 22, 2009	Sebastian Peremo	Male	1A 1B	34m 28m	Popondetta, PNG
July 22, 2009	Barry Silverback	Male	1	2h30m	Popondetta, PNG
July 22, 2009	Henry Nigel	Male	1	52m	Popondetta, PNG
July 23, 2009	Thomas Tamanabae	Male	1	1h27m	Popondetta, PNG
July 23, 2009	Arthur Jawodimbari	Male	1	1h19m	Popondetta, PNG
July 24, 2009	Ivan Avowari	Male	1	54m	Popondetta, PNG
July 24, 2009	Sylvestor Barai Nelson Barai	Male Male	1	1h16m	Popondetta, PNG
July 26, 2009	Robert Tamanabae Kingsford	Male Male	1	49m	Popondetta, PNG
July 28, 2009	Ai Wari Gabi Wari	Male Female	1	2h43m	Port Moresby, PNG
July 29, 2009	Geua (Wia) Wari*	Female	1	1h6m	Port Moresby, PNG
Aug. 2–5, 2009	Numba Puri*	Male	1A 1B 1C	2h18m 46m 12m	Lae, PNG

Interview Date	Name	Gender	Interviews	Time	Interview Location
Aug. 1 and 3, 2009	Peter Igarobae*	Male	1 2A 2B 2C 2D	1h18m 37m 1h6m 30m 42m	Lae, PNG
Aug. 8, 2009	Margaret Sete*	Female	1A 1B	1h37 54m	Port Moresby, PNG

*Indicates the interview transcripts that were included in the case study analysis.

APPENDIX B

Blessing of God in Genesis 1–11

Recipient	Created	Blessed	Fruitfulness	Dominion	Resources
Every living creature 1:21–22	"So God created the great sea monsters and every living creature that moves, of every kind, with which the waters swarm, and every winged bird of every kind. And God saw that it was good." (21)	"God blessed them, saying. . ." (22a)	"Be fruitful and multiply and fill the waters in the seas, and let birds multiply on the earth." (22b)		

Recipient	Created	Blessed	Fruitfulness	Dominion	Resources
Humanity 1:27–29	"So God created humankind in his image, in the image of God he created them; male and female he created them." (27)	"God blessed them, and God said to them. . ." (28a)	"Be fruitful and multiply, and fill the earth. . ." (28b)	". . .and subdue it; and have dominion over the fish of the sea and over the birds of the air and over every living thing that moves upon the earth." (28c)	"God said, "See, I have given you every plant yielding seed that is upon the face of all the earth, and every tree with seed in its fruit; you shall have them for food. And to every beast of the earth, and to every bird of the air, and to everything that creeps on the earth, everything that has the breath of life, I have given every green plant for food." (29)
Seventh Day 2:3		"So God blessed the seventh day and hallowed it. . ." (3)			
Humanity 5:1b–2	"When God created humankind, he made them in the likeness of God. Male and female he created them. . ." (2a)	". . .and blessed them and named them" (2b) "Humankind when they were created." (2c)"			

Recipient	Created	Blessed	Fruitfulness	Dominion	Resources
Noah and his Sons 9:1–7		"God blessed Noah and his sons, and said to them. . ." (1a)	"Be fruitful and multiply, and fill the earth." (1b) "And you, be fruitful and multiply, abound on the earth and multiply in it." (7)	"The fear and dread of you shall rest on every animal of the earth, and on every bird of the air, on everything that creeps on the ground, and on all the fish of the sea; into your hand they are delivered." (2)	"Every moving thing that lives shall be food for you; and just as I gave you the green plants, I give you everything." (3)

APPENDIX C

Abrahamic Blessing Motif in Genesis 12–50

Recipient	God's Command	Land/Nation	Blessing	Fruitful	Blessing to Nations
Abraham 12:1–4	"Now the Lord said to Abram, "Go from your country and your kindred and your father's house to the land that I will show you." (1)	"I will make of you a great nation. . ." (2a)	"and I will bless you, and make your name great, so that you will be a blessing. "I will bless those who bless you, and the one who curses you I will curse." (2b–3b)		". . .and in you all the families of the earth shall be blessed." (3c)
Abraham 12:7		"Then the Lord appeared to Abram, and said, "To your offspring I will give this land." (7a)			
Abraham 18:17–18	"The Lord said, Shall I hide from Abraham what I am about to do. . ." (17)			". . .seeing that Abraham shall become a great and mighty nation. . ." (18a)	". . .and all the nations of the earth shall be blessed in him?" (18b)

Recipient	God's Command	Land/Nation	Blessing	Fruitful	Blessing to Nations
Abraham 22:15–18a	"The angel of the Lord called to Abraham a second time from heaven, and said, "By myself I have sworn, says the Lord: Because you have done this, and have not withheld your son, your only son. . ." (15–16)		". . .I will bless you. . ." (17a)	". . .and I will make your offspring as numerous as the stars of heaven and as the sand that is on the seashore. And your offspring shall possess the gate of their enemies. . ." (17b–c)	". . .and by your offspring shall all the nations of the earth gain blessing for themselves. . ." (18a)
Isaac 26:2–3a		"The Lord. . . said, 'Do not go down to Egypt; settle in the land that I shall show you." (2)	"Reside in this land as an alien and I will be with you, and will bless you." (3a)		
Isaac 26:3b–4a		". . .for to you and to your descendant I will give all these lands. . ." (3b)	". . .and I will fulfill the oath that I swore to your father Abraham." (3c)	"I will make your offspring as numerous as the stars of heaven. . ." (4a)	
Isaac 26:4b–5		". . .and will give to your offspring all these lands. . ." (4b)			". . .and all the nations of the earth shall gain blessing for themselves through your offspring. . ." (4c)

Recipient	God's Command	Land/Nation	Blessing	Fruitful	Blessing to Nations
Jacob 28:12–14	"And the Lord stood beside him and said, I am the Lord, the God of Abraham you father and the God of Isaac." (12–13a)	". . .the land on which you lie I will give to you and to your offspring." (13b)		". . .and your offspring shall be like the dust of the earth, and you shall spread abroad." (14a)	". . .and all the families of the earth shall be blessed in you and in your offspring." (14b)

APPENDIX D

Extension of the Abrahamic Blessing in Genesis 12–50

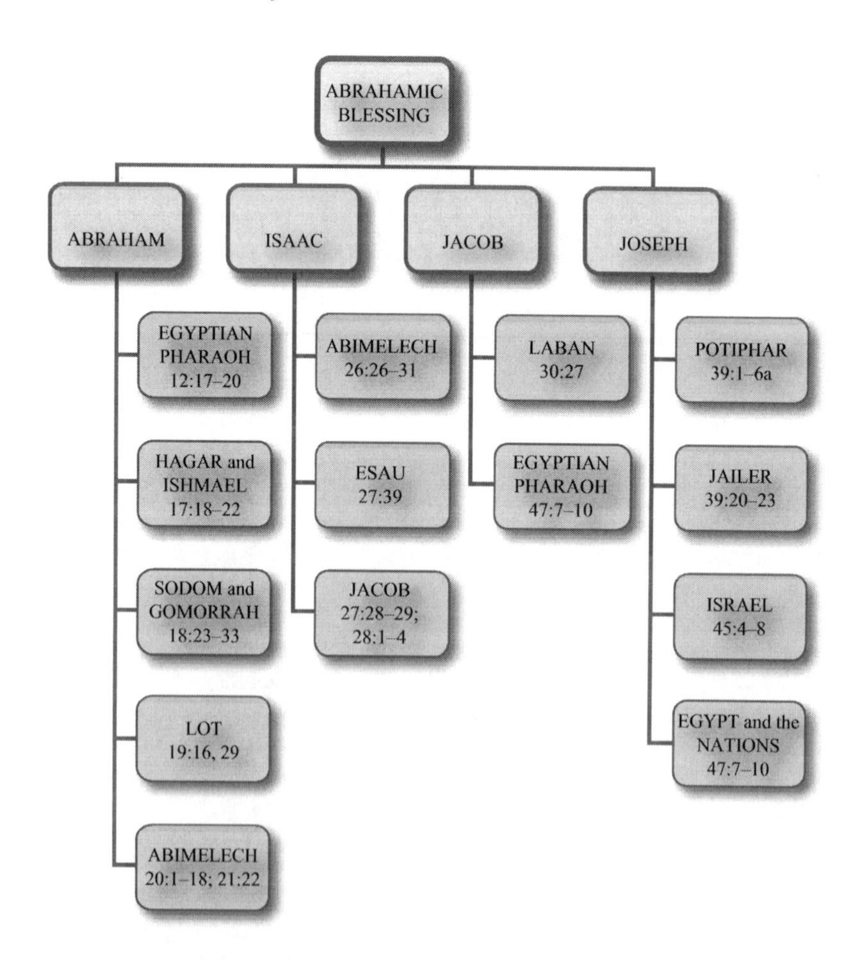

APPENDIX E

PNG CRC Church Growth Statistics[1]

Year	Number of Provinces with CRC Churches	Number of CRC Churches	Number of People in CRC	Number of Full-Time Training Schools	Estimated Number of People Trained/Year	Total Number of Ordained Pastors
1972	1	1	2	1	0	0
1973	1	1	30	1	0	0
1974	1	1	400	1	*	0
1975	1	*	1000	1	*	0
1981	2	40	3000	1	11	5
1984	6	60	7000	2	70	7
1985	10	85	10,000	*	*	*
1987	13	158	16,000	4	150	24
1990	17	218	24,000	6	150	66
1991	17	230	25,000	9	200	80
1993	19	350	30,000	13	*	*

*Statistics not available.

1. PNG CRC statistics have been compiled from Bethel Center's World Mission Office records; unfortunately, largely due to the Bethel Center fire in 1995, more detailed statistics were not available to the researcher.

APPENDIX F

List of PNG CRC Bible Schools[2]

School Name	Start Date	Location
Crusade Bible School (part–time)	Mar 1974	Port Moresby, PNG
Bible School (full–time)	Apr 1979	Port Moresby, PNG
Institute of Evangelism	Apr 1981	Port Moresby, PNG
Bethel Bible College	Feb 1984	Port Moresby, PNG
Vision Bible School	July 1984	Rabaul, ENBP, PNG
Oro Province Bible Training School	1986	Popondetta, Oro, PNG
Gulf Bible Training School	1988	Gulf Province, PNG
Sekolah Alkitab Bethel Abepura	July 1990	Irian Jaya, Indonesia
Western Prov. Bible Training School	1990	Western Province, PNG
Philippines School of Ministry	Sept. 1991	Legazpi, Philippines
Hailens Skul Bilong Evanselism	1991	Mala, Western Highlands, PNG
Milne Bay School of Discipleship	1991	Milne Bay Province, PNG
Bethel Women's School of Ministry	Aug 1993	Port Moresby, PNG
Peniel Bible School	1994	North Solomon Province, PNG
Enga Provins Disaipelship Trening Skul	1994	Enga Province, PNG
Fiji School of Discipleship and Christian Ministry	1994	Fiji
KarKar Ministry Training Center	1995	KarKar Island, Madang Province, PNG

2. This list of CRC (PNG) training schools has been compiled from Bethel Center World Mission Office records and in particular the document entitled "PNG Events in Papua New Guinea."

School Name	Start Date	Location
Sekolah Alkitab Bethel Manokwari	1995	Manokwari, Indonesia
World Mission Faith Training School	Mar 1996	Port Moresby, PNG
Lahai Roi Bible School	1997	Trobriand Islands, Milne Bay Province, PNG
Livingston Discipleship Training School	1997	Vanuatu
Christian Ministry Training Center	1997	Malaita, Solomon Islands
School of the Teacher	1997	Port Moresby, PNG

APPENDIX G

PNG CRC Missionary Service[1]

Name	Location of Missionary Service	Departure Date
Richmond and Leila Tamanabae	Samarai, Milne Bay Province, PNG	Nov. 1980
	Narrandara, Australia (Aboriginal Ministry)	Sept. 1988
Thomas and Grace Tamanabae	Popondetta, Oro Province, PNG	1980
Labu and Ovoa Tuakana	Popondetta, Oro Province, PNG	Jan. 1980
John Tobo	Kiunga, Western Province	April 1982
Caleb Kauma	Kiunga, Western Province	April 1982
Peter and Vami Igarobae	Manus Province, PNG	June 1983
	Rabaul, ENBP, PNG	Feb. 1986
	Lae, Morobe Province, PNG	*
Suckling Tamanabae	Kerema, Gulf Province, PNG	Jan. 1984
	Solomon Islands	1989
Kila and Poka Laena	Solomon Islands	Feb. 1985
Fuwe and Rhoda Hageyo	Manus Province, PNG	Feb. 1986
Greg Steven	Solomon Islands	Aug. 1987
Goina Tau	New South Wales, Australia	Sept. 1987

1. Missionary service locations and dates have been compiled from Bethel Center World Mission Office records and personal interviews by the author with PNG CRC missionaries (June–August 2009); due to Bethel Center's lack of archival records, there is no means to determine whether this list includes every missionary sent from PNG CRC churches between 1984 and 1997.

Name	Location of Missionary Service	Departure Date
Kila and Geua Wari	Rabaul, ENBP, PNG	1990–1994
Margaret Sete	Missionary on Doulos Ship	*
Elijah and Beverly Umeume	Kiunga, Western Province, PNG	*
	New Zealand	*
	Cook Islands	*
	Misima Island, MBP, PNG	*
	Philippines	*
	Fiji	1994
David and Manoka Jaruga	Fiji	1997**
Susan Beni	Fiji	1997**
Aria and Loa Hegame	Solomon Islands	1997**
Moses and Kari Daure	Australia	1997**
Mishael and Jennifer Zairere	Philippines	*
Jennah Gwaibo	Philippines	1997**
John Weimani	Philippines	1997**
Peter and Nellie Hauje	Philippines	1997**
Geno and Eleina Kanage	Vanuatu	1997**

*Dates not available.

**Year report was dated.

Bibliography

Achtemeier, Paul J., et al., eds. *Introducing the New Testament: Its Literature and Theology*. Grand Rapids: Eerdmans, 2001.

Albright, William F. "From the Patriarchs to Moses." *Biblical Archaeologist* 36 (1973) 7–15.

Alexander, T. Desmond. "Abraham Re-Assessed Theologically." *He Swore an Oath: Biblical Themes from Genesis* 12, 2nd ed., edited by R. S. Hess et al., 12–50. Grand Rapids: Baker, 1994.

Alter, Robert. *Genesis: Translation and Commentary*. New York: Norton, 1996.

Amani, Uvao. Interview by author. Cairns, Australia. June 14, 2009.

Angrosino, Michael. *Doing Ethnographic and Observational Research*. Sage Qualitative Research Kit 3. Los Angeles: Sage, 2007.

Barker, John, ed. "Christian Bodies: Dialectics of Sickness and Salvation among the Maisin of Papua New Guinea." *Journal of Religious History* 27 (2003) 272–92.

———. *Christianity in Oceania: Ethnographic Perspectives*. Lanham, MD: University Press of America, 1990.

Barr, John. "A Survey of Ecstatic 'Holy Spirit Movements' in Melanesia." *Oceania* 54 (1983) 109–32.

Bartle, Neville. *Death, Witchcraft and the Spirit World in the Highlands of Papua New Guinea*. Point Series 29. Goroka, PNG: Melanesian Institute, 2003.

Barton, John. "Disclosing Human Possibilities: Revelation and Biblical Stories." *Revelation and Story: Narrative Theology and the Centrality of Story*, edited by G. Sauter and J. Barton, 53–78. Aldershot, UK: Ashgate, 2000.

Bauckham, Richard. *Bible and Mission: Christian Witness in a Postmodern World*. Grand Rapids: Baker Academic, 2003.

Bergmann, Ulrich. "Old Testament Concepts of Blessing: Their Relevance for a Theological Interpretation of Cargo Cult." *Point* 3 (1974) 176–86.

Berkhof, Hendricus, and Philip Potter. *Key Words of the Gospel*. London: SCM, 1964.

Berlin, Adele. *Poetics and Interpretation of Biblical Narrative*. Winona Lake, IN: Eisenbrauns, 1994.

Bernard, H. Russell. *Research Methods in Anthropology*. Walnut Creek, CA: AltaMira, 1995.

Blauw, Johannes. *The Missionary Nature of the Church*. New York: McGraw-Hill, 1962.

Boice, James Montgomery. *Genesis: An Expositional Commentary*. Vol. 3. Grand Rapids: Baker, 1998.

Bosch, David. *Transforming Mission: Paradigm Shifts in Theology of Mission*. Maryknoll: Orbis, 1991.

———. *Witness to the World: The Christian Mission in Theological Perspective*. Atlanta: John Knox, 1980.

Bowling, Andrew. "Be a Blessing, or, So That You Will Be a Blessing: Implications for Old Testament Missiology." Theological Research Exchange Network (TREN), 2005.

"Brief Summary of Some of the Events in the World of the Christian Revival Crusade in Papua New Guinea." Unpublished Christian Revival Crusade report. No date.

Bruce, F. F. *The Epistles to the Colossians, to Philemon, and to the Ephesians*. New International Commentary on the New Testament. Grand Rapids: Eerdmans, 1984.

Brueggemann, Walter. *Genesis*. Atlanta: John Knox, 1982.

———. "The Kerygma of the 'Priestly Writers.'" *ZAW* 84 (1972) 397–414.

———. "Ministry Among: The Power of Blessing." *Journal for Preachers* 22 (1999) 21–29.

Burnett, David. *God's Mission: Healing the Nations*. Kent, UK: Sending the Light, 1986.

Calvin, John. *Genesis*. Edinburgh: Calvin Translation Society, 1847.

Cassuto, Umberto. *A Commentary on the Book of Genesis*. Vol. 1. Jerusalem: Magnes, 1989.

———. *A Commentary on the Book of Genesis*. Vol. 2. Jerusalem: Magnes, 1984.

Charmaz, Kathy. *Constructing Grounded Theory: A Practical Guide through Qualitative Analysis*. Los Angeles: Sage, 2006.

Childs, Brevard S. *Introduction to the Old Testament as Scripture*. Philadelphia: Fortress, 1979.

———. "Old Testament Theology." In *Old Testament Interpretation: Past, Present, and Future*, edited by J. L. Mays et al., 293–301. Nashville: Abingdon, 1995.

Christensen, Duane L. "Nations." In *The Anchor Bible Dictionary*, edited by D. N. Freedman, 1037–48. New York: Doubleday, 1992.

Christian Revival Crusade (PNG) Strategy in Relation to Other Countries. Port Moresby: Bethel Center.

Clements, Ronald. *Abraham and David: Genesis 15 and Its Meaning for Israelite Tradition*. Studies in Biblical Theology, 2nd Series. London: Cunningham, 1967.

Clines, David J. A. *The Theme of the Pentateuch*. JSOT Supplement 10. Sheffield, UK: University of Sheffield, 1978.

Coats, George. *Genesis: With an Introduction to Narrative Literature*. Grand Rapids: Eerdmans, 1983.

Cogan, Mordechai. *I Kings: A New Translation with Introduction and Commentary*. The Anchor Bible. New York: Doubleday, 2000.

Cogan, Mordechai, and Hayim Tadmor. *II Kings*. The Anchor Bible. New York: Doubleday, 1988.

Cohn, Robert L., ed. *2 Kings*. Berit Olam: Studies in Hebrew Narrative and Poetry. Collegeville: Liturgical, 2000.

Comfort, Philip W., and Walter A. Elwell, eds. *Tyndale Bible Dictionary*. Wheaton, IL: Tyndale, 2001.

Cooper, Dudley. *Flames of Revival: The Continuing Story of the Christian Revival Crusade*. Endeavour Hills, Australia: CRC National Executive, 1995.

"CRC (PNG) World Mission Department Annual Report." Port Moresby: Christian Revival Crusade (PNG), 1989.

Denoon, Donald. *Trial Separation: Australia and the Decolonisation of Papua New Guinea*. Canberra, Australia: Pandanus, 2005.

Dentan, Robert C. *The First and Second Books of the Kings*. Layman's Bible Commentary 7. Richmond, VA: John Knox, 1964.

De Ridder, Richard. *Discipling the Nations*. Grand Rapids: Baker, 1971.

DeVries, Simon John. *I Kings*. Word Biblical Commentary 12. Nashville: Nelson, 2003.

Driver, S. R. *The Book of Genesis*. London: Methuen, 1904.

Dunn, James D. G. *Romans 9–16*. Word Biblical Commentary 38B. Dallas: Word, 1988.

Dyrness, W. A., and V. M. Kärkkäinen, eds. "Theology of Mission." In *Global Dictionary of Theology*, 550–61. Downers Grove, IL: InterVarsity, 2008.

Ellingsen, Mark. *The Integrity of Biblical Narrative: Story in Theology and Proclamation*. Eugene, OR: Wipf & Stock, 2002.

Ellis, E. Earle. *The Gospel of Luke*. New Century Bible Commentary. Grand Rapids: Eerdmans, 1980.

Eskenazi, Tamara Cohn. "Torah as Narrative and Narrative as Torah." Chapter 1 of *Old Testament Interpretation: Past, Present, and Future*, edited by J. L. Mays et al. Nashville: Abingdon, 1995.

Fackre, Gabriel J. *The Christian Story*. Grand Rapids: Eerdmans, 1984.

———. "Narrative Theology: An Overview." *Interpretation* 37 (1983) 340–52.

———. "Narrative Theology from an Evangelical Perspective." Chapter 10 of *Faith and Narrative*, edited by K. E. Yandell. Oxford: Oxford University Press, 2001.

Fetterman, David M. *Ethnography: Step by Step*. 3rd ed. Applied Social Research Methods Series 17. Newbury Park, CA: Sage, 2010.

Flannery, Austin P., ed. *Documents of Vatican II*. Grand Rapids: Eerdmans, 1975.

Forbes, George. *A Church on Fire: The Story of the Assemblies of God of Papua New Guinea*. Mitcham, Australia: Mission Mobilisers, 2001.

Fritz, Volkmar. *I and II Kings*. Translated by A. Hagedorn. Continental Commentaries. Minneapolis: Fortress, 1984.

Fugmann, Gernot. "Salvation in Melanesian Religions." Chapter 9 of *An Introduction to Melanesian Religions*, edited by E. Mantovani. Goroka, PNG: Melanesian Institute, 1984.

Garao, Thelma. Interview by author. Cairns, Australia. June 14, 2009.

Gilding, Bruce L. "PNG Impressions." Unpublished report. Adelaide, Australia, 1978.

Glaser, Barney G. *Basics of Grounded Theory Analysis*. Mill Valley, CA: Sociology, 1992.

Glasser, Arthur F., and Donald A. McGavran. *Contemporary Theologies of Mission*. Grand Rapids: Baker, 1983.

Goldberg, Michael. *Theology and Narrative: A Critical Introduction*. Nashville: Abingdon, 1982.

Goldingay, John. *Israel's Faith, Old Testament Theology*. Downers Grove, IL: InterVarsity, 2006.

———. *Models for Interpretation of Scripture*. Grand Rapids: Eerdmans, 1995.

———. *Old Testament Theology: Israel's Gospel*. Vol. 1. Downers Grove, IL: InterVarsity, 2003.

Griffin, James, et al. *Papua New Guinea: A Political History*. Richmond, Australia: Heinemann Educational Australia, 1979.

Guiart, Jean. "The Millenarian Aspect of Conversion to Christianity in the South Pacific." Chapter 26 of *Cultures of the Pacific: Selected Readings*, edited by T. G. Harding and B. J. Wallace. New York: Free Press, 1970.

Gunkel, Hermann. *Genesis*. Translated by M. E. Biddle. Macon, GA: Mercer University Press, 1997.

Hageyo, Fuwe. Interview by author. Port Moresby, PNG. July 7–8, 2009.

Harbin, Michael A. *The Promise and the Blessing: A Historical Survey of the Old and New Testaments*. Grand Rapids: Zondervan, 2005.

Hedlund, Roger E. *God and the Nations: A Biblical Theology of Mission in the Asian Context*. Delphi: ISPCK, 1997.

Hiebert, Paul G. *Anthropological Reflections on Missiological Issues*. Grand Rapids: Baker, 1994.

Hobbs, T. R. *II Kings*. Word Biblical Commentary 13. Waco, TX: Word, 1982.

Holstein, James A., and Jaber F. Gubrium. *The Active Interview*. Qualitative Research Methods 37. Thousand Oaks, CA: Sage, 1995.

Hughes, R. Kent. *Genesis: Beginnings and Blessing*. Wheaton: Crossway, 2004.

Igarobae, Peter. Interview by author. Lae, PNG. August 2–5, 2009.

Janzen, J. Gerald. *Abraham and All the Families of the Earth: A Commentary on the Book of Genesis 12–50*. International Bible Commentary. Grand Rapids: Eerdmans, 1993.

Just, Arthur A. *Luke 1:1—9:50*. Concordia Commentary. St. Louis: Concordia, 1996.

Kaiser, Walter C., Jr. *Mission in the Old Testament: Israel as a Light to the Nations*. Grand Rapids: Baker, 2000.

Kidner, Derek. *Genesis: An Introduction and Commentary*. Tyndale Old Testament Commentaries. London: Tyndale, 1967.

Koenig, John. *Rediscovering New Testament Prayer: Boldness and Blessing in the Name of Jesus*. Harrisburg, PA: Morehouse, 1998.

Köstenberger, Andreas J., and Peter Thomas O'Brien. *Salvation to the Ends of the Earth: A Biblical Theology of Mission*. Downers Grove, IL: InterVarsity, 2001.

Kraft, Charles H. *Anthropology for Christian Witness*. Maryknoll: Orbis, 2007.

Langness, L. L. *The Life History in Anthropological Science*. Studies in Anthropological Method. New York: Holt, Rinehart & Winston, 1965.

Leke, Daniel K. "The Role of Churches in Nation Building in Papua New Guinea." In *Building a Nation in Papua New Guinea: Views of the Post-Independence Generation*, edited by D. Kavanamur et al., 283–308. Canberra, Australia: Pandanus, 2003.

Lincoln, Andrew T. *Ephesians*. Word Biblical Commentary 42. Dallas: Word, 1990.

Longenecker, Richard. *Galatians*. Word Biblical Commentary 41. Dallas: Word, 1990.

Ma, Julie C., and Wonsuk Ma. *Mission in the Spirit: Towards a Pentecostal/Charismatic Missiology*. Regnum Studies in Mission. Oxford, UK: Regnum, 2010.

Macky, Peter W. "Biblical Story Theology." *Theological Educator* 33 (1986) 22–31.

Magonet, Jonathan. "Abraham and God." *Judaism* 33 (1984) 162–63.

McGavran, Donald A. *The Bridges of God: A Study in the Strategy of Missions*. 2nd ed. New York: Friendship, 1955.

———. *Understanding Church Growth*. Edited by C. P. Wagner. Grand Rapids: Eerdmans, 1970.

Mead, Margaret. "The Rights of Primitive Peoples." In *Cultures of the Pacific: Selected Readings*, edited by T. G. Harding and B. J. Wallace, 419–30. New York: Free Press, 1970.

Missionaries (Etc) Overseas. Unpublished printed report by the CRC denomination in Papua New Guinea. Port Moresby: Bethel Centre, n.d.

Moberly, R. W. L. *Genesis 12–50*. Old Testament Guides. Sheffield, UK: JSOT, 1992.

———. *The Old Testament of the Old Testament*. Edited by W. Brueggemann et al. Overtures to Biblical Theology. Minneapolis: Fortress, 1992.

Moo, Douglas J. *The Epistle to the Romans*. New International Commentary on the New Testament. Grand Rapids: Eerdmans, 1996.

Mowinckel, Sigmund. *Religion and Kultus*. Göttingen, Germany: Vandenhoeck & Ruprecht, 1953.

Namunu, Simeon. "Spirits in Melanesian Tradition and Spirit in Christianity." In *The Gospel Is Not Western: Black Theologies from the Southwest Pacific*, edited by G. W. Trompf, 109–18. New York: Orbis, 1987.

Narokobi, Bernard. "What Is Religious Experience for a Melanesian?" In *Living Theology in Melanesia: A Reader*, edited by J. D. A. May, 69–77. Goroka, PNG: Melanesian Institute for Pastoral and Socio-Economic Service, 1985.

"Nation Aflame: Voice of Papua New Guinea." Printed pamphlet produced by the CRC in Papua New Guinea. Port Moresby: Bethel, 1989.

Neill, Stephen, et al., eds. *Concise Dictionary of the Christian World Mission*. Nashville: Abingdon, 1971.

"New Guinea News." *Revivalist*, June 1973, 10–13.

"New Guinea News." *Revivalist*, February 1974, 10–11.

Newbigin, Lesslie. *Open Secret*. Grand Rapids: Eerdmans, 1978.

"Newspoint." *Impact*, April–May 1980.

Okoye, James Chukwuma. *Israel and the Nations: A Mission Theology of the Old Testament*. American Society of Missiology Series. Maryknoll: Orbis, 2006.

Orona, Alkin. Interview by author. Mt. Hagen, PNG. July 2, 2009.

Orona, Celia J. "Temporality and Identity Loss Due to Alzheimer's Disease." In *Grounded Theory in Practice*, edited by A. Strauss and J. Corbin, 171–96. Thousand Oaks, CA: Sage, 1997.

Paterson, Dean. "Sorcery and Demonism in Papua New Guinea." *Revivalist*, August 1974, 11.

Patton, Michael Quinn. *Qualitative Evaluation and Research Methods*. Newbury Park, CA: Sage, 1990.

Peters, George. *A Biblical Theology of Mission*. Chicago: Moody, 1972.

Plummer, Alfred. *A Critical and Exegetical Commentary on the Gospel according to St. Luke*. International Critical Commentary. Edinburgh: T. & T. Clark, 1964.

Puri, Numba. Interview by author. Lae, PNG. August 2–5, 2009.

Rendtorff, Rolf. "Genesis 8 21 und die Urgeschichte des Yahwisten." *Kerygma and Dogma* 7 (1961) 69–78.

———. *The Old Testament: An Introduction*. London: SCM, 1985.

Rice, Gene. *I Kings: Nations under God*. International Theological Commentary. Grand Rapids: Eerdmans, 1990.

Robbins, Joel. "Introduction: Global Religions, Pacific Island Transformations." *Journal of Ritual Studies* 15 (2001) 7–12.

Robin, R. "Revival Movements in the Southern Highlands Province of Papua New Guinea." *Oceania* 52 (1982) 242–320.

Rosin, H. H. *Missio Dei: An Examination of the Origin, Contents and Function of the Term in Protestant Missiological Discussion*. Leiden, Netherlands: Inter–University Institute for Missiology and Ecumentical Research, 1972.

Ross, Allen P. *Creation and Blessing: A Guide to the Study and Exposition of the Book of Genesis*. Grand Rapids: Baker, 1987.

"Run with the Vision." Printed pamphlet produced by the CRC in Papua New Guinea. Port Moresby: Bethel, 1982.

Sarna, Nahum M. *Genesis*. JPS Torah Commentary. Philadelphia: Jewish Publication Society, 1989.

Scherer, James A. "Church, Kingdom and Missio Dei: Lutheran and Orthodox Correctives to Recent Ecumentical Mission Theology." In *The Good News of the Kingdom*, edited by C. E. Van Engen et al., 82–88. Maryknoll: Orbis, 1993.

Senior, Donald, and Carroll Stuhlmueller. *The Biblical Foundations for Mission*. Maryknoll: Orbis, 1983.

Seow, Choon–Leong, et al. *1 and 2 Kings, 1 and 2 Chronicles, Ezra, Nehemiah, Esther, Additions to Esther, Tobit, Judith*. New Interpreter's Bible 3. Nashville: Abingdon, 1999.

Sete, Margaret. Interview by author. Port Moresby, PNG. August 8, 2009.

Shaw, R. Daniel. "Melanesian Perspectives: The Need to Integrate Worldview, Translation and the Church." In *SIL Anthropology Workshop*, a compendium of workshop materials. Ukarumpa, PNG: 2010.

Shaw, R. Daniel, and Charles E. Van Engen. *Communicating God's Word in a Complex World: God's Truth or Hocus–Pocus?* Lanham: Rowman & Littlefield, 2003.

Sillitoe, Paul. *An Introduction to the Anthropology of Melanesia: Culture and Tradition*. Cambridge: Cambridge University Press, 1998.

Silverback, Barry. "Mission Update to CRC Churches." Photocopy of unpublished report. Adelaide, Australia, May 11, 1990.

———. "New Guinea News." *Revivalist*, October 1972, 17–18.

———. "New Guinea News." *Revivalist*, July 1974, 13–15.

———. "PNG Annual Report for Conference 1991." Photocopy of unpublished report. Adelaide, Australia, 1991.

———. "Report on Latest Patrol." Photocopy of unpublished report. Adelaide, Australia, 1977.

Skinner, John. *A Critical and Exegetical Commentary on Genesis*. International Critical Commentary 1. Edinburgh: T. & T. Clark, 1910.

"Some Dates and Statistics (CRC Training Programmes)." Unpublished Christian Revival Crusade report. July 21, 1997.

Speiser, E. A. *Genesis: Introduction, Translation, and Notes*. The Anchor Bible. Garden City: Doubleday, 1964.

Spradley, James P. *The Ethnographic Interview*. New York: Holt, Rinehart & Winston, 1979.

Steele, Les L. *On the Way: A Practical Theology of Christian Formation*. Grand Rapids: Baker, 1990.

Strauss, Anselm, and Juliet Corbin. *Basics of Qualitative Research: Techniques and Procedures for Developing Grounded Theory*. Thousand Oaks, CA: Sage, 1998.

Sundkler, Bengt. *The World of Mission*. Grand Rapids: Eerdmans, 1965.

Swain, Tony, and Garry Trompf. *Religions of Oceania*. London: Routledge, 1995.

Tabara, Barnabas. Interview by author. Mt. Hagen, PNG. June 30, 2009.

Tamanabae, Richmond. Interview by author. Port Moresby, PNG. July 13, 2009.

———. "Love Has Replaced Fear and Sorcery." *Impact*, August–September 1980, 13–14.

Tamanabae, Thomas. Interview by author. Popondetta, PNG. July 23, 2009.

Teague, Merrilyn. "The Outpouring of the Holy Spirit in Papua New Guinea (1965–1978)." Photocopy of unpublished report. Adelaide, Australia, May 2005.

Thomas, Nancy. "Following the Footprints." In *Footprints of God*, edited by C. E. Van Engen et al., 225–33. Monrovia, CA: MARC, 1999.

Tippett, Alan R. *The Deep Sea Canoe: The Story of Third World Missionaries in the South Pacific*. South Pasadena, CA: William Carey Library, 1977.

———. *People Movements in Southern Polynesia*. Chicago: Moody Bible Institute, 1971.

———. *Solomon Islands Christianity*. New York: Friendship, 1967.

Togawata, John. Interview by author. Port Moresby, PNG. July 13, 2009.

Togawata, Nellie. Interview by author. Port Moresby, PNG. July 13, 2009.

Turner, Ann. *Historical Dictionary of Papua New Guinea, Oceanian Historical Dictionaries*. London: Scarecrow, 1994.

Turner, Laurence A. *Genesis*. Sheffield, UK: Sheffield Academic, 2000.

Umeume, Beverly. Interview by author. Port Moresby, PNG. June 24, 2009.

Umeume, Elijah. Interview by author. Port Moresby, PNG. June 24, 2009.

Urbrock, William J. "Blessing and Curses." In *The Anchor Bible Dictionary*, edited by D. N. Freedman, 755–60. New York: Doubleday, 1992.

Van Engen, Charles E. *The Growth of the True Church*. Amsterdam: Rodopi, 1981.

———. *Mission on the Way: Issues in Mission Theology*. Grand Rapids: Baker, 1996.

Van Engen, Charles E., et al., eds. *Footprints of God: A Narrative Theology of Mission*. Monrovia, CA: MARC, 1999.

Verkuyl, Johannes. *Contemporary Missiology: An Introduction*. Grand Rapids: Eerdmans, 1978.

Vicedom, Georg. *The Mission of God: An Introduction to a Theology of Mission*. St. Louis: Concordia, 1965.

Vine, W. E. *Vine's Complete Expository Dictionary of Old and New Testament Words*. Nashville: Nelson, 1996.

Von Rad, Gerhard. *Genesis*. London: Jenkins, 1961.

———. *Genesis: A Commentary*. Old Testament Library. Philadelphia: Westminister, 1972.

Walsh, Jerome T. *1 Kings*. Berit Olam: Studies in Hebrew Narrative and Poetry. Collegeville: Liturgical, 1996.

Wari, Geua. Interview by author. Port Moresby, PNG. July 29, 2009.

Wellhausen, Julius. *Prolegomena to the History of Ancient Israel*. New York: Meridian, 1958. First published in German as *Prologomena zur Geschichte Israels*, 1883.

Wenham, Gordon J. *Genesis 1–15*. Word Bible Commentary 1. Waco, TX: Word, 1987.

———. *Genesis 16–50*. Word Bible Commentary 2. Waco, TX: Word, 1993.

Westermann, Claus. *Blessing in the Bible and the Life of the Church*. Philadelphia: Fortress, 1978.

———. *Genesis*. Interpretation: A Bible Commentary for Preaching and Teaching. Atlanta: John Knox, 1982.

———. *Genesis 1–11*. Minneapolis: Augsburg, 1984.

———. *Genesis 12–36*. Minneapolis: Augsburg, 1985.

———. *Genesis 37–50: A Commentary*. Translated by John J. Scullion. Minneapolis: Augsburg, 1982.

———. *Genesis: An Introduction*. Translated by John J. Scullion. Minneapolis: Fortress, 1992.

———. *The Promises to the Fathers: Studies on the Patriarchal Narratives*. Translated by D. E. Green. Philadelphia: Fortress, 1980.

Whiteman, Darrell. "Melanesian Religions: An Overview." Chapter 4 of *An Introduction to Melanesian Religions*, edited by E. Mantovani, 87–121. Goroka, PNG: Melanesian Institute, 1984.

Whybray, Roger Norman. *Introduction to the Pentateuch*. Grand Rapids: Eerdmans, 1995.

Wright, Christopher J. H. *The Mission of God: Unlocking the Bible's Grand Narrative*. Downers Grove, IL: InterVarsity, 2006.

Zimmerli, W. "Promise and Fulfillment." In *Essays on Old Testament Hermeneutics*, edited by C. Westermann, 89–122. Richmond, VA: John Knox, 1963.

Index